Big Enterprise in a Competitive System

Big Enterprise in a Competitive System / REVISED EDITION

by A.D.H. KAPLAN

The Brookings Institution, *Washington, D.C.*

© 1964 by

THE BROOKINGS INSTITUTION

Published November 1964

Library of Congress Catalogue Card Number 64-8754

THE BROOKINGS INSTITUTION is an independent organization devoted to nonpartisan research, education, and publication in economics, government, foreign policy, and the social sciences generally. Its principal purposes are to aid in the development of sound public policies and to promote public understanding of issues of national importance.

The Institution was founded December 8, 1927, to merge the activities of the Institute for Government Research, founded in 1916, the Institute of Economics, founded in 1922, and the Robert Brookings Graduate School of Economics and Government, founded in 1924.

The general administration of the Institution is the responsibility of a self-perpetuating Board of Trustees. The Trustees are likewise charged with maintaining the independence of the staff and fostering the most favorable conditions for creative research and education. The immediate direction of the policies, program, and staff of the Institution is vested in the President, assisted by the division directors and an advisory council, chosen from the professional staff of the Institution.

In publishing a study, the Institution presents it as a competent treatment of a subject worthy of public consideration. The interpretations and conclusions in such publications are those of the author or authors and do not purport to represent the views of the other staff members, officers, or trustees of the Brookings Institution.

Foreword

IN 1947 THE BROOKINGS Institution began an investigation of the place of large industrial enterprises in the American economy. Such an investigation had become increasingly important because of the rapid growth of big business and conflicting attitudes toward it. On the one hand, public conduct fostered this growth; on the other, public opinion was suspicious of bigness or hostile to it. The courts enforcing the antitrust laws shifted ground with the fashions of the times. The original study was undertaken in an attempt to improve public understanding of modern competition and the structure and performance of big business.

The first edition of A. D. H. Kaplan's *Big Enterprise in a Competitive System* was published in 1954. The book received widespread public attention and provoked considerable comment in professional articles. In large part, this interest reflected the pioneering quality of Dr. Kaplan's work. Although several reviews objected to details of his procedures and to some implications of his work, all tended to accept the basic concept of industrial turnover and its applicability to the analysis of industrial organizations.

Since the publication of *Big Enterprise,* Brookings has continued its interest in this area. Subsequent publications include *Pricing in Big Business: A Case Approach,* by A. D. H. Kaplan, Joel B. Dirlam, and Robert F. Lanzillotti; *The Price Discrimination Law: A Review of Experience,* by Corwin D. Edwards; *Competition As a Dynamic Process,* by John Maurice Clark; and *Competition and Monopoly: Legal and Economic Issues,* by Mark S. Massel. Additional studies are in process.

This revised edition of Dr. Kaplan's study brings the statistical material and text of the original work up to date to take account of developments in the last ten years. In addition, the exposition has been clarified at several points. It is not, however, a new study. The original volume, for which there has been continued public demand, is now out of print.

Dr. Kaplan is especially grateful to Charles H. Berry of the present Brookings staff for advice and assistance in the preparation of the second edition. Mrs. Betty Churchill assisted in the preparation of the statistical materials in Chapters 3 and 4. Morris A. Adelman of the Massachusetts Institute of Technology, Alfred E. Kahn of Cornell University, Merton J. Peck, formerly of the Brookings staff and now at Yale University, and Lee E. Preston of the University of California (Berkeley) read the updated manuscript and contributed many helpful comments and suggestions. Sheau-eng Lau, Irene Lurie, and Eleanor B. Steinberg prepared and checked the statistical data, and Alix L. Rycoff provided secretarial assistance. A. Evelyn Breck edited the manuscript and Virginia Haaga prepared the index. The revision was prepared under the supervision of Joseph A. Pechman, Director of Economic Studies.

The author again wishes to include his personal acknowledgment to the following consultants who collaborated in the field work undertaken in connection with the earlier volume: Joel Dean, Columbia University; Melvin G. de Chazeau, Cornell University; Ewald T. Grether, University of California, Berkeley; Clare E. Griffin, University of Michigan; Richard B. Heflebower, Northwestern University; Neil H. Jacoby, University of California, Los Angeles; John P. Miller, Yale University; Herluf V. Olsen, Dartmouth College; Russell A. Stevenson, University of Michigan; Lawrence H. Seltzer, Wayne State University. The author is also indebted to Alfred E. Kahn, who served as staff member of the project while on sabbatical leave from Cornell University, to Marie Thresher, his research assistant, to Esther Payson, his secretary, and to Francis Milliken, who served as statistical assistant.

The Brookings Institution wishes to acknowledge and express its appreciation for the generous financial assistance by the Maurice and Laura Falk Foundation of Pittsburgh and the Alfred P. Sloan Foundation of New York for the support of the original study. The revision was financed by a second grant from the Alfred P. Sloan Foundation. The foundations, of course, assume no responsibility for the findings of the study, and they are not to be understood as approving or disapproving the statements and views expressed herein. The views expressed are those of the author and do not purport to represent the views of the Brookings Institution, its trustees, officers, or other staff members, or of the individuals who read and commented on the original and updated study.

Robert D. Calkins
President

September 1964
The Brookings Institution
1775 Massachusetts Avenue, N.W.
Washington, D.C.

Contents

Tables

Charts

Introduction

THE AMERICAN PUBLIC simultaneously holds two contradictory views of big business. The products, jobs, and investment opportunities afforded by large-scale enterprise have found ready acceptance by the majority of the people. The managerial and technical know-how of the large corporations has also been recognized as a major resource in national defense. But these considerations have not lessened the fear that business has expanded beyond the requirements of advancing technology and efficiency, and that it wields a power too great to be trusted in private hands without public regulation. Many Americans with a faith in private enterprise nevertheless fear that increasing concentration of business organization is hastening the demise of capitalism.

The public image of big business has been influenced by the early history of its development through mergers of competitors and by the investigations and litigations in which the giant corporations have been defendants against public charges of monopoly and abuse of economic power. Most economic theorists have been reared in a tradition that considers competition in relation to a pure or "ideal" market—one in which no individual buyer or seller can have an appreciable influence on price or on the adjustments of supply and demand through the price mechanism. Departures from this market were considered as forms of monopolistic competition, becoming monopoly as buyers or sellers extended their influence on price and on the market adjustments of supply and demand. Much of the literature of big business has been focused on antitrust aspects of industrial organization and conduct, or on transgressions of the traditional norms of competition.

In recent years, there has been increasing dissatisfaction with such a setting for the study of big business. Concepts of dynamic

1

and workable competition have gained interest as points of departure, but criteria have not yet been developed which take into account the combined objectives that competition is intended to serve, nor have such criteria been applied to the prevailing practices of modern industry.

This study is concerned mainly with the nonregulated sector of big business. It deals with that field of private enterprise represented by firms engaged in manufacturing, mining, construction, distribution, and business services. Big business here includes multi-unit corporations with activities spread over the national market and, usually, international markets as well. Excluded from the study are the utilities and financial corporations operating under public franchises that grant certain immunities from competition and delimit the range of competitive action in those fields.

Altogether the sector of big business here considered generally accounts for a substantial fraction of the output or sales in its respective industries, and the decisions of the companies in this sector have a significant effect on the markets in which they chiefly operate. These corporate giants make up a segment of the American economy that must itself be competitive if the American system of private enterprise is to survive and flourish as a competitive system.

The problem of formulating public policy has been to find a way to retain the benefits of large business units without weakening the competitive forces that are an essential part of the enterprise system. This study is neither directly concerned with formulating such a policy nor with offering recommendations of specific laws affecting big business. The search for a better-informed rationale for the appraisal of public policy toward big business has its justification in the strategic impact of that sector on the economy, and in the significant conflicts and inconsistencies that have yet to be resolved. To the extent that objective empirical analysis can yield consistent and intelligent conclusions about the big business issue, it can contribute toward a broadening of common ground and a narrowing of the tendency to work at cross-purposes.

Thus the first step is a review of the changing facets of the big business issue as they have appeared on the American scene over the past three-quarters of a century. Attention is drawn to the main counts on which big business has from time to time been adjudged inimical to the healthy development of the private enterprise system. In Chapter 2, an attempt is made to define the prerequisites of industrial competition, and to suggest criteria by which the competitiveness of the economic order can be tested. The goals that are commonly accepted as desirable results of competition are considered, and the market conditions with which competition and monopoly have been identified are explored. Relevant postulates of economic theory are briefly reviewed to see their implications for the appraisal of our present economic structure.

Chapters 3 through 7 deal with quantitative measures of the position of big business in the national economy. Measurement of bigness requires a re-examination of the conventional statistics of concentration. The shares of big business in various industries and product groups are considered. A separate analysis is presented in Chapter 7 of the changes in the relative position of the 100 largest industrials during the past six decades to show the extent to which they are entrenched as leaders in their respective industries and markets.

These statistical presentations provide the basis for the more qualitative analysis of big business that follows in Chapters 8 through 10. Changes are noted in particular aims and methods of competition as the scale of the enterprise is enlarged. These aims are traced in the pricing policies of big corporations and the market behavior with which they are associated. The practices that are characteristic of big business and have accounted for its more positive contributions are discussed. Consideration is given to the tendency for big business to produce a progressively wider range of goods and services, and to the implications of continuing integration and diversification.

A summary chapter sets forth the author's conclusions regarding the net contribution of big business to American enterprise. The nation's economic welfare is now dependent on the performance of a business sector in which big business has come to play a vital role. In the interests of continued economic growth, of improved technology, and an ever-widening range of new products and processes, it is essential that the analysis of big business not be colored by unquestioning approval or by prejudice. It is toward increased understanding in this important area, and toward improved analysis of related public policy, that this study is directed.

1

Development of
Public Opinion and Policy

FOR MORE THAN a half century, the control of big business has
been a major theme of public policy discussion in the United
States. The progress of that discussion can readily be traced
despite its shifting emphasis. Economic conditions and public
attitudes have influenced immediate objectives and modified
underlying assumptions and conceptions, but whether the controversy has centered on administered prices, as much seems to
today, or on the abuse of monopoly, as it did fifty or more years
ago, big business has remained a central target.

In the past, many of the practices of big business, including the
merger of former rivals, as well as market manipulations to enforce
or maintain monopoly, have generally been decried as being inconsistent with the nation's economic and social objectives. The
cure has been seen in legislation to promote competition. Competition itself, however, has been variously interpreted. At times,
practices denounced as monopolistic have in reality been distaste-
ful because they were aggressively competitive, and injured competitors have sought a modified rivalry and the elimination of
overly aggressive or "cutthroat" techniques. Emphasis has been
placed on the maintenance of competition through the suppression of "unfair" practices. More recently, attention has focused on
the possibility that monopoly has been acquired, not by the exercise of specific unfair practices, but simply by virtue of the ad-

5

vantages of large-scale enterprise. Concern has correspondingly centered on efforts to maintain an effective degree of competition where industry is dominated by relatively few firms.

Policy toward big business has in turn been influenced by the level of prosperity, as well as by war and other threats to the national peace of mind. It has also responded to changing social standards for judging the performance of business in general, and big business in particular.

Monopoly As a National Issue

Prior to World War I, big business was identified in the public mind with monopoly achieved by merger or by the outright elimination of competitors. Two lines of attack are discernible in the history of attempts to deal with this problem. One is the attack on those forms of business organization that meant control of industry-wide policy, directed first against trusts and holding companies, and later against financial oligarchies. The other, of course, is the drive against business practices designed to limit competition. The latter gradually broadened from an initial condemnation of only the most ruthless and predatory business practices to a more general barring of all forms of business action considered to fall within the category of "unfair competition."

The big business controversy in the United States first emerged as part of the transition of the country from an agrarian to an industrial economy following the Civil War. Mechanization and urbanization, shifts in population, and changes in consumption patterns were not accomplished without and, in fact, contributed to, severe economic maladjustments. American industry in its adolescence was only learning how to mass-produce. In addition, business units were motivated to expand not only for technological reasons, but also to obtain and provide better and more complete control of their respective markets. By 1890, the acquisition of market control through mergers and other methods of eliminating rivals had created enough concern to give rise to a demand for federal action.

Early Legislation

Antimonopoly laws already existed in a number of states in the 1890's, but were inapplicable to business activities that expanded or originated beyond state boundaries. Businessmen as well as farm and labor groups were aroused by combinations such as the sugar, whisky, and oil trusts. Secret railroad rebates and rampant and destructive discriminatory practices did not go unnoticed, especially by those directly affected. Although the Interstate Commerce Act of 1887 prohibited railroads from granting special rates and other preferences to large shippers, a wide range of other monopolistic or monopoly-promoting devices did not come within its scope. Of these, the trust agreement gained special prominence as a means of uniting independent firms under unified control.

Under the trust form of combination, or the "voting trust," as it came to be known, competing companies assigned their shares of voting stock to a board of trustees in return for certificates of trust. The central board, or trust, thus was enabled to make policy decisions with respect to prices and markets, as well as finance, on behalf of the firms whose stock it controlled. The trust agreements usually left operational policy to the individual participating companies; production economies were not substantial.

Both the Republican and Democratic platforms of 1888 included recommendations for antitrust legislation. The Republican plank declared its opposition to "all combinations of capital, organized in trusts or otherwise, to control arbitrarily the condition of trade among our citizens; . . . [and to] all schemes to oppress the people by undue charges on their supplies, or by unjust rates for the transportation of their products to market." The Democratic plank declared that "the interests of the people are betrayed when . . . trusts and combinations are permitted to exist, which, while unduly enriching the few that combine, rob the body of our citizens by depriving them of the benefits of natural competition."[1]

[1] Eliot Jones, *The Trust Problem in the United States* (Macmillan, 1928), pp. 318-19.

Federal jurisdiction over trusts and other forms of monopoly was asserted in 1890. A bill, bearing the name of Senator John Sherman, later to become the Sherman Act of 1890,[2] passed the Senate with one dissenting vote and the House without recorded vote.[3] Framed in broad and general terms, this legislation declared illegal "any contract, combination in restraint of trade or commerce among the several states or with foreign nations" and also provided, in Section 2, that "who shall monopolize or conspire to monopolize ... shall be deemed guilty of a misdemeanor." Passage of this legislation, together with condemnation of the Sugar Trust by the New York courts in 1890, and the Standard Oil Company of Ohio by the Ohio courts in 1892, marked the end of the voting trust as a device for business consolidation.[4] However, the growth of business empires was far from halted by legal sanctions against this particular form of combination.

The Great Era of Consolidation

Although slowed by the monetary crisis of the early 1890's, consolidation again found favor, this time facilitated by a New Jersey law (1889) permitting companies incorporated in that state to hold stock in other companies. This statute enabled promoters to substitute the holding company, or the outright merger, for the voting trust. The holding company differed from the trust primarily in that it actually owned a controlling interest in the stock of its subsidiary enterprises. Through this ownership, the holding company could select, or elect, directors who would in turn cooperate in supporting the central policies and directives of the parent company.

[2] 15 U.S.C. 1.

[3] Clair Wilcox, *Public Policies Toward Business* (Richard D. Irwin, 1955), p. 58.

[4] The Standard Oil Company was condemned on two counts. First, it was controlled and managed by the Standard Oil Trust of New York, thus violating the law of Ohio requiring that "a corporation should be controlled and managed by its directors in the interests of its own stockholders"; and second, the object of the Trust was "to establish a virtual monopoly of the business of producing petroleum, and of manufacturing, refining and dealing in it and all its products, throughout the entire country, and by which it might not merely control the production, but the price at its pleasure." See Jones, *op. cit.*, pp. 314-15.

In 1893, commercial failures, including bank failures, reached unprecedented proportions. Prevention of a recurrence of this experience provided an additional motive in the development of the holding company movement. The route to stability appeared to be through combination and integration. Earlier consolidations, like American Sugar Refining and Standard Oil, stood out for their ability to weather the crisis with relatively little harm.[5]

With the close of the century, business activity recovered. Exports were high; the balance of international payments was favorable. Increased savings, which could not now find an outlet in railroad expansion, provided an additional basis for corporate investment. The United States was no longer a minor power in the world economy. Key industries were established. The capital market was interested; industrial consolidation was attractive.[6]

The combined impact of these conditions was a spectacular consolidation movement near the turn of the century. In the six-year period 1898 to 1903, the public record showed 243 new industrial consolidations capitalized at more than $1 million each, with a combined capitalization of over $7 billion. Heading the list was the steel promotion which, as the United States Steel Corporation, by 1901 had absorbed eleven major independent companies with nearly 800 separate properties. This firm alone was capitalized at $1.37 billion. Two years before, the Standard Oil Company of New Jersey, modestly capitalized at $97.5 million, had merged 400 companies into an oil empire which by 1904 controlled an estimated 84 percent of the domestic sales and 90 percent of the American export of refined petroleum products. The Consolidated Tobacco Company, founded in 1901 as a security-holding corporation with an initial capital of $30 million, was by 1904 capitalized

[5] The American Sugar Refining Company, established in 1891, paid dividends equivalent to 22 percent of its high common stock capitalization in 1893, and continued with 12 percent in the six years thereafter. *Ibid.*, p. 121.

[6] The rising rate of such activity was reflected in the expansion of bank loans against securities. Reports of the Comptroller of the Currency show an increase in such loans from $627 million in 1896 to $1,519 million in 1904. See Harold G. Moulton, *The Formation of Capital* (Brookings Institution, 1935), App. Table 3, p. 196.

at slightly over $500 million. Of 92 major trusts considered by
John Moody in 1904, 78 were estimated to control more than 50
percent of the products in their respective fields; 26 controlled
80 percent or more.[7]

Antagonism against such consolidations ran high because most
were obvious mergers of competitors for the purpose of effecting
monopoly.[8] This antagonism was intensified by the evidence of
ruthless tactics against remaining rivals and new entrants.

There were, however, offsetting advantages. Though promoted
for financial control and financial profit, the new consolidations
frequently served as a means of bringing capital and management
resources together for technological advancement and more efficient industrial production. Sereno S. Pratt, a Wall Street jour-
nalist, noted this conflict in 1903:

> This concentration has its undoubted advantages. It is an eco-
> nomic evolution of tremendous power. It has, among other causes,
> enabled this country in the past twenty years to develop more wealth
> than in all the preceding years since the discovery of America. It
> may be argued, however, that this concentration is too high a price
> to pay even for benefits such as these. Concentration of the control
> of wealth certainly presents problems, the gravity of which it is
> impossible to conceal or evade.
>
> How to preserve the advantages of concentration and at the same
> time to get rid of its evils; how to prevent the waste of competition
> without destroying it; how to secure stability and strength without
> loss of individual liberty; how to permit the railroads to combine
> and at the same time to provide for government regulation of rates;
> how to make possible the achievement of great enterprises, without
> resort to methods involving the violation of law, and the corruption
> of legislatures; how to encourage promotion without the evils of
> over-capitalization and over-speculation; how to secure comprehen-

[7] John Moody, *The Truth About the Trusts* (Moody Publishing Co., 1904),
pp. 86, 97, 111, 132, 486-87.

[8] It is interesting, for example, that Moody quotes S. C. T. Dodd, solicitor of the
Standard Oil Company, as follows: "The term 'Trust' . . . has [now] obtained a
wider signification, and embraces every act, agreement, or combination of persons
or capital *believed to be done, made, or formed with the intent, power, or tendency
to monopolize business, to restrain or interfere with competitive trade, or to fix,
influence, or increase the price of commodities.*" Moody calls this "the best known
definition of the Trust." *Ibid.*, pp. xiii-xiv.

sive publicity without disclosure of proper trade secrets — these form the one large problem before us that overshadows and includes all others.[9]

Anxiety over the net effect of these new industrial empires was undoubtedly reinforced by a number of conspicuous promotional failures. Overcapitalization showed up in the fading market values of the securities floated by the new giants. In a summary of the results of thirty-one large promotions, the *Commercial and Financial Chronicle* in September 1900 reported that sixteen promotions, with capitalization ranging from $8 million to $16 million, had suffered declines in the value of their securities of such proportions that even underwriters receiving stock bonuses of from 50 percent to 100 percent suffered net losses.[10]

In addition, there were spectacular corporate failures. By 1903, the National Asphalt Company, formed in 1900 as an almost absolute monopoly, had collapsed. Reorganization of the wreckage was only partially successful. Similar failures attended efforts to achieve monopoly in bicycles, cordage, cotton duck yarns, glucose, malt, salt, leather, and starch.[11]

Action to Circumscribe Big Business

In 1903 Congress established the Bureau of Corporations to investigate the leading firms engaged in interstate or foreign commerce. The early reports of the bureau on the Standard Oil Company and the American Tobacco Company have been credited

[9] Sereno S. Pratt, "Who Owns the United States," *World's Week,* Vol. 7 (1903), p. 4266.

[10] *Commercial and Financial Chronicle,* Sept. 15, 1900.

[11] See Arthur S. Dewing, *Corporate Promotions and Reorganizations* (Harvard University Press, 1920) for an extended account of the rise and fall of a number of important combines, including, in addition to the National Asphalt Company, the United States Leather Company, which at the time of its formation (1893) had a bigger capitalization than any other industrial combine; the National Cordage Company and the Glucose Sugar Refining Company, each of which controlled 90 percent or more of the output of its industry; the National Starch Company, which at one time accounted for 85 percent of domestic production; and the National Salt Company and the American Bicycle Company, controlling between 65 and 70 percent of their respective industries. Eliot Jones also cites asphalt, linseed oil, newsprint paper, paper bags, cutlery and silverware, wallpaper and whisky. *Op. cit.,* p. 539.

with supplying to the Department of Justice the main factual basis for the later dissolution suits against these companies.[12] Congress also appropriated a half million dollars for more vigorous enforcement of the Sherman Act and amended the Interstate Commerce Act to extend penalties for freight rate discrimination to favored shippers, as well as to the carriers. These measures, coming at a time when the stock market was in a mild recession, marked the close of a second era of spectacular business consolidation.

President Theodore Roosevelt took an active and aggressive interest in these developments. Underlying his efforts was a fundamental distinction, and an important one, between combinations and consolidations artificially created for the exploitation of monopoly, and consolidations that were, in his phrase, "the results of natural causes in the business world." Concerning the growth of great corporate enterprises, and their impact on economic life, Roosevelt's first message to Congress argued:

> The process has aroused much antagonism, a great part of which is wholly without warrant. It is not true that as the rich have grown richer the poor have grown poorer. On the contrary, never before has the average man, the wage-earner, the farmer, the small trader, been so well off as in this country and at the present time . . . *Much of the legislation directed at the trusts would have been exceedingly mischievous had it not also been entirely ineffective.*[13]

At the same time, Roosevelt advocated safeguards against the abuses of overcapitalization, monopoly, corporate interlockings, and financial dictatorship of industries. As a prelude to intelligent regulation, he recommended disclosure, full and complete, of the operation of large corporations:

> Artificial bodies such as corporations and joint stock or other associations, depending upon any statutory law for their existence or privileges, should be subject to proper governmental supervision,

[12] Thomas C. Blaisdell, Jr., *The Federal Trade Commission: An Experiment in the Control of Business* (Columbia University Press, 1932), p. 108.

[13] Italics supplied. See Theodore Roosevelt, Message to the Senate and House of Representatives, December 3, 1901, *Messages and Papers of the Presidents*, Vol. 15, pp. 6643-44, 6645.

and full and accurate information as to their operations should be made public regularly at reasonable intervals.[14]

In a later message to Congress, he recommended elaboration of the Sherman Act to distinguish between reasonable and unreasonable combinations and market practices.[15]

Legislation incorporating these recommendations did not appear until later. Nevertheless, the Roosevelt administration marked the first effective effort by the federal government to challenge big business through the courts. Suits initiated by the Department of Justice between March 1903 and July 1907 led to dissolution of four major consolidations: Northern Securities (a railroad holding company), Standard Oil of New Jersey, American Tobacco Company, and E. I. du Pont de Nemours Powder Company. There was general agreement in these decisions that the Sherman Act intended the court to go behind the form of the combination, "the garb in which such acts were clothed," to find the facts that disclosed illegal restraint.[16] But the Supreme Court shared the difficulties of the layman in trying to reconcile legitimate growth of the great business corporation with domination of the market and injury of small competitors. As it reached for a rule to distinguish legitimate from illegitimate restraints of trade, the court was divided.

Interpretation of the Sherman Act

The major provisions of the Sherman Act, it will be recalled, are contained in two sections: Section 1 forbidding contracts, conspiracies, and combinations in restraint of trade, and Section 2 making it unlawful to monopolize, or to attempt, conspire, or combine to monopolize. The first has proven by far the more power-

---

14 *Ibid.*, p. 6646.

15 *Ibid.*, Vol. 16, pp. 7421-22.

16 ". . . The first and second Sections of the law [Sherman Act], when taken together, embrace every conceivable act which could possibly come within the spirit or purpose of the law, without regard to the garb in which such acts were clothed." Chief Justice White, in *United States v. American Tobacco Co.*, 221 U.S. 181 (1911).

ful; the courts have consistently found it easier to act in the face of combinations or conspiracies than when confronted with the complete consolidations of accomplished monopolies.

Literally interpreted, the act by its very language forbids "every contract, combination ... or conspiracy, in restraint of trade." A looser interpretation, later to become familiar as the *rule of reason,* would forbid only unreasonable restraint. This rule of reason had precedent in earlier common law decisions where restrictive contracts judged reasonable within the context of some other and primary lawful purpose had been held enforceable through the courts. Early argument before the courts centered on the question whether the Sherman Act was new and overriding legislation, or merely a formal extension of the common law.

The case for literal and unequivocal interpretation of the act, an interpretation characteristic of the first twenty years of experience with this statute, is found in the decisions of Mr. Justice Harlan. "The Act," Judge Harlan argued in his majority decree of Northern Securities in 1904, "is not limited to restraints of interstate or international trade or commerce that are unreasonable in their nature, but embraces all direct restraints imposed by any combination, conspiracy or monopoly upon such trade or commerce."[17] In this case, however, the dissenting opinion of Chief Justice White and the concurrent dissent by Justice Oliver Wendell Holmes foreshadowed the rule of reason:

> According to popular speech, every concern monopolizes whatever business it does, and if that business is trade between two States it monopolizes a part of the trade among the States. Of course, the statute does not forbid that. It does not mean that all business must cease.
>
> ... the Act of Congress makes no discrimination according to size. Size has nothing to do with the matter. A monopoly of "any part" of commerce among the States is unlawful. The supposed company [Northern Securities] would have owned lines that might have been competing — probably the present one does. But the Act of Congress

[17] 193 U.S. 331-32. Harlan also made the point that Congress, after due consideration, had refused amendment of the act to exempt efforts to reduce "mutually destructive competition."

will not be construed to mean the universal disintegration of society into single men, each at war with all the rest, or even the prevention of all further combinations for a common end.

There is a natural feeling that somehow or other that statute meant to strike at combinations great enough to cause just anxiety . . . while it viewed such little ones as I have supposed with just indifference. This notion, it may be said, somehow breathes from the pores of the Act, although it seems to be contradicted in every way by the words in detail. And it has occurred to me that it might be that when a combination reached a certain size it might have attributed to it more of the character of a monopoly merely by virtue of its size than would be attributed to a smaller one.[18]

In 1911 the Supreme Court handed down decisions in the Standard Oil of New Jersey and American Tobacco cases. The rule of reason found formal support in the majority decision of Chief Justice White:

The Statute . . . evidenced the intent not to restrain the right to make and enforce contracts, whether resulting from combinations or otherwise, which did not unduly restrain . . . commerce, but to protect that commerce from being restrained by methods . . . which would constitute an interference — that is, an undue restraint.[19]

Dissolution of the petroleum and tobacco combines was dictated, not by the mere fact that restraint existed, but by practices deemed to constitute undue or unreasonable restraint combined with a belief that nothing short of dissolution would constitute an effective remedy.

The growth of big business was not, however, prohibited by these dissolution cases, although the wide discretion assumed by the courts under the rule of reason introduced a distinct element of uncertainty. It is instructive in this regard to follow the efforts of Judge Gary, chairman of the nation's largest industrial corporation, to act as big brother of the steel industry and forestall criticism of the overwhelming position of United States Steel in that industry.

[18] *Ibid.*, p. 407.
[19] *Standard Oil of New Jersey v. United States*, 221 U.S. 1, 60 (1911).

The "Gary Dinners," begun following the financial panic of 1907, were held for purposes of exchange of information among competing steel men to help stabilize prices and avoid "demoralization" of the industry. Public criticism of these dinners as a vehicle for fixing price and quota agreements drew from Judge Gary this statement of the place of the corporate giant in the social order:

> Large corporations [he wrote Attorney General Bonaparte in February, 1908] are confronted with two extreme opposite points of view. Public sentiment as well as the laws are opposed to combinations in restraint of trade which I suppose would include positive agreements between large interests to maintain prices, restrict output, divide territory, etc., etc. in accordance with the practice of other countries. On the other hand, public sentiment is bitterly opposed to such competition as will result in the destruction of the business of competitors whose opportunities or resources are weak in comparison, because in the end it is certain to secure an absolute monopoly and in the meantime bring great harm to the employees and others.
>
> We have endeavored to maintain a position between the two extremes. We are perfectly satisfied to limit the amount of our business to our proportion of capacity and to do everything possible we can to promote the interests of our competitors; and by frequent meetings and the interchange of opinions we have thus far been able to accomplish this result without making any agreements of any kind.[20]

Another example of the paternal attitude of the "good trust" was furnished by Judge Gary shortly after initiation of the Standard Oil and du Pont suits:

> It is clear that the United States Steel Corporation, with its extensive resources, could use its giant strength, like other corporations, to crush competition. But in the end would the game be worth the candle? The Corporation would become an object of attack. In my judgment such a policy would be the undoing of our Corporation in which billions of dollars are invested.[21]

[20] Ida M. Tarbell, *The Life of Elbert H. Gary* (D. Appleton & Company, 1925), p. 212.
[21] *Ibid.*, p. 205.

At no point did Judge Gary recognize that the assumption, by the industry's largest corporation, of an obligation to hold an umbrella over its competitors was incompatible with the principle of a market-determined economy. His efforts to stay within what he conceived to be the legal limits of the Sherman Act did not forestall suit by the federal government against the United States Steel Corporation in 1911, charging it with monopoly of the industry. It is significant, however, that the government failed to win its suit. The court found that Big Steel had become a "good trust"—that it had leaned backwards not to injure competitors. "The law," said the court, "does not make mere size an offense . . . [but] . . . requires overt acts . . . ." This company had "resorted to none of the brutalities or tyrannies that the cases illustrate of other combinations . . . ."[22] It was only later that the effect of Judge Gary's forebearance was evidenced in the relatively slow growth of his corporation. And to the successors of Judge Gary, it was painfully obvious that his management of U.S. Steel had overestimated the corporation's superiority and underestimated the capacity of other firms in the industry to challenge the leader with new technology and more effective offerings. Legal success in 1920 was not without its costs.

Definition and Control of Predatory Practices

The discretion exercised by the courts in these actions increased the unwillingness of Congress to leave in the hands of the judiciary alone the determination of what was reasonable and unreasonable. The consequent step was an attempt to remove the uncertainties of law by specifying in more precise terms the forms of financial integration and the types of trade practices deemed to be in restraint of trade. The drive to define illegal practices took legislative form in the Wilson Administration. There were two aspects to this development. The first was an effort to check the growth of the great financial oligarchies. The second attempted to distinguish clearly legitimate from illegitimate competitive business practice.

[22] *United States v. U. S. Steel Corp.*, 251 U.S. 417, 441 (1920).

CONTROL OF FINANCIAL "OLIGARCHIES". The presidential campaign of 1912 emphasized the line of cleavage between Wall Street and Main Street. Woodrow Wilson focused on the "money trusts," contrasting natural productive growth through competitive efficiency with bigness artificially created through financial manipulation. "A trust," he said, "is an arrangement to get rid of competition, and a big business is a business that has survived competition by conquering in the field of intelligence and economy."[23]

Shortly after Wilson took office, congressional sentiment to discourage business manipulation through high finance was spurred by the report of the Pujo (House Banking and Currency) Committee which pointed to a

> . . . well-defined identity and community of interest between a few leaders of finance . . . held together through stockholdings, interlocking directorates, and other forms of domination over banks, trust companies, railroads, public service and industrial corporations, and which has resulted in a vast and growing concentration of control of money in the hands of a comparatively few men.[24]

This determination to decentralize financial power was evident in the Federal Reserve Act of 1913, particularly in its provision for autonomous regional Federal Reserve banks.[25] This legislation was a modification of the original central bank plan previously prepared by the Senate Finance (Aldrich) Committee.[26]

Legislative measures to hold down the "communities of interest" created through stock ownership and control were also embodied in the Clayton and Federal Trade Commission Acts of 1914.[27] The former prohibited the acquisition by one corporation of the stock or shares of another corporation "where the effect of such acquisition may be to substantially lessen competition" between the two, or "tend to create a monopoly of any line of com-

---

[23] Woodrow Wilson, *The New Freedom* (Doubleday and Page, 1921), p. 180.

[24] *Money Trust Investigation*, Report of the House Banking and Currency Committee, 62 Cong. 3 sess. (1913), Vol. 3, p. 130.

[25] 12 U.S.C. 222.

[26] E. A. Goldenweiser, *American Monetary Policy* (McGraw-Hill, 1951), pp. 70-110.

[27] 15 U.S.C. 13; 15 U.S.C. 41.

merce," and placed similar restrictions on companies acquiring control of two or more competing corporations. Interlocking directorates among competing companies (non-financial) where any one had a net worth in excess of $1 million were outlawed.

Powers of investigation granted to the five-man commission under the Federal Trade Commission Act included the power to require annual or special reports "furnishing to the commission such information as it may require as to the organization, business, conduct, practices, management, and relation to other corporations, partnerships, and individuals of the respective corporations filing such reports or answers in writing."[28]

DEFINING UNFAIR COMPETITION. Complementing this program to decentralize the financial concentration was an effort to reduce the uncertainty in business circles regarding what constituted monopolistic or unfair competitive practices. President Wilson expressed the belief that monopolistic practices could not only be defined, but could be "explicitly and item by item forbidden by statute in such terms as will practically eliminate uncertainty."[29] It was, however, realized through extended congressional hearings on both the Clayton and Federal Trade Commission bills that no listing could keep up with changing practice. Congress instead gave power to administrative agencies to determine unfair practices and set limits within which business could legally move. The Clayton Act specifically prohibited price discrimination among customers and exclusive and tying contracts where the effect of such discrimination or contractual arrangements "may be to substantially lessen competition or tend to create a monopoly in any line of commerce."[30] The Federal Trade Commission Act simply outlawed "unfair methods of competition in commerce."

Subsequent events have demonstrated the difficulties in carrying out the intentions of antitrust and the literally innumerable ways in which the law might be circumvented. The position of the Standard Oil enterprises following the dissolution of the

[28] 15 U.S.C. 46.
[29] *President Wilson's State Papers and Addresses* (The Review of Reviews Company, 1917), p. 52.
[30] 15 U.S.C. 13.

parent company illustrates the difficulty of abolishing their interdependence by legal adjudication. The fiat of the courts did not limit the size of the separate pieces of the original Standard Oil Company nor did it prevent their becoming much larger than the combination that had been splintered. Nevertheless, on the eve of World War I, the administration felt that it had made substantial progress toward meeting the problem of the money trust and of the unfair competitive acts of big business. Following the passage of the Federal Trade Commission and Clayton Acts, President Woodrow Wilson had this to say in a public address:

> . . . Nobody is henceforth going to be afraid of or suspicious of any business merely because it is big. If my judgment is correct, nobody has been suspicious of any business merely because it was big; but they have been suspicious whenever they thought that the bigness was being used to take an unfair advantage. We all have to admit that it is easier for a big fellow to take advantage of you than for a little fellow to take advantage of you; therefore, we instinctively watch the big fellow with a little closer scrutiny than we watch the little fellow. But, bond having been given for the big fellow . . . that he will keep the peace, we do not have to spend our time and waste our energy watching him. The conditions of confidence being established, nobody . . . is going to throw a stone at him simply because he is a favorable target — always provided there is fair dealing and real service.[31]

Big Business in World War I and the 1920's

World War I marked the end of one era of big business. It was an era in which industrial empires had been built through trusts, holding companies, and direct mergers. Great financial power in the hands of a few men controlled production and guided the functioning of a host of key markets. It was a period of both private and public education in the risks as well as the economic advantages of corporate consolidation. It was also a period that revealed practical limitations on governmental efforts to delineate legitimate organization and practices.

The decades following World War I saw the rise of a more

[31] Wilson, *State Papers and Addresses*, p. 100.

rationally developed industrial giant, the large integrated corporation of coordinated management. Emphasis of public policy shifted. How was concentration of economic power in a few such undertakings to be limited without also penalizing technical efficiency and economic growth?

From the beginning of World War I to the end of the 1920's, the course of events evoked a more favorable public attitude toward large-scale enterprise and the exploitation of its potential. The war itself seriously impeded any full-scale launching of the Wilsonian program for defining fair competition or for the dismemberment of large-scale corporate networks. In the more compelling interest of mobilizing economic resources for war, the government encouraged integration. The War Industries Board fostered the pooling of orders with negotiated terms and fixed prices. Emphasizing joint mobilization by industries, the Board worked largely through industry trade associations.

This deviation from the letter and the spirit of antitrust met with some hesitancy in business circles. Judge Gary, on behalf of the United States Steel Corporation, requested an opinion by the Attorney General on the legality of what he feared as "inevitable consequences" of the unified effort that the War Industries Board and other governmental agencies were demanding.[32] The elimination of price competition impelled Charles Evans Hughes to say that "the war has compelled cooperation, and the Government, under this compulsion, has fostered what it previously denounced as criminal."[33]

Emphasis on Cooperation

The fear of unsettled markets immediately after World War I led to adoption of a policy directed toward economic stabilization rather than freer competition. A recession in 1919, followed by an inflationary boom with a severe setback in 1920-21, brought suggestions for business cooperation to reduce the violence of these fluctuations in trade, employment, and prices. Trade as-

[32] Grosvenor B. Clarkson, *Industrial America in the World War* (Houghton Mifflin, 1923), p. 313.

[33] Henry R. Seager, Charles A. Gulick, Jr., *Trust and Corporation Problems* (Harper, 1929), p. 306.

sociations were active in enlisting the aid of the government toward that end. The Fordney-McCumber tariff restored a high level of protective duties to check the unsettling effect of the postwar inflow of foreign goods. Herbert Hoover, as Secretary of Commerce, regarded it as a primary function of his department to help maintain stable business conditions. Under his leadership the department fostered conferences of industrial groups to stimulate cooperative effort in market analysis, standardization, and research as aids in reducing maladjustments between supply and demand and in tempering cyclical fluctuations.[34]

Concern for stability during the Harding and Coolidge administrations became less prominent with the accelerated industrial expansion of succeeding years. The vast increase in capital formation extended to virtually all lines of industry. Expanding foreign markets for American goods were sustained by the large extension of credit for the rehabilitation and reconstruction of Europe after the Reparation Agreement (Dawes Plan) of 1924. In the domestic economy, the war had built up a backlog of unsatisfied requirements for durable consumer goods, housing, and business construction. Technological development, whether postponed by the war, as in automobiles, or stimulated by the war, as in chemicals, gathered momentum. Annual private gross capital formation rose from $10.3 billion in 1922 to $17.6 billion in 1929.[35]

Renewal of Expansion and Mergers

In this favorable political and economic climate, big business experienced another major consolidation movement.[36] Giant firms appeared in the automotive, farm machinery, motion picture, chemical, and electric industries, as well as in related areas. This

---

[34] U. S. Department of Commerce, *Tenth Annual Report of the Secretary of Commerce* (1922), pp. 29-32 and succeeding *Annual Reports* to 1928.

[35] Board of Governors of the Federal Reserve System, *Federal Reserve Bulletin*, Vol. 31 (September 1945), p. 873. This compares with a $5.7 billion annual average of gross capital formation for the decade 1904-13 ($10.7 billion in equivalent 1929 dollars). Simon S. Kuznets, *National Product Since 1869* (National Bureau of Economic Research, 1946), p. 115.

[36] According to Markham, "Between 1919 and 1930 nearly 12,000 public utility, banking, manufacturing, and mining concerns disappeared from the American

growth was further stimulated by a booming stock market, and a re-emergence of the banks as a major factor in security flotations and promotions. In 1930 bank affiliates sponsored 54.4 percent of all new securities issued.[37]

The industrial mergers of the 1920's were of a different type from those of 1900. Some firms, such as Chrysler, were formed by a merging of smaller competitors to produce a single large corporation to meet the challenge of industry leaders. Others, such as Ford, further integrated to acquire their own sources of supply or better to coordinate similar productive processes. In general, however, the new consolidations, unlike those characteristic of many mergers at the beginning of the century, were not primarily designed to achieve sole domination of particular markets. Consolidations tended no longer to be limited to mergers within the branches of industry where the parent companies operated. Large diversified corporations appeared in the food industry, chemicals, electrical equipment, and in retail marketing. These corporations, huge in themselves, were frequently responsible for only a small part of the total output of most of their products.

Consolidation was further encouraged by court decisions that size as such, even when it involved control of over 80 percent of some lines of production, as in the case of United States Steel in 1920,[38] could not be held to constitute violation of the antitrust

---

economy through mergers, more than twice the number of *plants* absorbed in all the industrial combinations recorded up to 1904 . . . . The 11,852 absorptions included approximately 2,100 mergers, or about five times the number of mergers recorded for the earlier wave. (Jesse W. Markham, "Survey of the Evidence and Findings on Mergers, in National Bureau of Economic Research, *Business Concentration and Price Policy,* Princeton University Press, 1955, p. 168.) The merger wave of the 1920's was not small. However, for reasons developed below, and also because these mergers tended disproportionately to represent the utilities and financial areas, this merger wave is generally considered to be of substantially less importance from a public policy standpoint than the monopoly-oriented merger movement of the late nineteenth century. See also M. A. Adelman, "The Measurement of Industrial Concentration," in Richard B. Heflebower and George W. Stocking (eds.), *Readings in Industrial Organization and Public Policy* (Richard D. Irwin, Inc., 1958), pp. 40-43.

[37] Ray B. Westerfield, *Money, Credit and Banking* (Ronald Press, 1937), p. 339.

[38] George W. Stocking, Myron W. Watkins, *Monopoly and Free Enterprise* (Twentieth Century Fund, 1951), p. 38.

laws. Judicial interpretation held that abuse of power must be proved. Small business was prospering, and these decisions appear to have aroused little discontent.

The National Bureau of Economic Research, reporting to the Hoover Committee on Recent Economic Changes, noted this change in public attitudes:

> The great corporate development of business enterprise . . . has gone on to new heights. It may be creating, as some think, a new type of social organization, but in any case the open-mindedness of the public, and of the state which is its instrument, toward this growing power of business corporations appears to be novel in American history.[39]

The era from World War I to the end of the 1920's may be considered an interlude of increasing public faith in the efficiency of big business and its resourcefulness in stimulating economic progress.

Public Planning for Economic Security

The crash of 1929 abruptly halted the flow of capital into larger corporate units. The prolonged depression that followed shook public confidence in the efficiency of large-scale enterprise, in the economic justification of its expansion, and in its contribution to stability of output and employment. A series of exposures of poor business judgment, if not moral delinquency, undermined the faith the captains of industry had built during the 1920's, and dramatized the opportunities for manipulation of corporate structures. The collapse of elaborate pyramids established by public utility holding companies further reflected adversely on the whole big business sector.[40]

[39] National Bureau of Economic Research, *Recent Economic Changes*, Vol. 1 (McGraw-Hill, 1929), pp. 11-12.

[40] The hearings on the crash before the Senate Committee on Banking and Currency, reported about three years following the collapse of the stock market in

The Hoover Administration first tried to check the downward course of business through emergency measures. The President, in November 1929, sought the aid of the leading corporation executives in maintaining production schedules and wage levels. But voluntary action by individual concerns soon proved ineffective. The President's message to Congress of December 1931 called for public measures, in particular for the formation of a government-sponsored financing agency to bolster the capital structure of railroads, insurance companies, farm mortgage associations, and other strategic institutions. Public loans for self-liquidating public works were also recommended. The Reconstruction Finance Corporation was established in January 1932. Meanwhile, the decline persisted, and a further revision of the role of government in the national economy followed the 1932 election.

The National Industrial Recovery Act,[41] passed in June 1933 after nearly four years of depression, had objectives extending beyond purely immediate recovery. President Roosevelt had asked "that the Congress provide for the machinery necessary for a great cooperative movement throughout all industry in order to obtain wide re-employment, to shorten the working week, to pay a decent wage for the shorter week, and to prevent unfair competition and disastrous overproduction." [42]

On signing the act, the President said:

> It represents a supreme effort to stabilize for all time the many factors which make for the prosperity of the Nation and the preservation of American standards.
>
> Its goal is the assurance of a reasonable profit to industry and living wages for labor with the elimination of the piratical methods

---

1929, called forth comments of the following order in contemporary journals: "We wonder if it is really possible to read what . . . all the 'good' and the 'bad' capitalists did in the heyday of American prosperity and still have any confidence in capitalism. Surely it must be increasingly apparent that the system is morally as well as economically bankrupt and that it corrupts the souls of its beneficiaries as much as it destroys the bodies of its victims." (Editorial in *The World Tomorrow*, Vol. 16, March 8, 1933, p. 220.)

[41] 43 Stat. 195.

[42] *The Public Papers and Addresses of Franklin D. Roosevelt*, Vol. 2 (Random House, 1938), p. 202.

and practices which have not only harassed honest business but also contributed to the ills of labor.[43]

Although the Sherman Act remained on the statute books, NIRA provided for means of collaboration clearly at variance with the intention of the Sherman Act. Industries were placed under codes that abandoned the traditional emphasis on a free flow of goods and services with flexible competitive pricing. Direct government sanctions were applied to prevent "cut-throat underselling by selfish competitors unwilling to join in such a public-spirited endeavor." [44] In short, industry was asked to police itself, under the eye of the government, to achieve that stabilization of production and prices which the Sherman Act had sought to check.

The Recovery Act was declared unconstitutional in May 1935. The spirit of reform, however, continued. The National Labor Relations Act of 1935 [45] reinforced the principle of collective bargaining under government sponsorship. Dealer associations lobbied for fair trade laws preserving the price-fixing measures of the NRA codes. Pressure toward uniform pricing was buttressed at the federal level by passage of the Robinson-Patman Act in 1936,[46] amending and strengthening the anti-price-discrimination provisions of the Clayton Act. The Miller-Tydings Amendment [47] provided an exemption from the Sherman Act for fair trade contracts authorized by state law. Other special legislation continued to insulate large segments of the economy from the rigors of market competition. Agriculture, bituminous coal, and crude oil were each supported in one way or another by government control of price and output. Social security legislation to reduce hardship and cushion purchasing power during unemployment and old age was passed in 1935. All these confirmed the new emphasis on the function of government as provider of economic stability and security.

43 *Ibid.*, p. 246.
44 *Ibid.*, p. 202.
45 29 U.S.C. 167.
46 15 U.S.C. 21.
47 15 U.S.C. 1.

These actions and attitudes were accompanied by a greatly expanded program of public regulation and scrutiny. Early in 1933, an effort was made to force separation of banking and investment facilities to guard against recurrence of the financial license of the 1920's. The Securities Act of that year and the Securities Exchange Act of 1934 [48] helped to implement the principle that the operations of large-scale enterprise are a matter of public concern. These acts required full disclosure of pertinent data connected with the public offering of securities, the registration of securities issues, the filing of annual reports to stockholders, and the submission of financial statements and related information, including the interests held by executive officers and large stockholders in their companies or in affiliated enterprises.

The Securities and Exchange Commission (SEC) was given power to regulate the stock markets in an attempt to reduce the manipulation of corporate security prices by insiders, and also to "prevent the diversion into securities transactions of a disproportionate amount of the Nation's credit resources." [49] To support the SEC in its discouragement of speculation, the Federal Reserve Board was given the authority to set margin requirements on stock purchases, while the SEC itself was authorized to set limits on borrowing by stock exchange members, brokers, and dealers.

The Public Utility Holding Company Act of 1935 [50] extended detailed governmental regulation to gas and electric utilities, and corrected the abuses to which the jerry-built holding company had proved susceptible. The SEC was given the responsibility of reorganizing and simplifying the financial structure of public utilities. Meanwhile, the traditional forms of regulation in the public utility field were extended to new areas of large-scale enterprise by the Communications Act of 1934, the Federal Power Act of 1935, the Motor Carrier Act of 1935, the Natural Gas Act of 1938, and the Civil Aeronautics Act of 1938. [51]

[48] 15 U.S.C. 77; 15 U.S.C. 78.
[49] *Fifth Annual Report of the Securities and Exchange Commission* (1939), p. 35.
[50] 15 U.S.C. 79.
[51] 47 U.S.C. 151-609; 16 U.S.C. 791-825; 49 U.S.C. 301-327; 15 U.S.C. 717; 49 U.S.C. 401-722.

Resistance to the Concentration of Economic Power

After the Recovery Act was declared unconstitutional and the National Recovery Administration (NRA) liquidated, there was a resurgence of antitrust activity, stemming both from the Department of Justice and from the Federal Trade Commission.[52] Several convictions were obtained for the continuance of market practices that had been actively encouraged under NRA.[53] Nevertheless, the general belief persisted that the need for protection against the unregulated pursuit of private enterprise was greater than in previous decades.

From the view that big business was vested with a public interest because it sought capital from the public and affected large segments of the economy, the government was drawn into the position that bigness was of itself a threat to the survival of the competitive economy.

Critique by the Economists

In the development of this position, an influential factor was the work of economists who submitted the structure of industry to critical review. The climate of public opinion following the crash of 1929 was receptive to a re-examination of the American business system.

As early as 1928, work had begun on two important studies of the evolving business structure and its impact on competitive markets. *The Modern Corporation and Private Property*, by Adolf A. Berle, Jr. and Gardiner C. Means, was published in

---

[52] The number of suits brought by the Department of Justice under the Sherman Act rose from 10 in 1934 to 114 in 1940. For the same years, the number of restraint-of-competition cases handled by the FTC and decided by the courts increased from 5 to 51.

[53] For example, see *U. S. v. Socony Vacuum et al.*, 310 U.S. 150 (1940). This case was brought before the courts when twelve major oil companies continued the NRA practice of concerted buying of distress gasoline that flooded midwestern markets. The Supreme Court upheld a conviction of collusive interference, even though the interference was defended as reasonable and proved to be of only limited effectiveness.

1932; *The Decline of Competition* by Arthur R. Burns in 1936.

Berle and Means called attention to the influence of the large integrated corporation and to the progressive concentration of wealth, income, and economic power within the 200 largest corporations. To dramatize the potential of further big business expansion, they projected the trend as follows:

> If the wealth of the large corporations and that of all corporations should each continue to increase for the next twenty years at its average annual rate for the twenty years from 1909 to 1929, 70 percent of all corporate activity would be carried on by 200 corporations by 1950. If the more rapid rates of growth from 1924 to 1929 were maintained for the next twenty years, 85 percent of corporate wealth would be held by 200 huge units. It would take only forty years at the 1909-1929 rates or only thirty years at the 1924-1929 rates for all corporate activity and practically all industrial activity to be absorbed by two hundred giant companies. If the indicated growth of the large corporations and of the national wealth were to be effective from now until 1950, half of the national wealth would be under the control of big companies at the end of that period.[54]

Burns dealt with the prevalence in mass production industries of market controls inconsistent with the traditional concept of free competition. The restoration of the earlier forms of competition, with the loss of the technical benefits of large-scale production, he regarded as impractical. Hence, "All efforts to deal with the unsatisfactoriness of the outcome of the present organization of industry lead in the end to the acceptance by the state, in some form or other, of responsibility for participating in the exercise of economic power." [55]

Similar inferences could be drawn from the work of contemporary theorists. Reacting against classical theories of perfect competition, they constructed models to represent the behavior of the market and the firm under various patterns of "imperfect" or "monopolistic" competition. These were contrasted with free,

---

[54] *The Modern Corporation and Private Property* (Commerce Clearing House, 1932), pp. 40-41.

[55] *The Decline of Competition* (McGraw-Hill, 1936), p. 529.

market-determined competition. John Maynard Keynes cast doubt on the capacity of an autonomous market economy, unassisted by government spending, to maintain full employment. His American followers declared that capitalism had encountered a period of "secular stagnation."[56]

It was a short step from these explorations to a new political scrutiny of business structure and market behavior. After 1935 the administration had need of a rationale to bridge the gap between the government-sponsored centralization under NRA and a return to the rules of private competition. Big business policy was in part held responsible for the depth and persistence of the depression. The expansion of big business and its market leadership were felt to have deprived the economy of the automatic flexibility required to stimulate a natural recovery from the crisis. Monopoly restriction of output, price rigidity, reduction of purchasing power, and accentuation of the business cycle were regarded as components of the underlying threat of concentration.

Two prescriptions seemed to be indicated. First, in the interest of maintaining market flexibility, excessive concentration of business power should be eliminated. Second, insofar as the economic system appeared incapable of self-adjustment, it would become the direct function of government to restore the economic balance and to underwrite continuing high production and employment.

On the other hand, there was full realization that any comprehensive change in the antitrust laws, or in the structure of competition itself, would have to be predicated on broader knowledge

---

[56] Keynes found the key to "the paradox of poverty in the midst of plenty" — idle men and resources while wants remain unsatisfied — in an "insufficiency of effective demand" for consumption and investment goods. This insufficiency, he argued, was likely to be chronic in advanced economies already rich in capital. He concluded that the "State will have to exercise a guiding influence on the propensity to consume partly through its scheme of taxation, partly by fixing the rate of interest, and partly, perhaps, in other ways. Furthermore . . . I conceive . . . that a somewhat comprehensive socialization of investment will prove the only means of securing an approximation to full employment." *The General Theory of Employment, Interest and Money* (Harcourt, Brace, 1936), pp. 30-31, 378.

See also Alvin H. Hansen, "Economic Progress and Declining Population Growth," *American Economic Review*, Vol. 29 (March 1939), pp. 1-15.

than was then available.[57] This led to the launching of the Temporary National Economic Committee in 1938. In recommending the formation of this committee, President Roosevelt's message began:

> Unhappy events abroad have retaught us two simple truths about the liberty of a democratic people.
>
> The first truth is that the liberty of a democracy is not safe if the people tolerate the growth of private power to a point where it becomes stronger than their democratic state itself. That, in its essence, is fascism — ownership of government by an individual, by a group, or by any other controlling private power.
>
> The second truth is that the liberty of a democracy is not safe if its business system does not provide employment and produce and distribute goods in such a way as to sustain an acceptable standard of living.
>
> Both lessons hit home.
>
> Among us today a concentration of private power without equal in history is growing.
>
> This concentration is seriously impairing the economic effectiveness of private enterprise as a way of providing employment for labor and capital and as a way of assuring a more equitable distribution of income and earnings among the people of the nation as a whole.

The President's message ended on the same note:

> Once it is realized that business monopoly in America paralyzes the system of free enterprise on which it is grafted, and is as fatal to those who manipulate it as to the people who suffer beneath its impositions, action by the government to eliminate these artificial restraints will be welcomed by industry throughout the nation. For idle factories and idle workers profit no man.[58]

[57] See Edward S. Mason, "Monopoly in Law and Economics"; Donald H. Wallace, "Monopolistic Competition and Public Policy"; Arthur R. Burns, "The Organization of Industry and the Theory of Prices" in American Economic Association, *Readings in the Social Control of Industry* (Blakiston, 1949), pp. 47, 277-78, 396, 417.

[58] Temporary National Economic Committee, *Investigation of Concentration of Economic Power: Final Report and Recommendations*, S. Doc. 35, 77 Cong. 1 sess. (1941), p. 11.

The TNEC accumulated more than 20,000 pages of testimony covering the interrogation of 552 leaders of industry, 3,300 technical exhibits, and 43 monographs on significant economic problems of the day.[59] The final report was issued in March 1941, when the nation was already engaged in defense preparations. This report had obviously been put together in haste. There was little or no follow-up of the broad investigation, and moreover, the TNEC was able to reach agreement on only the most general statement of purpose. The committee agreed to recommend "the maintenance of free competitive enterprise by the effective suppression of the restrictive practices which have always been recognized as evil," but on specific recommendations, like one to place all corporations under national charter, the committee divided along party lines.[60] A recommendation to eliminate the Miller-Tydings amendment drew a dissent not only from minority members, but from the chairman of the committee as well. One specific recommendation retained in the Final Report was an amendment of the Clayton Act to give the Federal Trade Commission greater authority over mergers of competitors.[61]

World War II: Impetus to Increasing Concentration

Although World War I had set a precedent in mobilizing big business support for the military, this was hardly comparable to the use made of big business in World War II. The major contribution of big business to national security was undisputed. But wartime requirements also contributed to a marked increase in the scale of big business. Of the $18 billion of war plants constructed between 1940 and the end of 1943, nearly three-fourths were in units exceeding $10 million, and nearly one-third in units above $50 million. In addition, some $15 billion of war plants had been built and operated for the government by large private companies. Approximately $7.5 billion of government plant contracts were placed with thirty-one corporations, averaging over $200 million

---

[59] *Ibid.*, p. 696, 709.

[60] *Ibid.*, p. 9.

[61] Legislation to this effect was enacted in December 1950; 64 Stat. 1125.

per corporation. The great bulk of prime contracts went to the larger companies. The Federal Trade Commission reported that, during the period 1940-46, the process of war mobilization and demobilization saw the merging of not less than 1,658 companies: nearly one-third of these were absorbed by corporations having assets of $50 million or more.[62] These developments in turn implied that the disparity between big business and the rest of the economic structure had been accentuated by the wartime experience.[63] With the end of the war, containment of the economic power vested in the large corporations was again given a place of major importance in public policy.

Postwar Efforts to Reduce Business Concentration

In his State of the Union message of January 1947, President Truman emphasized the impact of the war on the concentration of industrial power:

> . . . In 1941 the Temporary National Economic Committee completed a comprehensive investigation into the workings of the national economy. The committee's study showed that, despite half a century of antitrust law enforcement, one of the gravest threats to our welfare lay in the increasing concentration of power in the hands of a small number of giant organizations.
>
> During the war, this long-standing tendency toward economic concentration was accelerated. As a consequence, we now find that to a greater extent than ever before, whole industries are dominated

[62] Federal Trade Commission, *Report on the Present Trend of Corporate Mergers and Acquisitions* (1947), p. 7.

[63] Gardiner C. Means has noted that "a disproportionately large proportion of contracts went to medium sized companies such as airplane makers while the big manufacturers . . . *as a whole* seem to have received less than their proportionate share of contracts [not of subcontracting]." (See "Thoughts on Concentration," in *Proceedings of the American Statistical Association*, 1962, p. 126.) Means' observation, which implies decreasing concentration within the industrial sector as a whole, is not, however, inconsistent with increasing concentration within individual manufacturing industries. His point is that those industries with medium sized firms were disproportionately favored in the awarding of wartime contracts, not that large firms fared less well than medium sized firms within particular industries.

by one or a few large organizations which can restrict production in the interest of higher profits and thus reduce employment and purchasing power.[64]

The new postwar problem of business concentration thus visualized, the government proceeded to attack it on two fronts. Under the Surplus Property Act of 1944,[65] Congress hoped to redistribute competitive strength by the sale of wartime plants to newer or smaller companies, rather than to firms already dominant in their respective industries. Simultaneously, the Federal Trade Commission and the Department of Justice moved to enlist the aid of the courts in reducing the market power of industrial giants.

War Plant Disposal

An effort to broaden the area of competition under the Surplus Property Act was made in several important industries. The aluminum plants built for the government by the Aluminum Company of America were leased or sold to two other companies, Kaiser and Reynolds, on terms designed to promote their development as substantial competitors. The huge Willow Run plant constructed by the Ford Company for airplane manufacture was leased to Kaiser-Fraser for manufacture of automobiles. The Geneva steel mill in Utah built by U.S. Steel was acquired by that company only when other practicable bids for the $200 million plant failed to materialize.[66]

Overall, however, the nature of disposable facilities was frequently such that they were most salable to those firms which had operated them during the war, and only in a few instances was industrial structure materially affected by the disposal program.

[64] Harry S. Truman, "The State of the Union," in *Vital Speeches of the Day,* Vol. 13 (Jan. 15, 1947), p. 196.

[65] 58 Stat. 765.

[66] The subsequent acquisition by U. S. Steel of fabricating facilities on the Pacific Coast for steel produced at Geneva was permitted by the Supreme Court after being challenged by the Department of Justice on the grounds that U. S. Steel already possessed a third of the nation's steel capacity. See *United States v. Columbia Steel Co. et al.,* 334 U.S. 495 (1948).

Judicial Determination in the Postwar Period

In the postwar period, the courts continued to be faced with the necessity of defining the limits of legitimate corporate growth. Initially, the period was one of tighter judicial interpretation of antitrust. More recent decisions appear to have eased the rigidity of the early postwar years. In general, the period has been one of increased maturity and sophistication in the application of antitrust. A few key decisions illustrate the pattern.

MONOPOLY. In 1945, the now famous Alcoa decision [67] broke a quarter century's reliance on the rule of reason in the judicial application of the Sherman Act. Earlier, in 1920, the Supreme Court had ruled that "the law does not make mere size an offense. . . . It requires overt acts." [68] In the Alcoa case, Judge Hand disagreed: "The law did not condone 'good' trusts and condemn 'bad' ones; it forbade all." [69] Specific acts of monopoly behavior were not required; the essential initial question was whether Alcoa had monopolized the aluminum industry. Judge Hand, reviewing Alcoa's 90 percent control of virgin aluminum, found the answer to be yes. In this light, Judge Hand considered the corporation's intent, and the possibility that monopoly could have been "thrust upon" the defendant, but rejected this argument, citing Alcoa's planned and coordinated expansion of facilities to meet the increasing domestic consumption of aluminum products.[70]

[67] United States v. Aluminum Co. of America et al., 148 F. 2d 416 (C.C.A. 2d 1945).

[68] United States v. U. S. Steel Corp., 251 U.S. 417 (1920).

[69] Because of the disqualification of four justices, the Supreme Court was unable to hear this case. Enabling legislation designated the Court of Appeals for the Second Circuit as the final court of appeal.

[70] In view of the government war plant disposal program, the court postponed any dissolution or other remedial action. In 1950, the District Court to which the case was returned for the preparation of a remedy found, with Kaiser and Reynolds established, that "the weakening of any aluminum producer would lessen the bouyancy of the market as a whole." United States v. Aluminum Co. of America, 91 F. Supp. 333 (S.D.N.Y. 1950). Alcoa, though divested of its Canadian affiliate, Aluminium Ltd., was permitted to stand. The court considered the presence of new competitors and the "fierce competition with articles com-

Similarly, in 1953, Judge Charles E. Wyzanski found that the United Shoe Machinery Corporation had "not based its growth solely on ability, economies of scale, research, and adaptation." [71] Wyzanski, however, extended Learned Hand's definition of the "thrust upon" exception to cover a defendant who could prove that monopoly is owed

> . . . solely to superior skill, superior products, natural advantages (including accessibility to raw materials or markets), economic or technological efficiency (including scientific research), low margins of profit maintained permanently and without discrimination, or licenses conferred by, and used within, the limits of law (including patents on one's own inventions, or franchises granted directly to the enterprise by a public authority).[72]

Even granting the behavior content of the "thrust upon" exemption, this interpretation of the legality of monopoly, and of the act of monopolization, remains a far cry from that of the prewar era.

CONSPIRACY. Both in the postwar period and before, the courts have moved with caution and conservatism when the legality of large single integrated firms has been challenged. Action with respect to combinations and agreements among independent firms has been more direct. Recent experience is no exception. The attack on "conscious parallel action" by competing firms, sustained in the American Tobacco case in 1946, was strengthened by the basing point decisions of the later 1940's.[73] The American Cement Institute decision declared a concerted basing point pricing system a technique of unfair competition.[74] In the Triangle Conduit case, the court went further to find that individual companies could violate the Federal Trade Commission Act by adherence to a

---

posed of other materials" to be sufficient to negate the need for dissolution of the American company.

[71] *United States v. United Shoe Machinery Corp.*, 110 F. Supp. 295 (1953).

[72] Carl Kaysen, *United States v. United Shoe Machinery Corporation* (Harvard University Press, 1956), p. 303.

[73] *American Tobacco Co. v. United States*, 328 U.S. 781 (1946). For a discussion of basing point pricing, see Fritz Machlup, *The Basing Point System* (Blakiston, 1949).

[74] *Federal Trade Commission v. Cement Institute*, 333 U.S. 683 (1948).

basing point pricing system without agreement, but simply with the knowledge that others "did likewise." [75] In 1954, however, the Supreme Court rejected the argument that common activity by distributors in limiting first runs of motion pictures constituted something more than independent action under similar business conditions. The court asserted it had "never held that . . . parallel behavior conclusively establishes agreement." [76] The court thus set itself the task of distinguishing between parallel behavior that is innocent, reflecting only judicious managerial decisions, and parallelism that can be considered rational only on the grounds that the actions of other firms are identical. Although the line of demarcation between the legitimate and the illegitimate is fuzzy, the intent of the court was and is clear. Where established, agreement with respect to price or market share constitutes a *per se* violation of antitrust.[77]

MERGERS. Mergers have been subject both to new legislation and to tighter judicial interpretation in the postwar period. In March 1962, final judgment of divestiture was entered in the government's writ of 1954 charging the du Pont Company with the illegal acquisition in 1917-19 of 23 percent of the shares of the General Motors Corporation. In so doing, the Supreme Court held that the Clayton Act was applicable not only to the acquisition of stock, but also to the holding or use of stock previously acquired.[78] At the same time, the court emphasized its view that the statute

[75] *Triangle Conduit and Cable Co. Inc. et al. v. Federal Trade Commission,* 168 F. 2d 175 (1948).

[76] *Theater Enterprises, Inc. v. Paramount Film Distributing Corp.,* 346 U.S. 537, 540 (1954).

[77] In the most spectacular conspiracy action of recent years, 30 executives of the heavy electrical equipment industry received jail sentences, 7 of which were served, and fines totaling almost $2 million were levied, as pleas of guilty or *nolo contendere* were entered in some 20 cases of conspiracy. See *United States v. Westinghouse Electric Corp. et al.* (D. C. Eastern Pa. 1960), *CCH Trade Cases,* Par. 69,699.

Although guilty pleas eliminated the need for judicial interpretation, the case is nevertheless significant for the penalties imposed and for the public outcry the action stimulated. For a fascinating account, see Richard Austin Smith, "The Incredible Electrical Conspiracy," *Fortune,* Vol. 63 (April 1961), p. 132.

[78] *United States v. E. I. du Pont de Nemours and Co.,* 353 U.S. 586 (1957).

was equally applicable to the acquisition of a customer or supplier as to the traditional merger of directly competing corporations. The vulnerability of the vertical merger as well as the traditional horizontal combination was clearly established.

The Celler Amendment of 1950 extended the antimerger provisions of the Clayton Act to cover the acquisition of assets as well as stock, and in 1962 the Supreme Court, in its first interpretation of this "new" section 7, found that the proposed acquisition of the Kinney Corporation, a shoe retailer, by the Brown Shoe Company, a manufacturer, would tend substantially to lessen competition even though the combined firm would account for only about 4 percent of the national production of footwear. The court relied heavily on the argument, clearly developed in the du Pont case, that this merger foreclosed a substantial portion of the final market to outside producers.[79] The court also found a tendency to lessen competition between Brown and Kinney retail outlets in local markets.

The Brown Shoe decision, and earlier District Court decisions including the Pillsbury Mills and Bethlehem Youngstown cases, emphasized the power of Section 7. The courts were willing to define markets narrowly, both in terms of products and region, to find a lessening of competition in both vertical and horizontal combination, and to look for that lessening of competition beyond the immediate boundaries of the combining firms. However difficult the dissolution of established giants, the merger route to corporate concentration appears substantially blocked. The only general justification for modern merger—at least where participants are large factors within their respective markets, or where competitors are "foreclosed" from a substantial market—appears to be financial distress, a justification that has been accepted both by the regulatory agencies and the courts.[80]

While the big business issue has been persistent, public and

[79] *Brown Shoe Co., Inc. v. United States,* 370 U.S. 294 (1962).

[80] In the case of the postwar major automobile mergers, the Department of Justice issued no complaint, evidently regarding the merger of smaller companies essential to the development of corporations better able to compete with the "Big Three." The Supreme Court, in the Brown Shoe case, noted "no mitigating factors, such as the business failure or the inadequate resources of one of the parties that may have prevented it from maintaining its competitive position, nor

governmental attitudes have been subject to change. As noted, the merger of competitors to achieve *total* monopoly has now essentially ceased. Cutthroat tactics of discrimination, boycotts, and price wars aimed at destruction of individual competitors have similarly lost their significance as identifying marks of the corporate giant. The phase in which a few giant bankers determined the organization and operating policies of large-scale industry is part of the past. The financial condition of the large corporation is now a matter of public record; the modern great industrials can scarcely be regarded as the dependents of financial institutions. The problem today arises from the dominant position of giant firms, singly on occasion, more often in small groups. This, in the economist's terminology, is oligopoly.

In much current economic and political argument, the point is nevertheless made that these firms are still effective monopolies. The giants are presumed to be so strongly entrenched that outsiders can have little hope of breaking into the markets pre-empted by these established leaders. In this context, the protection of the law has on occasion been employed to curb big business, to insulate the small competitor, and to prevent real or imagined discrimination favoring large enterprise. Ostensibly, to make competition "fairer," the government has introduced controls, like those of the National Industrial Recovery Act, the Robinson-Patman Act, or the McGuire-Keogh Act, all tending to some degree to limit individual competitive activity.

The interpretation of the Sherman Act, with its generalized prohibition of restraint of trade, has been an obligation of both the courts and the Department of Justice. In large part, these institutions have had to "play by ear," reacting to political interpretations, to the eloquence of counsel, and to their own economic predilections. The court itself has asserted that "precedents have fallen short of definite specifications as to the requirements of effective competition." [81]

---

a demonstrated need for combination to enable small companies to enter into a more meaningful competition with those dominating the relevant markets." *Ibid.*, p. 1551.

[81] *United States v. Aluminum Co. of America*, 91 F. Supp. 333, 340 (S.D.N.Y. 1950).

Behind us is more than half a century of big, big business. Notwithstanding the Sherman Act and related antitrust, the scale of American enterprise has continued to increase. In 1904, only three industrial corporations had assets of more than $200 million.[82] In 1960, there were twenty-nine with assets exceeding the billion dollar mark.[83] More than twice that number reported assets above the half billion dollar level.[84]

In one sense, this suggests that attitudes toward big business have changed very little over the last half century. The concentration of economic power has produced waves of genuine concern, but despite the broader scope for prosecution under the antitrust laws, a thread of tolerance may be discerned in the responses of the public to large-scale enterprise. The public by its conduct—as investor, consumer, and employee—continues to accept the role of large business.

In seeking to move behind these outward signs of split personality, it seems pertinent to ask whether the competitiveness of big business has been correctly evaluated. A large part of the difficulty has been in achieving agreement on what is meant by competition, and what is wanted of the economic system along with competition. The succession of laws, their interpreters and administrators, have failed to supply a standardized definition of the term "competition." There is all the more reason to seek criteria that may fairly determine the validity and adequacy of the competition the business structure provides.

[82] Moody, *op. cit.*, p. 453.

[83] "The 500 Largest Industrial Corporations," *The Fortune Directory* (Time, Inc., August 1961), pp. 2-19.

[84] Unfortunately, there is no easy basis for judging whether the *relative* concentration of assets in these few largest firms has also increased. The limited data available suggest that the opposite is more likely. For example, Goldsmith and Lipsey estimate the total current dollar value of all nongovernment assets at $150 billion in 1900 and at $3,416 billion in 1958. This increase of roughly 2,000 percent is larger than the growth of the total assets of the largest 10 or 20 industrial firms. See Raymond W. Goldsmith and Robert E. Lipsey, *Studies in the National Balance Sheet of the United States* (Princeton University Press, 1963), Vol. I, p. 43.

2

The Rationale of
Competitive Enterprise

THE AMERICAN ECONOMIC SYSTEM is commonly characterized as one of free private enterprise. The meaning of this term is
widely sensed through habitual usage. It is seldom precisely defined. Modern free enterprise can perhaps best be viewed as the
economic counterpart of a broader social and political philosophy
giving high priority to freedom of opportunity for the individual.
Such a system leaves the fulfillment of economic wants largely to
the private action of individuals or voluntary groups of individuals
competing in the production and exchange of goods and services
in open markets. This emphasis on private initiative may be contrasted with the patterns of those societies where the economic
life of the individual is largely subordinated to the state or to
groups of enterprises associated in formal cartels.[1]

Freedom of enterprise demands equality of opportunity in the
economic sphere in keeping with the "natural rights" of the indi-

[1] It should be obvious that the American economy has never relied exclusively
on private enterprise. The public functions of police protection, national defense,
navigation aids, official records, highways, and schools, as well as welfare programs
to safeguard health, security, and recreation are not only familiar but even now are
traditional. And the government may add to the list of its services as the technology of our economic life becomes more complicated. It is only in comparison
with more centralized economies that the term "free enterprise" gains its
applicability.

vidual to life, liberty, and the pursuit of happiness.[2] There must be room for exercise of individual initiative; there must be freedom for the pursuit of self-interest in offering labor or produce, employing capital, or making expenditures, with minimal interference from a vested authority. But additional limitations on individual effort are encountered as an economy evolves from a simple agrarian society to a modern industrial or corporate state. At the same time, another freedom of opportunity progressively gains recognition—the freedom of association. Joint effort in the voluntary pooling of capital and manpower becomes a device for more effective production and marketing.

The fears created by the rise of big business reflect the problem of reconciling the freedom of opportunity for the individual entrepreneur and the freedom of association for joint economic endeavor. There is always the danger that the one may undermine or overwhelm the other. In a changing society, the balance can be delicate; and the traditional esteem for freedom of individual enterprise as the best means for organizing economic activity is challenged from time to time by the criticism that energy lost in the battle of individual competition might better be devoted to the search for lower costs or to the development and improvement of product. Competition, in this context, may involve a duplication of facilities and costs that could be reduced or eliminated by a reduction in the number of competitors and cooperation among the remaining firms. Though large numbers of competitors may be forced to a minimum margin of profit, this does not necessarily guarantee the production and distribution of goods and services at least cost compared with what might be possible with fewer and better equipped establishments.[3]

In Adam Smith's view, the advantages of voluntary association

[2] For a general account of the development of this concept of natural right in American economic thought, and its roots in religion, politics, and the law, see *The Course of American Democratic Thought*, by Ralph Henry Gabriel (Ronald Press, 1940).

[3] The basic question here relates to the presence and degree of real economies of scale in modern production and distribution. To the extent that realized costs always decline with increased corporate size, these costs will be lower the fewer the firms in the relevant industry. In the extreme, competition is inconsistent with efficiency in the presence of economies of scale. Indeed, monopoly would be the

were mainly in the efficiencies of specialization, that is, the division of labor which accompanied mechanization. Since Adam Smith, however, the evolution of productive technology has been matched by a parallel evolution in business organization. It is exemplified in the modern multi-unit corporation with many central offices, subsidiaries, and diversified plants. The technology of management—the coordination of financial and human resources and market facilities—has been pushed no less vigorously than the technology of physical production.

Although the gains from association are exploited to enlarge total output, the net benefit for a free enterprise system is determinable only after taking into account the loss or gain in opportunities that new large-scale enterprise has generated for individual enterprise and independent action. Free enterprise has not only its historical (laissez-faire) implication of freedom from excessive control by the state; it also implies freedom from restrictive controls imposed by private domination of markets. The two are interdependent. The exercise of restrictive power by one segment of private enterprise over another must almost inevitably lead to intervention by government. The American tradition of reliance on a system of checks and balances to preserve political freedom has, as its counterpart in the economic sphere, a reliance on market competition. The preservation of competition may be viewed as a device for limiting the economic power of privileged groups to exploit others.

---

end result of active and effective competition in such circumstances—the largest firm would always be the most able competitor and the ultimate survivor. The rationale for direct government regulation of public utilities is generally based on the argument that significant economies of scale are present in these industries, ruling out free competition as an efficient means of economic organization. Elsewhere in the economy, the presence of such economies can be, and is, debated. Some economies of this sort unquestionably exist and are apparent even to the casual observer. The more important question is whether these economies extend beyond the level of purely optimal plant size to form an economic justification for the multi-plant organization characteristic of big business. In industries where economies of scale *are* important, these may be exhausted at fairly small plant sizes in terms of actual plant construction. The evidence, however, is inconclusive. See, for example, Caleb A. Smith, "Survey of the Empirical Evidence on Economies of Scale" in *Business Concentration and Price Policy* (National Bureau of Economic Research, 1955).

The Concept of Competition

Business competition can be broadly defined as the process of exchanging goods or services in a market where there is a choice among rival bids and offers. But this general definition leaves room for extreme differences, as well as various shadings, of opinion. Economists have considered business practices under theoretical concepts of pure or perfect competition, and under models of imperfect, monopolistic, and oligopolistic competition. Both theoretical and applied concepts of "workable competition" have been developed. There are uncounted variations of market action surrounding these terms, and common ground cannot be reached by a mere listing of formal conditions. Acceptable criteria may be agreed upon—"adequate" numbers of buyers and sellers, "market determination" of price and volume, "freedom" of entry, and so forth—and yet permit vastly different content to be given these terms. While certain of these criteria may be used as a general frame of reference, their meaning becomes clear only as they are considered in relation to the overall patterns of business structure and of production and markets, to compulsion to compete, and indeed, to their total economic consequence.

The primer of traditional economics holds that in a fully competitive economy, the sole arbiter is the market. Values are determined through the price mechanism. The market organizes, integrates, and directs the activities and decisions of buyers, sellers, producers, and consumers. Through competition and the drive for profit, activity tends to be directed into socially desirable channels as sellers seek their most favorable markets and buyers make their choices among alternative sources of supply. Thus competition, working through free markets, aims to reconcile self-interest with public interest, and to bring about the most satisfactory allocation and use of available private resources.

The determination of resource use is left, therefore, under a competitive system, to the spontaneous interaction of voluntary offers and responses. Competitors are presumed to be able to choose freely, and in the economic sense, intelligently, among the available alternatives for the acquisition and sale of materials, services, and products. From such contesting for economic reward in the face of available alternatives emerges the organization of productive effort and satisfaction of wants. Thus, both in terms of the way competition works and the results it is supposed to achieve, the more numerous, varied, and significant the market alternatives, the more convincing the objective evidence of effective competition.

It is not to be expected, however, that a progressive enlargement of choice will inevitably be realized merely by allowing competition to take its own course. The sequence, from pursuit of self-interest to the attainment of the maximum common welfare, is never perfect. The economy is vitally concerned with the manner in which, and the conditions under which, this competing is done. With faith in the ability of competition necessarily goes faith in the ability of men to create institutions, or an environment, within which such competition may work effectively.

Few economists displayed greater optimism regarding the potential good of competition than John Bates Clark. He hailed it as a force in the continued improvement of the productive arts:

> Competition is the assured guarantee of all such progress. It causes a race of improvement in which eager rivals strive with each other to see who can get the best result from a day's labor. It puts the producer where he must be enterprising or drop out of the race. He must invent machines and processes or adopt them as others discover them. He must organize, explore markets, and study consumers' wants. He must keep abreast of a rapidly moving procession if he expects to continue long to be a producer at all.[4]

But this high optimism was qualified with the eloquent warning:

> In our worship of the survival of the fit under free natural selection, we are sometimes in danger of forgetting that the conditions of the struggle fix the kind of fitness that shall come out of it; that survival in the prize ring means fitness for pugilism; not for bricklaying nor philanthropy; that survival in predatory competition

[4] John Bates Clark, *Essentials of Economic Theory* (Macmillan, 1907), pp. 533-34.

is likely to mean something else than fitness for good and efficient production; and that only from a strife with the right kind of rules can the right kind of fitness emerge. Competition . . . is a game played under rules fixed by the state to the end that, so far as possible, the prize of victory shall be earned, not by trickery or mere self-seeking adroitness, but by value rendered. It is not the mere play of unrestrained self-interest; it is a method of harnessing the wild beast of self-interest to serve the common good—a thing of ideals and not of sordidness. It is not a natural state, but like any other form of liberty, it is a social achievement, and eternal vigilance is the price of it.[5]

How do we determine that balance where the competitive process is strengthened, but not destroyed, by control ensuring that "the prize of victory shall be earned by value rendered"?

Under free enterprise it is essential that the competitive process itself be largely self-sustaining. Indeed, a significant measure of the effectiveness of competition is its ability to economize in the use of direct government intervention. To the extent that private enterprise is socially efficient, it relieves government from the task of engaging in economic activity except where, by common consent or for special reasons, such activity must be removed from the private sector. Public participation in the remaining activities may then be chiefly limited to the encouragement and protection of a climate in which competition serves to advance the common interest. But what is simply said is less easily accomplished. A changing economy requires continual resetting and re-examination of the elusive boundary between wanted and unwanted forms of competition.

The debate has many sides, but among the market conditions more frequently stressed as conducive to desirable competition are the following:

1. The number of buyers and sellers should be sufficient to provide a real and meaningful choice among alternative sources or outlets.

2. The position of any individual must not be so secure that he can dictate the conduct of others.

[5] John Bates Clark, John Maurice Clark, *The Control of Trusts* (Macmillan, 1912), pp. 200-01.

3.   The position of any seller must not be so strong that incentive to increase profits by reducing costs, altering prices, or improving product or service is materially reduced.

4.   There must be opportunity for individual buyers and sellers to make decisions independently, without coercive pressure to join in agreements tending to restrict or narrow competition.

5.   Entry or access to markets must not be hindered by deliberate restrictions or collusive measures, nor can the opportunities of individual buyers and sellers to act independently be hampered by private agreement.

6.   There must be no discrimination among similarly situated buyers and sellers.

These conditions, and the legal sanctions sought to enforce them, are frequently held to be violated by the concentration of resources in big business. This fear stems from a number of commonly accepted propositions about big business. It is widely held, for example, that in many industries, sellers and buyers are so few in number and so great in size that they provide no real choice among alternative sources; that these industrial giants dictate the conduct of competitors; that the entrenched position of the dominant corporations reduces incentive to increase profits by reducing costs and prices; or by improving product and service, that entry of new competitors is barred by the impracticability of matching the resources of the established firms; that small buyers or suppliers are satellites bound by conditions set by the dominant firm.

Neither the conditions listed above for a workably competitive market, nor this statement of the respects in which big business appears to do violence to them, is unambiguous. However, each has acquired special meaning with successive climates of thought, and from experience with a succession of institutions and practices.

Classical Competitive Markets

Classical theory concentrated on two examples of market conduct: pure competition and pure monopoly. The purely competitive market was described and rationalized as one in which supply and demand were brought into balance at a price yielding maximum turnover: at a higher price less would have been demanded; at a lower price, less offered. Buyers and sellers were considered to be of such numbers and so nearly alike that no single individual or firm could appreciably influence the market. Under monopoly, the bulk (or all in the case of pure monopoly) of the output entering the market was controlled by a single firm. There being no ready alternative to the monopolist's offering, price and volume could be manipulated to yield profits in excess of those attainable in a purely competitive market.[6]

The influence of the concept of pure competition is the more notable for the fact that it is so patently an ideal. Like all theories, it abstracts from detail. It is applicable, in the extreme, where differences in the products of competitors are negligible, where it does not matter who is the seller and who is the buyer. Thus, it is not a description of the day-to-day competition of actual markets. It does not ask how business firms could grow or live through periods of gluts, store up resources, or contrive counter measures against other contingencies. It neglects institutions. It does not contemplate the growth of large aggregates of capital, equipment, and technology, which by their very dimensions reduce the number of firms or sellers required to meet the total demand for given products. The essential theoretical distinction of the classical models was between "pure" competition, where no firm can substantially influence market supply, industry demand, or price, and

---

[6] Note that in classical theory, both pure competitors and pure monopolists are assumed to be profit maximizers. The pure competitor, however, faces a market of many buyers, each in turn with many alternative sources of supply. If a competitor's product is offered at a price above the market price, his sales will be zero. Sales at prices below the prevailing market price violate the assumed behavior of profit-maximization. The "pure" competitor is small relative to the market. His entire output can be absorbed without influencing the market price. The profit-maximizing price is the market price. The "pure" monopolist, on the other hand, confronts buyers who can find only imperfect alternatives for the monopolist's product. A range of prices exists at which sales can be made. Price is variable to the monopolist, not to the pure competitor. A profit-maximizing monopolist therefore takes account of the effect on price which increased offering on his part will induce. The pure competitor need not. This is the essential difference between the two in market behavior. Equivalent differences on the buying side distinguish the monopsonist from the pure competitor.

monopoly, where market power is absolute, and where price is variable at the monopolist's discretion.[7]

Imperfect Competition

The limited applicability of these models to the real world prompted economists to develop a theory of the firm under "imperfect" or "monopolistic" competition.[8] This work recognized the power of individual firms to influence markets. A series of models represented various degrees of market control between pure competition and classical monopoly. These models were used to explain, or to try to explain, how rational businessmen would determine price and output where each must take account of the actions expected from the other. But these models have also been subject to criticism with regard to their reality: they represent situations that do not help to explain actual markets where each firm must act individually on the basis of its detailed estimate of the special conditions it faces.[9] Nevertheless, this theoretical

[7] The early models did, of course, show a monopolist's sales to be dependent on price. In this regard, the power of monopoly was limited. What the classical theory, with one or two exceptions, did not postulate was the response of one large firm to actions taken by another where both price and product were weapons of competition.

[8] The first development in this direction is generally associated with Joan Robinson, *The Economics of Imperfect Competition* (Macmillan, 1933) and Edward H. Chamberlin, *The Theory of Monopolistic Competition* (Harvard University Press, 1933). Models of the interaction of business decisions were published, however, as early as 1838. See Antoine A. Cournot, *Researches into the Mathematical Principles of the Theory of Wealth*, translated by N. T. Bacon, 2d. ed. (Macmillan, 1927).

[9] Economists are not unaware of the interplay of forces making it difficult, if not impossible, for a firm to follow the cost-price policy leading to maximum profit. Edward H. Chamberlin, for example, recognizes the uncertainty of rival action; that, given these uncertainties, "no assumption as to the intelligence which the sellers apply to the pursuit of their maximum gain, short of omniscience, would render the outcome determinate." (*Op. cit.*, p. 53.) Shubik attributes the "failure" of these models of oligopoly to a "strait-jacket" imposed by the application of the wrong analytic tools. See Martin Shubik, ed., *Readings in Game Theory and Political Behavior* (Doubleday, 1954), pp. 2-3.

Others go further. Gerhard Tintner denies the strict relevance of profit-maximization under uncertainty, arguing that the appropriate act by the firm is

work has served to focus attention on a number of factors influencing the behavior of markets—the number of buyers and sellers, the rigidity or elasticity of cost and demand for both the firm and industry, the degree of standardization or differentiation of product, and the communicability of market information.

The resultant conclusions regarding business conduct in markets that deviate from the purely competitive have helped to rationalize public regulation. The use of the term "monopolistic competition" to express deviation from "pure competition" has introduced overtones associating the big and the few with monopoly. An examination of this aspect of the theory reveals these social implications.

Oligopoly

The models of oligopoly have frequently lent themselves to the interpretation that it is rational for members of the oligopoly to act in concert. Each producer is a large and powerful influence on the market. If one chose to reduce his price, others would be forced to follow. Any reduction below the prevailing (profit-maximiz-

---

maximization of a preference function, not necessarily leading to a maximization of net income. *Studies in Mathematical Economics and Econometrics* (University of Chicago Press, 1942), pp. 92-109.

According to Carl Kaysen, strict profit maximization is not even the goal of modern corporate management. "No longer the agent of proprietorship seeking to maximize return on investment, management sees itself as responsible to stockholders, employees, customers, the general public, and perhaps most important, the firm itself as an institution. . . . . Its responsibilities to the general public are widespread: leadership in local charitable enterprises, concern with factory architecture and landscaping, provision of support for higher education, and even research in pure science, to name a few." "The Social Significance of the Modern Corporation," American Economic Association, *Papers and Proceedings*, Vol. 47 (May 1957), p. 313.

Alchian, on the other hand, views profit maximization more as an evolutionary matter, related to the survivorship of firms. See Armen A. Alchian, "Uncertainty, Evolution and Economic Theory," in Richard B. Heflebower and George W. Stocking (eds.), *Readings in Industrial Organization and Public Policy* (Richard D. Irwin, 1958), pp. 207-19. See also Edward S. Mason, *The Corporation in Modern Society* (Harvard University Press, 1960), Chap. 1, especially pp. 4-5 and 9-19, and M. A. Adelman, "Some Aspects of Corporate Enterprise," in Ralph E. Freeman (ed.), *Postwar Economic Trends in the United States* (Harper, 1960), pp. 291-307.

ing) price would therefore reduce net revenues for all concerned. Similarly, when one large seller, usually the largest, sets a higher price to yield higher profits, others can follow to take advantage of this opportunity for joint enrichment.[10] Price competition thus becomes self-defeating as a means of obtaining additional net income. In the end, prices then tend to be fixed, as though by a single seller, at the point which maximizes profits for the joint membership of the oligopoly.[11]

In what circumstances would business men be likely to set prices in this fashion? A first condition usually must be that the judgment of the market coincides among members of the oligopoly. Each seller, guessing as best he can how a changing market will behave, must reach a verdict about price which is also reached by the others. Alternatively, each must act, without collusion or disciplinary action, as though this were the case.

Each must, to a point, be satisfied with his share. Each seller in the oligopoly, whether a high-cost producer or low, old or young, enterprising or conservative, must see self-interest in conformity with the group in matters concerning price. There must be no divergence among the producers great enough to tempt an aggressive member to get more business by making his own special pricing decisions.

To achieve this parallelism, each oligopolist must be confident of common action with regard to price.[12] There must be reason-

[10] This is true, of course, only if the market price is initially below the point of joint maximization.

[11] This interpretation is narrow and perhaps more characteristic of early writing than of contemporary work in this area. Nevertheless, it is still influential in the development of attitudes and public policy. For a more careful and balanced interpretation of oligopoly, see William J. Fellner, *Competition Among the Few* (Knopf, 1949). See also George J. Stigler, "A Theory of Oligopoly," *Journal of Political Economy*, Vol. 72 (February 1964), pp. 44-61, for a perceptive analysis of collusive behavior where undetected violation of implied or actual inter-firm agreement is possible. Stigler extends the analysis to provide a model of price behavior related to market structure in both the buying and the selling side. In spite of the insight of these and other more modern analysts, the earlier identification of oligopoly with full and complete tacit agreement continues to be popular in nonprofessional circles.

[12] Emphasis on price is important. Joint maximization of income with respect to price will typically, under oligopoly, lead to prices markedly above marginal costs of production. This divergence between price and cost at the margin pro-

able certainty in the mind of each seller that others will not under-
cut him, are not secretly doing so, and that when one makes a
price change, others will promptly go along.

The products in this setting must also be reasonably uniform.
Substantial immunity from outside substitute products is required. And the market must be under control in other respects
as well. Each member of the oligopoly must know in general
what is being done by others. Among the buyers, none may be
so powerful that he can play one seller against another to force
competitive price concessions within the industry.

These postulates of oligopoly theory are given in extreme
form. As such, however, they clearly indicate the manner in
which the structure and motivations of big business appear to deviate from those that make for pure competition. Thus stated,
they pose the issue whether the deviations from competition are
correctly mirrored by this theory, or whether new or offsetting
elements of competition have developed that contribute to the
attainment of the total objectives of the competitive economy.

Applicability of the Postulates

To the extent that the conditions of formal oligopoly are not
met, uniformity of action is less likely, and fewness of sellers—
even big sellers—may not be taken for granted as a barrier to
effective competition. Business management would be quick to
say that the market situation is characteristically complex and
uncertain, that each firm's conception of it is unique, and that
adjustments made by the individual firm to the pattern of long-
and short-term factors will vary according to the particular circumstances of the individual firm.

Economists admit these complexities. It has long been recognized, for example, that positive leadership in market organiza-

---

vides a powerful incentive to nonprice techniques of competition—competition
through service, product design, advertising, and so forth. This competition can
be as ruthless and devastating as any contest with respect to price. Indeed, one
great economist regarded it as the most devastating of all. See Joseph A. Schum-
peter, *Capitalism, Socialism and Democracy*, 3d ed. (Harper, 1950), pp. 81-87.
Nonprice competition is not, however, the equivalent of competition with respect
to price.

tion may be essential for effective competition in order to over-
come declining profits in a stagnant industry, or to build a broad
market for new products.[13] It is further realized that when all the
hypothetical prerequisites of pure or perfect competition are not
present—if products are differentiated, if patents are obtainable,
or if there are a few outstanding buyers among many small ones—
that satisfactory "workable competition" may nonetheless be
achieved through the interplay of rival company policies.[14] Nevertheless, the popular presumption prevails that market structure
must clearly approach that of pure competition if the central objective of competition is to be attained—namely the achievement
of the optimal use of resources within the bounds of feasible
alternatives.[15]

If the performance of contemporary industry is to be judged on
its merits, it should be reviewed not against the standards of a
mythical or unattainable market structure, but against the requirements of a degree of competition that is both feasible and
effective in continuing the search for a more economic means of
satisfying the material wants of society.

[13] See, for example, R. A. Gordon, *Business Leadership in the Large Corporation*
(University of California Press in cooperation with the Brookings Institution, 1961),
esp. pp. 67-98.

[14] John Maurice Clark, "Toward a Concept of Workable Competition," *American Economic Review*, Vol. 30 (June 1940) and *Competition as a Dynamic
Process* (Brookings Institution, 1961), esp. pp. 24-88. Clark concerns himself both
with market structure and performance. Edward S. Mason, another leading
proponent of "workable competition," has emphasized performance: "a progressive
technology (and) the passing on to customer of the results of this progressiveness
in the form of lower prices, larger output, improved products"; see Mason in
Dexter M. Keezer, ed., "The Antitrust Laws: A Symposium," *American Economic
Review*, Vol. 39 (June 1949), p. 712.

John Kenneth Galbraith has argued that additional advantages stem from the
interplay (and potential interplay) of giant organizations. See *American Capitalism*
(Houghton Mifflin, 1952). See also Joe S. Bain, "Workable Competition in Oli-
gopoly," American Economic Association, *Papers and Proceedings*, Vol. 40 (May
1950), pp. 35-47; Jesse W. Markham, "An Alternative Approach to the Concept of
Workable Competition," *American Economic Review*, Vol. 40 (1950); and
Edward S. Mason, "The Current Status of the Monopoly Problem in the United
States," *Harvard Law Review*, Vol. 62 (June 1949), p. 1265.

[15] This position has its professional proponents as well. See George W. Stocking,
Workable Competition and Antitrust Policy (Vanderbilt University Press, 1961),
pp. 1-17.

Evolution in the Competitive Setting

Big business today represents a type of organization and a pattern of competitive practice that differ from those earlier accepted as exemplary of competitive behavior. This changing character of competition does not of itself signify either improvement or retrogression. Shifts in competitive practice, and in the order of priority of the several aims of competition, are a part of the evolution of technology and market organization. Big business has subordinated some traditional forms of competition; it has revitalized others.

The economic transition from control by the feudal lord, craft guild, church, merchant league, or state, to relatively free markets occurred gradually between the Crusades and the nineteenth century. Only as men acquired the means to multiply goods readily did markets and competitive pricing begin to steer economic activity. The increasing availability of capital, and the development of technology which made the capital meaningful, created an opportunity for an expansion of output that was both desired and profitable. Improvements in transportation and communications helped to extend trade, broaden markets, and break down barriers rooted in local practice, tradition, and scarcity.

Expanding markets required larger and more efficient economic institutions. Increased volume of goods called for corresponding progress to achieve regularity of supply. More complex relationships between primary producers and fabricators, and between wholesalers and retailers, placed greater reliance on the market for adjusting prices to equate supply and demand.

In turn, the market has itself encouraged the initiation of new ventures and broadened the base of competition with new supplies and new demands. The impressiveness of this achievement is reflected in a representative observation that "during the first half of the nineteenth century the competitive system was probably more generally in effect than ever before or since."[16]

Nevertheless, even the comparatively unfettered and expand-

---

[16] John Maurice Clark, "Monopoly," *Encyclopedia of the Social Sciences*, Vol. 10 (1933), p. 625.

ing markets of the nineteenth century produced only rare examples of "pure" competition, mainly in the markets of finance and international trade. Even these could at best be said only to approximate the automatic competition with which students embellished the classical tradition. Aside from the special protection and privileges afforded by the state, custom and habit continued to influence the distribution of goods and services. John Stuart Mill, spokesman of the classical tradition in the golden age of free trade, reminded his readers of 1850 that substantial market competition was a phenomenon of recent origin. He cautioned, even in regard to conditions then current, lest his colleagues be blind to the facts in their preoccupation with pure competition as a tool of theory:

> They are apt to express themselves as if they thought that competition actually does, in all cases, whatever it can be shown to be the tendency of competition to do. This is partly intelligible, if we consider that only through the principle of competition has political economy any pretension to the character of science. So far as rents, profits, wages, prices, are determined by competition, laws may be assigned for them. Assume competition to be their exclusive regulator, and principles of broad generality and scientific precision may be laid down, according to which they will be regulated. The political economist justly deems that his proper business; and as an abstract or hypothetical science, political economy cannot be required to do, or indeed cannot do, anything more. But it would be a great misconception of the actual course of human affairs, to suppose that competition exercises in fact this unlimited sway.[17]

Since Mill's time, the pendulum has swung between free markets and greater institutional controls, but the volume and variety of goods and services have continued to grow.

The development of technology and newer forms of economic organization have inevitably tended to change the character of competitive effort. Such shifting has occurred repeatedly, bringing to the fore different features of the competitive drive. A system of fraternal business discipline was provided by the medieval

[17] John Stuart Mill, *Principles of Political Economy*, W. J. Ashley, ed. (London: Longmans, Green, 1929), p. 242.

guild. Craftsmen operated within narrow limits of discretion in the specifications and sale of their products, yet found various ways to vie with each other for the customer's favor. A different frame for operation was later provided by the great chartered trading companies. These were state protected monopolies. Still, they served to break down the limitations on competition set by local monopolies and guild restrictions. Through the trading companies, the scope of market competition was extended far beyond its previous range, paving the way for the industrial revolution and an era of international free trade. The expanding enterprises of the industrial revolution further altered the focus of competition. The concentration of investment and enterprise produced cheap products in large quantity, products which became available to more of the people of the world, giving greater scope to less personal forms of competition.

The great markets of the commercial and early industrial revolutions were chiefly in staple products—wool, sugar, rum, timber, grains, bullion, coal, cotton piece goods. The general conception of competition was then of competition in standard products. Competition was characterized by individual producers not specifically identified with the product. Farmers sending wheat to market were not engaged in direct rivalry with each other, but were bystanders, waiting to learn their take as price settled to that point where the offered supply of the commodity was absorbed. As long as commerce was chiefly confined to the exchange of uniform commodities, competition was conceived primarily in terms of price adjustments for the same commodity.

During the last half century, big business effected drastic changes in the scope and form of business by simultaneously expanding both the range of products and the range of quality specifications. The technological progress that enlarged the scale of enterprise also led business firms, and big firms in particular, to become agencies for the continuous creation of product variations and consequent redistribution of markets. Steel-making today is a whole complex of metal production. It involves light sheets for automobiles, stainless steel for cutlery, coated plate for tin cans, and so on through a long list of steels by specification. With big-scale production, the traditional boundaries of established industries are more frequently crossed; new groups of competitive commodities make for realignments of firms in market rivalries. Another accompaniment of technological development has been the participation of big-scale enterprise in related phases of supply and distribution—in the succession of pipelines through which the mass-produced output is made to flow to the customer.[18]

This continual remaking of markets has tended more than ever to render academic the simplest models of competitive behavior. If competition is dynamic—and it must be to serve the total objective of a competitive system—market equilibria will be attained at progressively advancing levels of economic output and want satisfaction. The "creation" of demand, the planned use of mass productive capacity, the maintenance of inducements for profitable investment, have all meant a more active role for the company in influencing the market.

Coordination of Multiple Objectives

The case for the competitive system must, as it operates today, ultimately rest on its ability to satisfy a set of objectives, no one of which the consuming public would willingly forego. A wide choice of available goods and services is an end in itself for a free society. Room must be provided for individual opportunity, but an attempt must also be made to raise the plane of living. This requires the organization of manpower and capital for joint effort. The scale of such effort often requires coordination of production and distribution for mass output. Regulation of prices, processes, and contractual arrangements between suppliers and users may in turn be required. While a dynamic and innovative competition, with recurring inducements to risk-taking is a desirable goal, it is also desirable that business rivalry be tempered by social ethics; and that public goods and services be directly administered or provided under the auspices of government.

[18] Some of the problems to which this development gives rise are discussed in Chap. 10.

The organization, coordination, and allocation of responsibility for the maximum realization of these ends are continual problems. Big business has its legitimate place in this complex only insofar as it makes a contribution to the total economy that cannot be made by smaller-scale enterprise and that involves activities that preferably should not be added to the burden of the state.

The American economy can be viewed as the composite of three fields of enterprise—small and medium-sized business, big business, and public enterprise.

Small business furnishes the prototype of competitive enterprise. Each proprietor is a center of individual initiative; the decisions are his; the consequences, favorable or unfavorable, fall mainly on him. With millions of such small-scale ventures, the success or failure of one is not directly noticeable in the economy as a whole. Among the millions of self-employed is an open range of new ideas, individual trial and error, and flexibility of independent adjustment to changing market conditions. The government has endeavored to serve this area of individual initiative in the role of monitor, aide, and equalizer of bargaining strength.

At the opposite pole is that area of economic effort legally vested with special public interest. Here the community either directly provides a public service or, alternatively, supervises the private operation of a franchised monopoly. Publicly operated enterprises—postal service, urban water supply, elementary and secondary education, and others—are generally removed from the private sector on the grounds that these services must be generally available to the community and that the private economy is better able to focus on competitive behavior elsewhere when these basic services have been guaranteed by public operations. Many, if not all, of these services would, under private operation, create a divergence between the private interests of individual buyers and/or sellers and the public interest of society as a whole. In other words, significant external effects are associated with the provision of these services.[19] Similar considerations of efficiency

[19] For a general review of public enterprise, see Clair Wilcox, *Public Policies Toward Business*, rev. ed. (Richard D. Irwin, Inc., 1960), pp. 781-884. See also Richard A. Musgrave, *Theory of Public Finance* (McGraw-Hill, 1959), pp. 6-17, 136-59.

and protection of essential services underlie the regulation of public utilities and financial institutions.

The area of industrial big business has features of both private and public enterprise. It has some of the freedoms associated with the former; it is subject to the disciplines and responsibilities of the latter. It has been described as "managerial enterprise" to connote that it is management, not owner, operated on behalf of an aggregation of interests directly as well as indirectly involved with big business. This management is directly responsible to owners and investors who for the most part do not participate in management. This management is also clearly, if not intimately, involved with large labor groups, with thousands of independent or not so independent suppliers and distributors, and with the innumerable consumers on whose acceptance of the output the success of the entire operation ultimately depends. The planning and policy decisions of big business management are an adaptation to this complex. Indeed, the label "big business" becomes applicable when the dimensions of an enterprise have reached a point where a major decision affecting production, pricing, or operating methods will have a significant effect on the total market of one or more industries. Increasingly in recent years, big business has been enlisted by the government for operations involving national security in which the know-how, facilities, and product of the large enterprise are reserved without resort to the usual procedures of competitive bidding and market price and profit determination.

The division into these three categories of enterprise is neither clear-cut nor unchanging. A growing economy cannot be expected to take the present allocation of functions and responsibilities as definitive. Enterprises in these three fields, doing business with each other, are expected to challenge as they cooperate. If competition is to thrive, no field of opportunity or responsibility should irrevocably be regarded as the exclusive domain of any one type of organization or form of competition. In like manner, the body of laws designed to attain the multiple objectives of the competitive system must be kept sensitive to changes in the relative market position of competing elements. Protection designed to bolster the weak must be modified when the weak wax strong and can stand the full brunt of the market. A large measure of regulation need not weaken the essential drives of a competitive society if, for the bulk of economic wants and satisfactions, the market remains the final arbiter.

Points of Reference for Analysis

How and in what proportion the three sectors—small business, big business, and public enterprise—have grown is developed in the statistical tabulations of succeeding chapters. Data comparing the growth of big business with that of the other sectors of the economy are examined in an attempt to assess the degree to which big business is supporting or suppressing a climate of fair and dynamic competition. The statement that big business represents an excessive concentration of economic power, should be explained in terms of "power to do what?" The balance of economic power should be considered as reflected in the extent of growth of big business in relation to the rest of the economy. If the number of buyers or sellers in a given industry is found to be small, a test of the competitive access to market sources is applied. When big business occupies a dominant position in an industry, the effect of its position on the conduct of its competitors, or on the range of alternatives open to consumers, is considered.

In this regard, the apparent entrenchment of a giant corporation in a position of leadership is translated into the effect of that entrenchment on its incentives as a competitor and on the markets in which it competes. To what extent, for example, are other members of the industry, or those directly competitive with it, prevented from making decisions except under the coercive pressure of the dominant firm? Has the presence of these giants barred lesser companies from entering the market in competition with them? How has the growth of big business affected equality of bargaining power between buyers and sellers similarly situated, or the opportunity of buyers or sellers to shop around for the most favorable bids or offers? The conditions surrounding the operation of big business in the economy may or may not be found suited to the kind of aggressive and innovative competition required, to the continued multiplication and improvement of goods and services, and to the expansion and direction of production in accordance with ultimate consumer preference.

3

Big Business in the Business Population

THE INDUSTRIAL CORPORATION large enough to be considered a part of big business is one of only a few hundred firms. If the lower limit of size by total assets is set at $100 million, 400 corporations would qualify.[1] If size is based on number of employed persons, with 5,000 as the lower limit, about 450 to 500 firms would be included. By either measure, the number is not large. Nevertheless, many of the organizations included by these definitions would be smaller than a number of the subsidiaries of the nation's largest corporations, where assets may run into the billions of dollars, and where employment may exceed 100,000. The composition of the big business sector is varied.

This chapter, and the four that follow, contain a summary of the statistical evidence of the degree of concentration of economic power in large corporations. The remaining chapters are concerned with the performance of big business in various types of markets, and with efforts to assess the degree to which practices of big business diverge from the socially desirable. Structure will be discussed first. Subsequently, the behavior of big business within particular institutional settings will be analyzed.

---

[1] U.S. Internal Revenue Service, *Statistics of Income, 1960-61: Corporation Income Tax Returns* (U.S. Government Printing Office, 1963), Table 4, pp. 62-96. Industrial firms are here considered to include corporations in mining (31), manufacturing (304), construction (1), wholesale and retail trade (53), and services (11).

The Distribution of Employed Persons

The 1960 decennial census of population of the United States showed nearly 64 million persons to be receiving remuneration as employees, proprietors, or other self-employed individuals. The distribution of this total employment is shown in Table 3-1, both by class of worker and by industrial division.[2]

Business firms account for about 71 percent of all employment. The manufacturing division alone accounts for 28 percent. Nearly 19 percent of total employment is in wholesale and retail trade, and about 11 percent is in finance, insurance, transportation and other public utilities. Personal repairs and other services performed by business firms account for 6 percent.

Of the 29 percent of all employment in industrial divisions usually considered outside the realm of business firms, government employees constitute the largest single component, slightly exceeding the combined employment of agriculture and professional services.

Proprietors and self-employed persons represent only about one-eighth of total employment. As Table 3-1 shows, proprietors out-number paid employees only within the agriculture division. Proprietors constitute roughly one-fifth of the labor involved in services, trade, and construction (combined with mining) divisions, but are of negligible importance within all other major industrial divisions.

Comparisons of the 1960 employment pattern with those of ten and thirty years earlier are provided by Table 3-2. In 1950 the proportion of total employment in business firms was 71 per-

[2] A conspicuous feature of this table is the large group (nearly 4 percent of all employees) for whom employment status and class of worker were ascertained, but for whom information was insufficient to permit classification by industry. The data in this table do not agree precisely with data from other sources (see, for example, Table 3-2) because of differences in timing, method, and concept. For a statement of the derivation of these data, see *U.S. Income and Output*, Supplement to the *Survey of Current Business* (November 1958), Table VI-16, p. 214, note 1; and *Measuring Employment and Unemployment*, President's Committee to Appraise Employment and Unemployment Statistics (U.S. Government Printing Office, 1962), App. I, pp. 359-70.

cent—six percentage points higher than in 1929; gains in the proportion of persons engaged in manufacturing and in trade more than offset a small decline in the finance, transportation, and com-

TABLE 3-1. *Civilian Employment by Industry and Class of Worker, April 1960*[a]

(Number in thousands)

Industry	Total Employment		Wage and Salary Employees		Proprietors and Self-employed	
	Number	Percent of Total [b]	Number	Percent of Total [b]	Number	Percent of Total [b]
Business firms	43,379	70.6	38,881	63.3	4,498	7.3
Mining and construction	4,001	6.5	3,240	5.3	761	1.2
Manufacturing	17,279	28.1	16,913	27.5	366	.6
Trade	11,514	18.8	9,608	15.6	1,906	3.1
Finance, transportation, communications	6,641	10.8	6,195	10.1	446	.7
Services	3,944	6.4	2,925	4.8	1,019	1.7
Other	18,023	29.4	14,676	23.9	3,347	5.5
Agriculture, forestry, fisheries	4,007	6.5	1,422	2.3	2,585	4.2
Professional services	3,429	5.6	2,724	4.4	705	1.1
Religious and other nonprofit organizations	814	1.3	781	1.3	33	.1
Private households	1,912	3.1	1,888	3.1	24	—
Government	7,861	12.8	7,861	12.8	—	—
Total known by industry	61,402	100.0	53,557	87.2	7,845	12.8
Unknown by industry	2,565		2,507		58	
Total civilian employment	63,967		56,064		7,903	

Source: U.S. Bureau of the Census, *U.S. Census of Population: 1960*, Detailed Characteristics, United States Summary. Final Report PC (1)-1D, Table 214.

[a] Excludes 2½ million persons in the armed forces and roughly 700,000 unpaid family workers. Unpaid family workers are found chiefly in agriculture and retail trades.

[b] Based on total known by industry for all industry groups.

munication sectors. The employment share of the business sector and its divisions remained quite stable in the years following 1950.

Although marked and continuing declines in the number of persons employed in agriculture and as paid workers in private households occurred over the past thirty years, these have been matched by larger increases in employment in professional services, nonprofit organizations, and in government. Overall, however, employment in business firms rose by 55 percent between 1929 and 1960, while civilian employment elsewhere increased little more than 15 percent.

TABLE 3-2. *Number of Persons Engaged in Production, by Industry, 1929, 1950, and 1960*[a]

Industry	Thousands of Persons			Percent of Total		
	1929	1950	1960	1929	1950	1960
Business firms	29,814	40,444	46,178	64.9	70.9	71.3
Mining and construction	3,323	4,343	4,912	7.2	7.6	7.6
Manufacturing	10,556	15,163	16,549	23.0	26.6	25.5
Trade	7,821	11,439	13,525	17.0	20.1	20.9
Finance, transportation, communications	5,643	6,139	7,092	12.3	10.8	10.9
Services	2,471	3,355	4,096	5.4	5.9	6.3
Rest of the world	0	5	4	—	b	b
Other	16,141	16,593	18,611	35.1	29.1	28.7
Agriculture, forestry, fisheries	9,205	6,546	5,133	20.0	11.5	7.9
Professional services	1,314	2,070	3,240	2.9	3.6	5.0
Religious and other nonprofit organizations	351	581	831	.8	1.0	1.3
Private households	2,348	1,710	1,600	5.1	3.0	2.5
Government [c]	2,923	5,686	7,807	6.4	10.0	12.0
Total	45,955	57,037	64,789	100.0	100.0	100.0

Source: 1929: *National Income 1954*, Supplement to *Survey of Current Business* (1954), Table 28; 1950: *National Income, 1957, Supplement* (1957), Table VI-16, p. 214; 1960: *Survey of Current Business* (July 1963), Table VI-16.

a Based on estimated man-years of full-time employment for wage and salary workers and active proprietors.
b Less than .01 percent.
c Excludes military personnel.

The Business Population[3]

Growth in the number of business firms exceeded that of the United States population generally between 1900 and 1940. This reflected increased per capita demand for goods and services, a decline of agriculture and domestic services, and, of course, added specialization within the business sector. This upward trend in the number of firms per thousand persons is indicated in Table 3-3.

TABLE 3-3. *Number of Firms, U.S. Population, and Number of Firms per Thousand Persons, 1900 to 1960*

Year	Number of Firms (Millions)	U.S. Population (Millions)	Firms per 1,000 Persons
1900	1.6	76.1	21
1930	3.0	123.2	24
1940	3.3	132.6	25
1950	4.0	152.3	26
1960	4.7	180.7	26

Source: U.S. Bureau of the Census, *Statistical Abstract of the United States: 1956*, Table 577, p. 485; *Statistical Abstract of the United States: 1962*, Table 645, p. 487 and Table 2, p. 5.

Since 1940, the number of business firms has risen approximately in proportion to population. In both 1950 and 1960, there were 26 firms for every 1,000 people in the United States.

For the 1948-56 period, growth of firm, by size of firm, is shown in Table 3-4.[4] During this eight-year interval, a gain of about half

---

[3] The discussion of trends in the number and distribution of business firms in the remainder of this chapter is based primarily on business population estimates prepared by the U.S. Department of Commerce, Office of Business Economics, published from time to time in the monthly *Survey of Current Business*. In business population statistics, there is no cutoff based on size of firm except that a self-employed person is excluded unless he has either at least one paid employee or an established place of business. A multi-plant establishment, or an outlet firm, is counted once, with all classifications based on the firm as a whole.

[4] Distributions of firms by size are available only for 1945-49, 1951, and 1956. Table 3-4 compares the latest available year, 1956, with 1948 to avoid, insofar as possible, the distorting effects of the war and recovery period.

TABLE 3-4. *Firms in Operation and Paid Employment, by Size of Firm, 1948 and 1956*

Employee Size Classes	Firms in Operation January 1		Paid Employment Mid-March	
	1948	1956	1948	1956
All size classes	3,872,900	4,381,200	36,475,000	40,667,000
0-19	3,681,600	4,164,400	8,485,000	9,621,000
20-99	156,300	179,100	6,267,000	7,126,000
100-499	28,660	31,310	5,713,000	6,171,000
500-999	3,310	3,310	2,291,000	2,271,000
1,000-9,999	2,810	2,880	7,101,000	8,237,000
10,000 or more	230	220	6,618,000	7,240,000
	Percent (Cumulative)		*Percent (Cumulative)*	
0 or more	*100.00*	*100.00*	*100.0*	*100.0*
20 or more	*4.94*	*4.95*	*76.7*	*76.3*
100 or more	*.90*	*.86*	*59.6*	*58.8*
500 or more	*.16*	*.15*	*43.9*	*43.6*
1,000 or more	*.08*	*.07*	*37.6*	*38.1*
10,000 or more	*.01*	*.01*	*18.1*	*17.8*

Source: Betty C. Churchill, "Size of Business Firms," *Survey of Current Business*, Vol. 39 (September 1959), Table 1, p. 15.

a million business firms was shared by all size classes except the largest (10,000 or more employees) and that with 500-999 employees. Paid employment increased in all classes except for firms with 500-999 employees. The average size of firm both within this class and all smaller size classes declined, at least slightly, between these two dates. On the other hand, the average employee size among firms with 1,000 to 9,999 employees rose from 2,527 in 1948 to 2,860 in 1956. Among firms in the largest category, average size rose from 28,774 to 32,909 employees. Particularly in the latter case, change can in part be attributed to business mergers. It also should be noted that the business population statistics distinguish separately incorporated companies, and changes within a few large enterprises from a subsidiary to a division form of organization (or vice versa) can have a marked effect on these statistics.

In general, the business population largely comprises small firms. Ninety-five percent of all firms have fewer than 20 employees. Roughly 40 percent have no employees at all. Most of these small firms are unincorporated. Table 3-4 shows more than 4 million firms with fewer than 20 employees in 1956; the total number of corporations in that year was only 886,000.[5] But nine-tenths of all corporations are also small, tending to be closely, or even individually controlled enterprises, adopting the corporate form of organization only to gain legal, investment, or tax advantages.[6] Similarly, virtually all business turnover is among firms with fewer than 20 employees. This category includes between 98 and 99 percent of all newly acquired or newly established businesses.[7]

Of these small firms, nearly two-thirds are in the two major industry divisions serving consumers most directly—retail trade and services. Construction, however, accounts for 10 percent of firms with fewer than 20 employees.

In a study of big business, greater interest attaches to the other end of the scale—firms with 1,000 or more employees. The percentage of total employment in firms with 1,000 or more employees by major industry division and by the subgroups of the manufacturing, retail trade, and services is shown in Table 3-5. These companies represent less than one-tenth of 1 percent of the firms in the business population as a whole. This percentage ranges among the major industry divisions from a high of about one-half of 1 percent in manufacturing to a low of one one-hundredth of 1 percent in services.

These few firms, nevertheless, account for substantial proportions of total employment. More than two-thirds of all persons employed in transportation and more than half of those in manufacturing are employed by firms with 1,000 or more employees.

[5] U.S. Internal Revenue Service, *Statistics of Income, 1956-57: Corporation Income Tax Returns* (U.S. Government Printing Office, 1959), Table 4, p. 33.

[6] Almost 90 percent of all corporations reporting to the Internal Revenue Service in 1960-61 had assets of less than $500 thousand. See U.S. Internal Revenue Service, *Statistics of Income, 1960-61, op. cit.*, Table 4, pp. 62-96.

[7] Betty Churchill, "Size of Business Firms," *Survey of Current Business*, Vol. 39 (September 1959), Table 4, pp. 14-18.

Among the manufacturing groups, this proportion ranges from nearly 90 percent in transportation equipment to approximately 13 percent in apparel and other finished textile products. The average employment size of the larger firms shows a similar variability among the industry divisions.

Employment is only one of a number of yardsticks. For example, a given firm might be relatively larger (or smaller) when classified by employment than when classified by investment in plant and equipment. Chapter 6 provides some alternative measures of size where assets are the basis of classification. The summary statistics of the business population presented here suggest that the status of the giant firm has grown with the economy. The changes that have taken place reflect primarily a move to a more advanced stage of industrialization. The movement of individual or family enterprises from the farms and villages to the urban centers of highly organized industry has been a movement from less to more attractive opportunities of employment. The rural area has in turn been transformed by the mechanization enabling the smaller numbers of those who continue in agriculture to keep the total farm production abreast of the increase in total population.[8]

The sector of heavy industry, including mines, manufactures, and construction, has added directly to employment at about the same rate as that of the general population increase since 1929 (see Tables 3-2 and 3-3). So far as growth in numbers of employees is concerned, the highest and most consistent rate of expansion is found in trade, finance, and service lines. Government services in the last quarter century have also absorbed employees at a higher rate than the rate of population increase.

In the period since World War II, big business has continued to represent a minor fraction of the total number of economic outlets. At the same time, in some industries, big business continues to include the bulk of total employment. Concentration is

---

[8] The 1959 Census of Agriculture showed that between 1920 and 1959, farms of 1,000 acres or over increased from 1 percent to 3.7 percent of all farms, and from 23.1 to 49.2 percent of total farm acreage. U.S. Bureau of the Census, *Census of Agriculture, 1959*, Vol. 2, pp. 390-92.

TABLE 3-5. *Firms with 1,000 or More Employees, and Average Employment per Firm, by Industry, 1956*

Industry	Firms with 1,000 or More Employees		Percent of Industry (Total) in Firms with 1,000 or More Employees	
	Number of Firms	Average Employment per Firm	Firms	Employment
All Industries	3,100	4,992	.07	38.05
Mining and quarrying	90	3,100	.22	36.37
Contract construction	70	2,571	.02	6.97
Manufacturing	1,780	5,246	.54	52.87
Food and kindred products	160	4,131	.42	43.15
Textile mill products	160	3,244	2.00	47.79
Apparel, other finished textile products	80	2,000	.22	12.76
Leather, leather products	30	4,000	.54	30.00
Lumber, basic timber products	40	2,375	.08	13.34
Furniture, finished lumber products	20	2,750	.15	14.86
Paper, allied products	90	3,467	2.19	54.26
Printing and publishing	100	2,280	.22	26.67
Chemicals and allied products	110	5,982	.91	70.22
Petroleum, coal products	30	9,833	2.50	85.75
Stone, clay, and glass products	70	3,800	.54	46.26
Primary metal industries	140	7,764	2.50	77.04
Fabricated metals [a]	120	3,650	.45	36.59
Machinery except electrical	250	3,776	.89	54.82
Electrical machinery	140	6,993	2.26	75.60
Transportation equipment	120	16,017	1.88	88.90
Professional, scientific, and controlling instruments	60	3,583	1.36	65.55
Rubber products	40	6,050	2.66	75.86
Miscellaneous [b]	50	2,840	.20	24.23
Transportation, communication, and other public utilities	440	6,254	.22	67.22
Wholesale trade	80	3,087	.03	10.23

Table 3-5 (continued)

Industry	Firms with 1,000 or More Employees		Percent of Industry (Total) in Firms with 1,000 or More Employees	
	Number of Firms	Average Employment per Firm	Firms	Employment
Retail trade	330	5,206	.02	21.71
General merchandise	130	6,977	.18	67.73
Food	90	5,855	.02	35.85
Motor vehicles, parts, and accessories	c			2.40
Filling stations	c			2.40
Apparel	20	2,850	.02	10.55
Shoes	10	1,200	.05	11.32
Lumber and building materials	c			0.42
Hardware and farm implements	c			1.60
Home furnishings	10	800	.02	3.12
Eating and drinking places	30	2,733	.01	5.58
Drugs	20	1,750	.04	10.61
Liquor	c			
Miscellaneous retail [d]	10	5,400	.00	7.50
Finance, insurance, and real estate	210	3,448	.06	31.13
Service industries	100	2,380	.01	8.18
Hotels, other lodging places	20	2,250	.02	9.18
Barber and beauty shops	c			
Other personal services	10	2,000	.01	2.86
Business services	40	2,775	.03	16.69
Automobile repair	c			
Miscellaneous repair	10	1,500	.01	10.20
Motion pictures	20	2,050	.15	18.30
Other amusements	c			

Source: Betty C. Churchill, "Size of Business Firms," *Survey of Current Business*, Vol. 39 (September 1959), Table 5, p. 19.
[a] Includes ordnance and accessories.
[b] Includes tobacco manufactures.
[c] Fewer than 5 firms.
[d] Includes appliances and radios.

present, but no major recent shifts in this pattern are discernible. This conclusion, however, is based on statistics of overall employment. The following chapter is concerned with the concentration of output and employment within very large firms and within particular industrial areas. Later chapters are devoted to an analysis of the significance of these measures.

4

Concentration of Employment and Production

THE PROPORTION of business employment concentrated in a relatively small number of large firms suggests a similar concentration in terms of output. However, the significant measures are those that throw light not on total concentration, but on the relationship among rival sellers within given markets. This chapter considers first the proportion of employment in giant firms—those with 10,000 or more employees—within more narrowly defined industrial areas and, secondly, the proportion of manufacturing production accounted for by the four largest producers within their particular markets. Data available from the U.S. Bureau of the Census are employed for this purpose, and include the mining, manufacturing, trade, and service divisions. These divisions account for roughly two-thirds of the national income originating in the business population. The remaining one-third is of relatively little importance to a study of industrial concentration.[1]

Census data are gathered by establishments, usually plants in

---

[1] Contract construction, a component of this one-third, is characterized by a large number of small concerns, and a considerable amount of heavy construction for mining and manufacturing companies is accomplished outside the construction industry by employees of the companies for whom the work is done. Although large and at least locally dominant companies are engaged in most of the remaining divisions—finance, transportation, communication, public utilities—these areas are subject to varying degrees of direct public control through regulatory agencies.

the case of manufacturing, and stores, shops, or outlets in the trade and service divisions.[2] Information on the ownership or control of each establishment within the scope of the 1958 Census material permits a company classification of the basic establishment data.[3] Companies operating a single establishment present no industry classification problems in this respect, and account for 97 percent[4] of all firms included. The larger companies, however, tend to operate many establishments and to cross the 855 detailed industry lines. Use of this detailed classification for company statistics would necessitate unrealistic "forcing" of the large multiunit, multi-industry firms in narrow industrial groups. The classification system has accordingly been regrouped into 135 categories reflecting the more common patterns of activity of the diversified companies. These data are employed for the closer examination of industrial concentration which follows.

Concentration of Employment

Table 4-1 summarizes employment and value of sales and receipts for major industry divisions by broad size classes of companies and establishments in 1958. Although a comparatively

[2] The Census defines an establishment as

". . . each location where business was conducted, including each location of multi-unit organizations. . . . Where two or more activities were carried on at a single location under a single ownership, all activities generally were grouped together as a single establishment, and the entire establishment was classified on the basis of its major activity.

". . . An establishment is classified as a single unit if it is operated by a firm which operated only one establishment in a particular kind-of-business group. An establishment is classified as a multi-unit if it is one of two or more establishments in the same general kind of business operated by the same firm." U.S. Bureau of the Census, *United States Census of Business, 1958* (U.S. Government Printing Office, 1961), Vol. I, App. D., pp. 11, 12.

[3] Discrepancies between Census *Enterprise Statistics* and business population data of Chapter 3 arise not only from the differences in industrial scope noted above, but also, in the case of Census statistics, from the combination into one concern of establishments under common ownership or control. (Separately incorporated subsidiaries are separately counted in the business population statistics.) Additional differences between the two sets of data are introduced by the absence of a size-of-firm cutoff for the business population, while the Census data exclude firms with no paid employment and which had sales volume of less than $2,500 in the Census year.

[4] See Table 4-1.

TABLE 4-1. *Distribution of Companies, Establishments, Employees, and Value of Sales and Receipts, by Industry Division and by Size of Firm, 1958*

Industry Division	Number of Companies (Thousands)				Number of Establishments (Thousands)				Number of Employees (Thousands)				Value of Sales and Receipts (Billions of Dollars)			
	All Size Classes	Firms Employing			All Size Classes	Firms Employing			All Size Classes	Firms Employing			All Size Classes	Firms Employing		
		Less Than 100	100- 9,999	10,000 or More		Less Than 100	100- 9,999	10,000 or More		Less Than 100	100- 9,999	10,000 or More		Less Than 100	100- 9,999	10,000 or More
All companies	3,151.6	3,125.2	26.22	.223	3,493.8	3,255.4	161.9	76.5	30,952	12,781	11,064	7,106	742.2	362.1	228.2	152.0
Single-unit	3,060.3	3,046.2	14.08	.002a	3,060.3	3,046.2	14.1	—	14,295	11,313	2,983	d	364.8	316.2	48.6	d
Multi-unit	91.3	79.0	12.15	.221	433.5	209.2	147.8	76.5	16,657	1,469	15,188	d e	377.5	45.9	331.6	d e
Mineral industries	30.1	29.5	.63	.002b	36.6	31.9	4.5	.2	575	252	323	d	11.6	4.2	7.4	d
Manufacturing	269.8	252.3	17.32	.181	379.9	259.6	69.7	50.7	17,273	3,559	7,957	5,756	331.5	57.9	149.3	124.3
Public warehousing	7.5	7.4	.11	—	8.6	8.0	.6	—	100	68	32	—	1.7	.8	.9	—
Wholesale trade	213.1	211.1	1.99	—	246.2	233.4	12.8	—	2,101	1,650	452	—	168.6	136.7	31.9	—
Retail trade	1,688.3	1,684.7	3.61	.087	1,839.2	1,757.2	57.0	25.0	8,034	5,285	1,503	1,273	196.9	140.4	29.9	26.7
Selected services	942.8	940.2	2.56	.003c	983.3	965.3	17.4	.6	2,869	1,994	875	d	31.9	22.2	9.7	d

Source: U.S. Bureau of the Census, *Enterprise Statistics: 1958*, Pt. 1, General Report, Table 8, pp. 105-08.

a Both companies are aircraft manufacturers.

b One company in each of two categories: metal mining, and bituminous coal and lignite mining.

c Two companies in hotels and other lodging places, and one company operating motion picture theaters.

d Combined with 100-9,999 employee-size class to avoid disclosure.

e Of the 221 companies in this class, 3 in manufacturing and 2 in retail trade together operate 502 establishments which do not cross the industry categories established within these industry divisions. Each of the remaining 216 companies operates in more than one detailed industry category and may cross industry divisions as well; this group of companies has 76,001 establishments, 6,918,000 employees, and $148 billion sales and receipts.

small proportion of all companies—3 percent—operated more than one establishment, these companies accounted for 12 percent of all establishments, 54 percent of total employment, and 51 percent of all sales and receipts. Multi-unit companies were a major factor among all firms with as many as 100 employees and almost completely dominated the group with 10,000 or more employees. Warehousing and wholesale trade, however, contained none of these large companies, and only five appeared in the mineral and service industries combined.

The table strongly suggests that the most concentrated areas are within manufacturing and, to a lesser extent, retail trade. On the average, manufacturing concerns with 10,000 or more employees each operated 280 establishments. Together these accounted for one-third of all employment and more than one-third of the value of all sales and receipts of the category as a whole. For retail trade, the average number of establishments per largest size-class firm was about 675. These firms accounted for roughly 15 percent of both total employment and sales within the retail trade sector.

Of 91 manufacturing industry categories for which Census *Enterprise* data are available, 44 included no company with as many as 10,000 employees. These categories are grouped together in Table 4-2, which shows the employment shares and average size of the largest firms by industry. In 25 instances, the number of companies in this large class is only one or two, and publication of employment information is restricted for reasons of disclosure. These are also grouped as a single entry. Nine of 15 retail trade categories included no company with 10,000 employees, 3 included one or two companies this large, and 3 a sufficient number to permit publication of the employment data.[5]

There is considerable variation in the concentration of employment among these industrial categories. Although the categories with substantial employment tend to be those with three or more of the largest companies, there are exceptions. Total employment exceeded 200,000 in 29 of the 91 manufacturing

[5] U.S. Bureau of the Census, *Enterprise Statistics: 1958,* Pt. 1, General Report, Table 9, pp. 109-31.

categories. Eighteen of these, including the top 5, are listed in Table 4-2. However, 7 of the 29 categories had no company with 10,000 or more employees. Fourteen of 29 manufacturing categories with employment of from 100,000 to 199,999 and 23 of the 33 categories with total employment of less than 100,000 similarly contained no company with more than 10,000 employees. Of the 25 categories each with one or two companies with 10,000 or more employees (not shown individually in Table 4-2), 4 had total employment of at least 200,000, while the remainder were nearly equally divided between firms with 100,000 to 199,999 employees and firms with fewer than 100,000 employed persons.[6]

Total employment exceeded 100,000 in each of the 15 business classifications used for *Enterprise Statistics* within retail trade. The largest group in this respect—eating and drinking places—had total employment of more than 1.5 million, but in no company did employment reach 10,000. In the grocery store field, second in total employment rank, the 11 largest chains accounted for 35 percent of all employment with an additional 26 percent reported in all smaller multi-unit companies. Only one company with more than 250 employees operated a single grocery store; individual outlets of the 11 largest chains average fewer than 30 employees. Limited price variety stores were eleventh by total employment, and 8 companies with 10,000 or more employees reported nearly 70 percent of the total employment within this category. The three categories with one or two of the largest companies were sixth, tenth, and fifteenth in order of total employment size.[7]

In addition to the patterns of business concentration at the national level, there is, given the regional nature of many markets, the secondary issue of regional concentration. Available census data yield only limited information in this regard. Of the 181 largest manufacturers, two companies were clearly concentrated at single locations—each operated one establishment. The activities of each of three additional companies were confined to one detailed industry classification, but with operations divided among 35 establishments, presumably at as many, or nearly as many,

[6] *Ibid.*
[7] Data are from Table 4-2 and *Ibid.*

locations. For the remaining 176 large manufacturers, all of which were active in more than one of the 855 detailed industry classes, an average of 280 establishments per firm indicates not only the geographical dispersion that may exist, but also the extent of

TABLE 4-2. *Number of Companies, Establishments, and Employees, in Companies with 10,000 or More Employees, by Industry, 1958*

Industry	Total Industry Employment (Thousands)	Companies with 10,000 or More Employees			
		Number of Companies	Number of Establishments	Number of Employees (Thousands)	*Percent of Total Employment*	Average Employment per Firm (Thousands)
All manufacturing	17,273	181	50,651	5,756	*33*	31.8
Meat packing	267	3	1,014	119	*45*	39.7
Dairy products	353	5	1,862	108	*31*	21.6
Bakery products	316	5	1,149	82	*26*	16.4
Broadwoven fabrics, yarn, thread, and finishing (except wool)	569	10	837	205	*36*	20.5
Pulp, paper, and board	305	7	772	129	*42*	18.4
Newspapers	312	3	173	44	*14*	14.7
Basic chemicals, fibers, plastics and rubber	517	13	2,063	381	*74*	28.6
Integrated petroleum extraction and refining	508	15	22,652	438	*86*	28.3
Rubber products	294	4	2,591	173	*59*	43.2
Footwear (except rubber)	250	4	1,725	82	*33*	20.5
Glass products	152	5	666	96	*63*	19.2
Blast furnaces and steel mills	721	13	2,070	615	*85*	47.3
Nonferrous primary metals	324	6	755	159	*49*	26.5
Farm machinery and equipment	148	3	524	95	*64*	31.7
General industrial machinery	189	3	148	35	*19*	11.7
Office machines n.e.c.ª	251	4	1,163	178	*71*	44.5
Radio and TV receiving equipment	572	7	696	316	*55*	45.1
Electrical machinery n.e.c.	808	6	3,281	402	*50*	67.0
Motor vehicles and equipment	938	8	1,065	720	*77*	90.0

TABLE 4-2 (continued)

Industry	Total Industry Employment (Thousands)	Companies with 10,000 or More Employees				
		Number of Companies	Number of Establishments	Number of Employees (Thousands)	Percent of Total Employment	Average Employment per Firm (Thousands)
Aircraft	462	10	117	436	94	43.6
Aircraft engines, propellers and equipment	391	10	389	249	64	24.9
Ships and boats	120	3	135	40	33	13.3
Manufacturing categories with 1 or 2 companies with 10,000 or more employees (25 categories included) b	3,191	34	4,804	655	21	19.2
Manufacturing categories with no company with 10,000 or more employees (44 categories included)	5,318	0	—	—	—	—
All retail trade	8,034	37	24,989	1,273	16	34.4
Department stores	990	14	3,941	608	61	43.4
Limited price variety stores	342	8	4,838	231	68	28.9
Grocery stores	1,095	11	13,547	387	35	35.2
Retail trade categories each with 1 or 2 companies with 10,000 or more employees (3 categories included) c	986	4	2,668	52	5	12.0
Retail trade categories with no company with 10,000 or more employees (9 categories included)	4,621	0	—	—	—	—

Source: U.S. Bureau of the Census, *Enterprise Statistics: 1958*, Pt. 1, General Report, Tables 8 and 9, pp. 105-131.

a Not elsewhere classified.

b Includes 9 Census Industry Categories with 2 companies, and 16 Census Industry Categories with 1 company.

c Includes 1 Census Industry Category with 2 companies, and 2 Census Industry Categories with 1 company.

product and activity diversification within these companies.[8]

The two industry categories showing the greatest employment concentration in Table 4-2 also offer the greatest contrast with re-

[8] *Ibid.*, Table 8, p. 106.

spect to the average number of establishments per large firm. Two of the 10 largest aircraft companies each operated only one establishment. The other 8 together reported 115 establishments, or only about 14 each on the average. At the other extreme, each of the large integrated petroleum extraction and refining companies had at least two establishments, one in mining and one in manufacturing, with an average for the group of over 1,500 establishments, representing 86 percent of all employment within the industry as a whole.[9] In the aircraft industry, companies with 10,000 or more employees accounted for 94 percent of total employment. The nature of the market for aircraft encourages production in large plants. There was also a less than average tendency toward diversification among companies in this category: 79 percent of all employment by firms in this area was in the aircraft industry itself. In contrast, only 40 percent of all employment in the integrated petroleum companies was in petroleum extraction and refining. An exceptionally high proportion of employment—33 percent—was in central administrative offices, auxiliaries, and sales branches.[10]

Concentration of Output

Table 4-3 provides concentration statistics based on the 1958 *Census of Manufactures,* including a comparison with earlier years where possible.[11] In 1958, in more than half of the 443 industries for which concentration ratios are available, the proportion of shipments accounted for by the four largest companies is less than 40 percent. Concentration ratios are between 40 and 60 percent in about one-quarter of the industries, and 60 percent or more in one-fifth.

Industry size, as gauged by value of shipments, bears only a

[9] *Ibid.,* Table 9, pp. 109-31.

[10] *Ibid.,* Table 4, pp. 63, 68.

[11] Concentration ratios shown in Table 4-3 are based on an allocation of each establishment's total sales to the Census 4-digit industry to which the establishment's most important product belongs. This can produce misleading results in the case of large, multiproduct establishments.

TABLE 4-3. *4-Digit Census Manufacturing Industries, by Concentration Ratio, and by Value of Shipments and Number of Companies, 1958 and Earlier Years*

Year and Industry Group	Total Number of Industries	Concentration Ratio				
		0-19 Percent	20-39 Percent	40-59 Percent	60-79 Percent	80-100 Percent
All Industries (1958)	443	100	140	113	61	29[a]
Value of shipments (millions of dollars)						
1,000 and over	77	22	32	11	9	3
500-999	69	26	22	10	8	3
200-499	115	30	33	28	17	7
100-199	63	10	18	19	8	8
50- 99	59	7	18	21	9	4
Under 50	60	5	17	24	10	4
Number of Companies						
0- 25	36	0	0	3	19	14
25- 69	65	0	5	30	20	10
70-199	112	3	36	53	16	4
200-699	129	29	71	25	4	0
700 and over	101	68	30	2	1	0
All Industries[b]						
1958	361	82	113	88	52	26
1954	361	77	118	85	54	27
1947	361	70	134	84	47	26
All Industries[c]						
1958	113	16	40	29	17	11
1954	113	13	39	33	16	12
1947	113	12	42	33	18	8
1935	113	15	38	28	23	9

Source: *Concentration Ratios in Manufacturing Industry, 1958,* Report prepared by the U.S. Bureau of the Census for the Subcommittee on Antitrust and Monopoly of the Senate Judiciary Committee, 87 Cong. 2 sess. (1962). Based on Table 9, p. 457 and Table 2, pp. 10-42.

[a] Includes 4 industries clearly within this size class for which concentration ratios were withheld to avoid disclosure.

[b] Includes 5 industries assumed to be in the 80-100 percent class for which concentration ratios were withheld to avoid disclosure.

[c] Of the 443 industries for which data were available for 1958, 113 had data available for 1954, 1947, and 1935.

loose relationship to the level of concentration. Ratios of 60 percent or more are relatively most frequent in the $100-$199 million class, but the proportion of industries with high concentration is not markedly different for industries with shipments of $500 million or more from those with shipments of below $100 million. At the other end of the scale, the proportion of industries with concentration ratios below 40 percent is 70 percent in each of the top size classes, and drops consistently to 37 percent for industries with shipments totaling less than $50 million.[12]

With size measured by number of companies, the relationship to concentration is somewhat clearer. Concentration ratios must, of course, be high if the number of companies in the industry is sufficiently small. Of the 36 industries with fewer than 25 companies, no industry shows concentration of less than 40 percent, and concentration is 60 percent or more in all but 3 of the 36 industries. The proportion of industries with concentration of 80 percent or more decreases as the number of companies increases. Of 101 industries with 700 or more firms, none showed concentration exceeding 80 percent, and only one showed concentration in the 60 to 79 percent range. Although no industry with from 200 to 699 companies showed concentration exceeding 80 percent, 4 of these showed concentration of between 60 and 79 percent.[13]

[12] Comparatively few of the industries with sales of $1 billion or more manufacture final durable products such as automobiles, farm or construction machinery, radios, or photographic equipment. Most of these larger industries produce chemical, wood, or metal materials having wide application in other manufacturing industries or in construction. Roughly a third produce nondurable goods, purchases of which are frequently made in markets that are far from nationwide. Although concentration ratios of effective market areas are not available, examination of these industries on regional and state bases shows, as would be expected, somewhat higher concentration in the case of regions and markedly higher concentration for states than for the country as a whole. In the case of fluid milk, the concentration ratio is 23 percent for the nation, regions show ratios ranging from 17 to 43 percent, and states 19 to 86 percent. For newspapers, the overall concentration ratio of 17 percent compares with regional ratios of from 23 to 52 percent, and state ratios ranging from 33 to 98 percent. (See *Concentration Ratios in Manufacturing Industry, 1958*, Report prepared by the U.S. Bureau of the Census for the Subcommittee on Antitrust and Monopoly of the Senate Judiciary Committee, 87 Cong. 2 sess. (1962), Table 36, pp. 495 and 501.

[13] In these tabulations, each company is counted in each detailed industry in which it operates one or more establishments, so that the number of companies

Attempts to examine trends in concentration ratios over time are complicated by problems of comparability primarily arising from changes which are made from time to time in the industry classification system. Changes in definition of detailed industries are necessary if currently useful economic data are to be made available, but comparisons with earlier years are often irrevocably lost in the process. And it may be argued that the most dynamic segments of a dynamic economy are lost when attention is confined to the industries for which definitions have remained the same or for which slight modifications have had an insignificant effect.

The 443 industries for which 1958 ratios are available drop to 361 for comparison with 1947 and to 113 for comparison with 1935. Table 4-3 shows little difference in the distribution of industries by concentration ratios between 1947 and 1958. For the 113 industries for which concentration ratios are available back to 1935, Table 4-3 shows an increase from 53 to 56 in the number of industries with concentration ratios below 40 percent, and a decline from 32 to 28 in those with concentration of 60 percent or more. A better comparison, however, is available in Table 4-4. Here, change in concentration is measured in terms of the proportion of gain or loss of the top four firms in the previously unconcentrated sector of the industry (i.e., the shares held by firms other than the top four). For example, a change in share of the top four from 90 to 92 percent is considered equivalent to a change from 50 to 60 percent. Both changes represent a capture by the top four producers of 20 percent of the market previously served by competitors.

Between 1947 and 1958, concentration ratios showed changes of less than 8 percent in 39 of the 113 industries for which data are available for the full twenty-three year period. Gains of more than 8 percent were registered in 33 industries, while losses of

---

by detailed industries contains considerable duplication. Of the 100 largest manufacturing companies, 2 appear among the 4 largest producers in 20 or more detailed industries, and 5 make from 10 to 19 such appearances. Only 5 of the 100 largest companies fail to appear as one of the top 4, and only 18 appear only once. Specific data are lacking, but substantially more duplication of the 100 largest companies must arise from appearances in industries for which they are not among the top 4. This point is developed further below.

TABLE 4-4. *Change in Detailed Industry Concentration Ratios, 1947-1958 and 1935-1947*

Detailed Industry Concentration	Total Number of Industries	Changes in Concentration[a]				
		21 Percent or more Loss	9 Percent Loss to 20 Percent Loss	8 Percent Loss to 8 Percent Gain	9 Percent Gain to 20 Percent Gain	21 Percent or more Gain
Concentration ratio in 1947 (percent)		1947 to 1958				
0- 20	12	0	2	8	1	1
20- 39	44	3	9	22	10	0
40- 59	32	8	6	6	3	9
60- 79	18	3	5	3	4	3
80-100	7	5	0	0	1	1
Total	113	19	22	39	19	14
Concentration ratio in 1935 (percent)		1935 to 1947				
0- 20	15	0	0	12	3	0
20- 39	40	1	5	28	4	2
40- 59	27	9	3	8	5	2
60- 79	24	10	2	5	2	5
80-100	7	2	2	2	1	0
Total	113	22	12	55	15	9

Source: *Concentration Ratios in Manufacturing Industry, 1958,* Report prepared by the U.S. Bureau of the Census for the Subcommittee on Antitrust and Monopoly of the Senate Judiciary Committee, 87 Cong. 2 sess. (1962). Computed for all Census 4-digit industries available for 1935, 1947, 1954, and 1958 from Table 2A, pp. 43-73.
[a] Concentration based on percent of total shipments accounted for by the four largest firms.

this amount or more occurred in 41. Classified by concentration ratios in 1947, 14 of 56 industries with initial concentration of less than 40 percent showed losses over this period of more than 8 percent, as opposed to 12 industries with equivalent gains. Fourteen of 32 industries with 1947 concentration of from 40 to 60 percent showed losses of more than 8 percent; 12 showed corresponding gains. Of 25 industries with 60 percent or more concentration in 1947, 13 declined by more than 8 percent over the 11-year period, and 9 gained more than 8 percent.

For the period 1935 to 1947, 55 of the 113 industries showed shifts in concentration of less than 8 percent. Only 24 gained by more than 8 percent; 34 showed declines in concentration by more than 8 percent.

This analysis is extended in Table 4-5 where these 113 industries are cross-classified by change in concentration between 1935 and 1947, and by change in concentration in the 1947 to 1958 decade. Only 24 of the 113 showed change of less than 8 percent in both periods. In 28 industries, gains or losses of more than 8 percent in the early 12 years were offset by corresponding losses or gains between 1947 and 1958. In only 5 instances were gains of more than 8 percent in the first period followed by gains of more than 8 percent in the second. Ten industries showed losses of 8 percent or more in both periods. If 8 percent is accepted as a measure of significant change in concentration, the experience over this twenty-three-year period is not one of extreme rigidity. There appears, from these data, to be no significant trend toward a greater concentration of output among the largest firms.

Concentration Within Detailed Product Classes

This pattern of change is also borne out by the recent Census review [14] of an earlier Temporary National Economic Committee (TNEC) study of 1,800 detailed product classes in 1937.[15] Of these 1,800 product classes, the Bureau of the Census found only 198 for which data could be made substantially comparable to 1937. The 1937-58 changes in concentration for these commodities are summarized in Table 4-6.

The list of commodities available for comparison greatly over-

[14] See *Concentration Ratios in Manufacturing Industry, 1958,* Report prepared by the U.S. Bureau of the Census for the Subcommittee on Antitrust and Monopoly of the Senate Judiciary Committee, 87 Cong. 2 sess. (1962), Table 35, pp. 486-91.

[15] Temporary National Economic Committee, *Investigation of Concentration of Economic Power, The Structure of Industry,* Monograph 27, 76 Cong. 3 sess. (1941).

TABLE 4-5. *Change in Concentration, 1947 to 1958, by Change in Concentration, 1935 to 1947, 113 Industries*

Change in Industry Concentration 1947 to 1958	Total Number of Industries	Change in Industry Concentration, 1935-1947				
		Over 20 Percent Loss	9 Percent Loss to 20 Percent Loss	8 Percent Loss to 8 Percent Gain	9 Percent Gain to 20 Percent Gain	Over 20 Percent Gain
Over 20 percent loss	19	3	1	7	4	4
9 percent loss-20 percent loss	22	2	4	10	5	1
8 percent loss-8 percent gain	39	7	3	24	4	1
9 percent gain-20 percent gain	19	3	2	10	2	2
Over 20 percent gain	14	7	2	4	0	1
Total	113	22	12	55	15	9

Source: *Concentration Ratios in Manufacturing Industry, 1958,* Report prepared by the U.S. Bureau of the Census for the Subcommittee on Antitrust and Monopoly of the Senate Judiciary Committee, 87 Cong. 2 sess. (1962). Computed for all Census 4-digit industries available for 1935, 1947, and 1958 from Table 2A, pp. 32-73.

represents food items (52 of the 198 total), nearly half of which represent specific canned fruits or vegetables. The same varieties of food in frozen form are not available for comparison. Such omissions of new commodities are, of course, inevitable. However, the intricacies of changing classification systems also result in the omission of commodities usually thought of as standard, at least over the period involved. Bread and all varieties of fresh meat do not appear; even cigarettes are not among the five specific tobacco products listed. Nor does the table include any commodities of the major manufacturing groups of lumber, textiles, apparel, or printing and publishing.

Despite these limitations, Table 4-6 is of considerable interest. Overall, losses in concentration of more than 8 percent slightly exceed corresponding gains. Table 4-6 shows 87 instances of such loss, as opposed to 81 gains. On the other hand, 72 product classes showed losses of more than 20 percent, while only 48 showed

TABLE 4-6. *Change in Product Concentration, 1937 to 1958, by Concentration and Growth in Value of Shipments*[a], *198 Product Classes*

Classification	Total Number of Product Classes	1937-1958 Percent Gain or Loss in Concentration				
		Over 20 Percent Loss	9 Percent Loss to 20 Percent Loss	8 Percent Loss to 8 Percent Gain	9 Percent Gain to 20 Percent Gain	Over 20 Percent Gain
All commodities	198	72	15	30	33	48
Concentration in 1937 (percent)						
Under 20	3	0	0	1	2	0
20-39	26	1	2	6	7	10
40-59	61	10	7	13	16	15
60-79	56	26	5	6	6	13
80-100	52	35	1	4	2	10
Ratio of value of shipments in 1958 to production for sale in 1937[b]						
Under 2.0	38	10	2	5	8	13
2.0-2.9	40	9	4	5	10	12
3.0-3.9	34	10	1	9	5	9
4.0-5.9	34	9	4	5	7	9
Over 6.0	52	34	4	6	3	5

Source: *Concentration Ratios in Manufacturing Industry, 1958*, Report prepared by the U.S. Bureau of the Census for the Subcommittee on Antitrust and Monopoly of the Senate Judiciary Committee, 87 Cong. 2 sess. (1962), Table 35, pp. 486-91.
a Concentration is based on shipments of the four largest producers. Change in concentration is 1958 concentration less 1937 concentration divided by the complement of 1937 concentration.
b Value of shipments differs from production for sale by amount of inventory change. Corresponding totals are not available for the two years.

equivalent gains. When classified by initial concentration, losses tend to be high where concentration in 1937 was high, and correspondingly, product classes with low initial concentration registered more frequent gains in concentration over the twenty-one year period. In part, this is a consequence of the measure of change in concentration adopted.[16] It probably also represents

16 As already indicated, change in concentration ratios are expressed as a per-

a general tendency for high concentration ratios to fall through time, and *vice versa*.

The latter half of the table shows change in concentration by growth in product shipments. Again, a wide range in experience is indicated. Although the evidence is far from decisive, there does seem to be some tendency for product growth to be negatively associated with change in concentration. Thirty-four of 52 products with a more than 600 percent growth in value of shipments between 1937 and 1958 showed losses in concentration of more than 20 percent. Thirteen of 38 industries with growth of less than 200 percent showed gains in product concentration of 20 percent or more. Note that the growth measure here employed is simply the ratio of the value of shipments in 1958 to the value of sales in 1937, both in current dollars. An increase of 200 percent therefore probably implies an absolute decline in the volume of shipments during the twenty-one year period. The index of wholesale prices increased from 47.2 in 1937 to 100.4 in 1958.[17]

In general, however, these data conceal a vast heterogeneity of market activity. Table 4-7, for example, summarizes one aspect of diversification among the truly large firms and their impact on these statistical measures of industrial concentration. This table, employing concentration ratios based on *product* classes, traces the number of appearances by the 100 largest industrial firms among the top 4 producers in these detailed product classes.[18] As shown, there is at least some participation by the 100 largest manufacturing companies among the top producers in more than

---

centage of the share of the market controlled by firms other than the top four. For example, a change from 90 percent to 92 percent is considered a 20 percent change.

[17] Council of Economic Advisers, *Economic Report of the President, January 1963* (U.S. Government Printing Office, 1963), Table C-41, p. 220.

[18] The product concentration ratios are defined on a "wherever made" basis. Unlike the earlier detailed industry ratios, this procedure does not make the assumption that the output of each establishment falls within a single industry, but rather defines an industry as the sum total of all the relevant products, wherever made; the products of a single establishment will frequently be divided among two or more industries.

TABLE 4-7. *Appearances by the 100 Largest Manufacturers Among the 4 Largest Producers of 1,014 Product Classes, by Product Concentration Ratios, Size of Product Class, and Class of Product, 1958*

Product Class	Total Number of Product Classes	Number of Product Classes in Which Firms Among the 100 Largest Are				
		Not Among 4 Largest	1 of 4 Largest	2 of 4 Largest	3 of 4 Largest	4 of 4 Largest
All classes	1,014	464	231	197	89	33
Concentration ratio[a]						
Under 20	144	105	28	8	3	0
20-39	344	186	72	65	17	4
40-59	283	112	68	65	31	7
60-79	151	38	46	35	20	12
80-100	92	23	17	24	18	10
Size of Product Class[b]						
1,000 and over	39	5	6	8	13	7
500-999	79	16	14	25	16	8
200-499	264	103	67	57	28	9
100-199	263	114	66	56	21	6
50-99	266	155	55	44	10	2
Below 50	103	71	23	7	1	1
Class of Product[c]						
Durable goods	495	215	121	92	51	16
Nondurable goods	519	249	110	105	38	17

Source: *Concentration Ratios in Manufacturing Industry, 1958*, Report prepared by the U.S. Bureau of the Census for the Subcommittee on Antitrust and Monopoly of the Senate Judiciary Committee, 87 Cong. 2 sess. (1962), Tables 29, 30, and 31, pp. 478-82.

[a] Percent.

[b] By value of shipments, in millions of dollars.

[c] Obtained by combining data shown by 20 major product groups as follows: durable includes 24 lumber, 25 furniture, 32 stone, clay, and glass, and 33 through 38 metals and metal products; nondurable includes 20 food, 21 tobacco, 22 textiles, 23 apparel, 26 paper, 27 printing, 28 chemicals, 29 petroleum, 30 rubber, 31 leather, and 39 miscellaneous manufactures.

half of the product classes. In 33 product classes, divided about equally between durable and nondurable goods, all 4 of the 4 largest producers are among the 100 largest concerns. The proportion of product classes in which the largest manufacturers appear among the 4 most important producers is high for product classes with concentration ratios of 60 or more (75 percent), and for those in which value of shipments exceeds $500 million (82 percent).

Overall, for 1,014 5-digit product classes, the largest 100 appear among the largest 4 producers within product classes an average of more than 10 times per company. The diversification indicated by this fact is, however, highly variable between companies. One of the largest companies fails to appear as one of the top 4 producers in any product class, 4 companies make only one appearance, and 11 only two or three such appearances. On the other hand, 10 companies each appear 20 or more times; 36 companies are among the top 4 producers in 10 to 20 product classes.[19]

Industrial Concentration and Market Performance

This chapter has included an analysis of available measures of industrial concentration. But the link between structure and performance is far from hard and fast. Even where concentration is low, performance is not necessarily adequate. Alternatively, monopolistic pricing, or price inertia, may be found in markets where sellers are many and small, just as aggressive rivalry may occur among only a few. Moreover, a single census by itself does not reveal the dynamics of growth and decline, or of innovation and obsolescence. A product line or commodity represented by important patents or first-in-the-market positions of leading firms—as in farm machinery, aluminum, processed cheeses, electric lamps, nylon, diesel locomotives, titanium—may move down from an initial 100 percent concentration and yet retain a major fraction of output in the hands of the innovator. Indeed, every real prod-

[19] *Concentration Ratios in Manufacturing Industry, 1958, op. cit.,* Tables 31 and 32, p. 482.

uct innovation introduces a new monopolist. In other lines, where concentration has risen, as in men's apparel or food processing, it may still be far below the average.

The concentration of output of individual products gives some indication of the market impact of large producers in distinct, well-defined products like automobiles or gasoline. These measures for individual products are, however, inadequate for revealing concentration in firms that carry a multitude of related product lines. Chemicals and building materials, for example, illustrate fairly common situations where the number of different products in which the firm is a factor may be a much more significant indication of leadership in its industry than the percentage of any single product that it might command. The integrated firm may be an important factor in the industry by virtue of the fullness of its lines of substitutable products.

These and similar qualifications suggest that appraisal of the concentration of market power must be supplemented by examination of particular industries illustrative of monopoly or oligopoly situations. Three such examples are presented in Chapter 5.

5

Interindustry Competition:
Three Illustrations

THE ILLUSTRATIONS that follow suggest the difficulty of drawing valid conclusions about the nature of competition from simple measures of industrial or market structure. Each is taken from a situation where one or a few large companies have dominant positions in recognized industries. Each, however, is also chosen to represent a different type of market, and each illustrates a different way in which the competitive process can continue to operate in concentrated industries.

The first is aluminum. Once a virtual monopoly in America, this is now an industry of seven firms. This case shows the influence of close substitutes outside the industry on the behavior of an otherwise close oligopoly. The second is tires. Substitutes for tires are not available. Here, competitive pressure, or the pressure of potential competition, has been brought to bear by large and powerful buyers. The third is the linoleum industry, more generally known as the floor and wall coverings industry. In the complex and changing structure of this industry, the difficulties of defining, let alone interpreting, concentration ratios are readily apparent.

Aluminum: Competition with Substitutes

Only one firm produced primary aluminum in the United States until 1940. Until then, the Aluminum Company of America was a classic illustration of industrial monopoly. The disposal of government plants constructed during the war added two more companies. Another three firms entered the industry in the 1950's. The seventh appeared in 1963. Despite these new entrants, aluminum still ranks at the top of the list of the highly concentrated industries.

The history of aluminum production has been shaped by the fact that the product itself has few natural or exclusive uses. The scope of product variations that have a bearing on its usability may be sensed from the long list of properties, ranging from weight to ductility and hardness, regarded by the industry as decisive in the competition of aluminum with other materials.[1]

The market for aluminum has been determined in almost every case by the success of the metal in its struggle for preference over established materials and in withstanding competition of new ones. In the 1890's, aluminum got its start by invading the household utensil market, where iron, copper, glass, and other familiar materials covered the field. It has had to compete with copper for a position in the electrical transmission industry. It has met the competition with wood, steel, and other metallic and nonmetallic materials in the building industry. In some of these markets, it has made a successful entry only to be again supplanted; in others it has been able to maintain, improve, or completely secure its position.

There have, however, been radical shifts in the importance of various industries as outlets for aluminum products. Aluminum in transportation equipment is a good example. In 1909, less than one-fifth of the 34 million pounds of aluminum consumed was used in the transportation industry. By 1920, the transporta-

[1] The list of properties includes:

Weight	Ability to form alloys
Heat conductivity	Compressive strength
Adaptability to casting	Coefficient of expansion
Ease of machining	Adaptability to extrusion
Malleability	Tensile strength
Corrosion resistance	Electrical conductivity
Reflectivity	Elasticity under varying
Adaptability to forging	temperatures and pressures
Appearance	Hardness
Ductility	

tion industry accounted for 50 percent of consumption—primarily as a result of the use of aluminum in automobile bodies. In 1939 this percentage had fallen to 37; by the close of the 1940's it was down to 21. For the most part, this decline reflected the fact that, while in 1920 the weight of aluminum per automobile averaged 50 pounds, by 1939, when steel had replaced aluminum in the automobile body, the average car used only 5 pounds of aluminum.[2] But the trend again reversed itself. By 1956, when aluminum was more extensively used in engineering parts, the average had risen to 35 pounds.[3] Indications are that this figure has since increased. In 1962, the automotive industry accounted for more than 41 percent of the end use of custom produced aluminum die casting; the transportation industry as a whole accounted for 23.4 percent of all aluminum shipments.[4]

This uncertainty of the automobile market, and later the fluctuation of demand in the aircraft market, induced the aluminum industry to look to other fields. A major opportunity emerged in the building industry. Prior to 1920, only a negligible fraction of the output of the aluminum industry went to the building industry. In 1930, 4 percent of aluminum consumption was in building materials.[5] By 1962 the building industry equaled transportation as an industrial consumer of aluminum, accounting for 23.4 percent of total annual shipments.[6] Early in this period aluminum was used in building and construction chiefly for siding and roofing, where it was directly competitive with galvanized iron sheet. More recently, of course, aluminum hardware and finishings of all sorts have become prominent, again competing directly with corresponding and older products fabricated from iron and steel.

[2] Data supplied by the Aluminum Company of America.

[3] Merton J. Peck, *Competition in the Aluminum Industry* (Harvard University Press, 1961), p. 27.

[4] The Aluminum Association, *Aluminum Industry Annual Statistical Review, 1962*, pp. 29, 33. Data relate to all aluminum shipments, including scrap and imported scrap.

[5] Data supplied by the Aluminum Company of America.

[6] U.S. Department of Commerce, Business and Defense Services Administration, *Aluminum Factbook* (1963), p. 16.

Similarly, in the expansion of power transmission lines, aluminum has had to wage a prolonged, but successful, battle to share the market with copper. In the early years of this century, copper accounted for more than 70 percent of the electrical transmission wiring. The positions have now been reversed, aluminum currently accounting for well over half of the kilowatt miles of electrical wiring.[7]

The bundles of properties of aluminum that have pitted it against copper, lead, tin, steel, and their alloys, or against wood and plastics must be scrutinized in the light of comparative costs. The market price of aluminum is in part a result of its ratings for various purposes. In 1909, when the market contest between aluminum and copper was under way, the price per pound of aluminum (24 cents) was nearly twice that of copper (13 cents). Since then, its price has undoubtedly been influenced not only by competition with copper, but also by the drives for entry and the holding of position in other markets. The price of aluminum has been lower than that of copper since 1950.

Table 5-1 provides a historical price series for these two competing metals. Aluminum prices rose markedly during World War I, remained relatively stable during the 1920's, and then fell almost continuously until the introduction of new competitors after World War II. The industry, even with Kaiser and Reynolds in addition to Alcoa, was not immune to the general inflationary pressure of the late 1940's and early 1950's. Aluminum prices rose continuously from 1945 to 1957, and remained relatively stable until 1960. The substantial decline in the early 1960's is striking. The postwar period has been one of rapid development of new products and processes in the industry. These have ranged from the mass delivery of molten aluminum under five- or even ten-year contracts, to the fabrication of outdoor telephone booths, to the use of aluminum in automobile engine blocks and transmissions, and even to kitchen foil.[8] This is now an active industry, characterized perhaps more than any of the other metals,

---

[7] Data supplied by the Aluminum Company of America.
[8] See Peck, op. cit., pp. 121-43, esp. 134-43.

TABLE 5-1. *Average Annual Prices of Aluminum and Copper, 1909-1962*

Year	Aluminum [a] Cents per Pound	Copper [b] Cents per Pound
1909	24.0	13.1
1915	24.6	17.5
1920	33.3	17.5
1925	28.2	14.2
1930	23.8	13.1
1935	19.5	8.8
1940	18.7	11.4
1945	15.0	11.9
1950	17.6	21.5
1951	19.0	24.4
1952	19.4	24.4
1953	20.9	28.9
1954	21.8	29.8
1955	23.7	37.4
1956	26.0	41.9
1957	27.5	30.0
1958	26.9	26.1
1959	26.9	30.8
1960	27.2	32.2
1961	25.5	30.1
1962	23.9	30.8

Source: U.S. Geological Survey, *Mineral Resources of the United States*, Pt. 1; Bureau of Mines, *Mineral Resources of the United States*, Pt. 1; Bureau of Mines, *Minerals Yearbook*, Vol. 1.

[a] 99 percent ingot.
[b] Copper ingot, electrolytic, f.o.b. New York.

regardless of the number of competitors, by the invasion of new fields and the displacement of old competitors.

It may be argued that the case of aluminum is one of almost infinite opportunities for substitution, and hence not representative of a truly isolated oligopoly. Nevertheless, the line between product differentiation and product substitution is not a sharp one. Differences in types of users can also generate intra-product competition not dependent on the number of producers. The tire industry, where there is as yet no ready substitute for rubber casing, is illustrative in this latter case.

Tire Industry: Oligopoly With Rival Markets

Considering that roughly 70 percent of new tire output is in the hands of four large manufacturers, the concentration ratio appears high enough to provide a favorable setting for a controlled market at stable prices.[9] Here again, the structure of the market supplies only a partial answer to the presumption of any blueprint for control by a Big Four oligopoly.

Table 5-2 illustrates the product structure of this market in 1962. The "original equipment" component accounts for about 25 percent of total sales. New tire replacements account for about another 53 percent. This replacement market for new tires is, in turn, divided between those sold under manufacturers' brands and those sold under private brand names. Manufacturers' brands are handled chiefly by the dealer agencies of tire producers.

TABLE 5-2. *Percentage Distribution of Passenger, Truck, and Bus Tire Sales, by Market Sector, 1962*

Market Sector	Percent of Total Market
Original equipment	24.8
Replacement: new tires	52.7
Manufacturer-owned brands 33.8 percent	
Private brands 18.9 percent	
Retreads	22.5
Total	100.0

Source: Data from a tire company and the Rubber Manufacturers Association.

Private brands, although made by the same tire manufacturers, compete with the manufacturers' own brands in sales by mail-order houses, filling stations, and automobile equipment chains, as well as by independent dealers.

The marked change in the relative importance of the three

[9] *Concentration Ratios in Manufacturing Industry, 1958,* Report prepared by the U.S. Bureau of the Census for the Subcommittee on Antitrust and Monopoly of the Senate Judiciary Committee, 87 Cong. 2 sess. (1962), Table 4, p. 135. See also Table 5-4.

replacement market sectors over the past forty years is shown by Table 5-3. In 1926, nearly all replacement sales were in manufacturers' brands. Private brands were just getting started; recapping had not yet emerged. By 1962, private brands and retreads accounted for more than 55 percent of the total replacement volume; retreads alone accounted for 30 percent.

TABLE 5-3. *Percentage Distribution of Replacement Tire Sales, by Market Sector, 1926 to 1962*

Market Sector	1926	1933	1941	1947	1952	1962
Manufacturers' brands: new	90.4	74.2	56.4	59.1	49.4	44.9
Private brands: new	9.6	20.0	27.1	27.5	22.7	25.1
Retreads		5.8	16.5	13.4	27.9	30.0
Total	100.0	100.0	100.0	100.0	100.0	100.0

Source: Data from a tire company, the Rubber Manufacturers Association, and Warren W. Leigh, *Automotive Tire Sales by Distribution Channels,* University of Akron Bureau of Business Research, Study 5 (1948).

A major component of competition in the tire industry arises from the fact that the tire manufacturers deal with customers who are at least as resourceful as themselves. In the original equipment market, tire manufacturers must contend with the enormous power of the large automobile manufacturers. In the replacement market, terms have to be made with large mail-order houses, oil companies, department stores, and other large firms promoting their private brands.

Though the Big Four produce roughly two-thirds of the domestic output of new tires, this overall percentage is not applicable to the individual sectors of the market. As shown in Table 5-4, the Big Four, in 1962, had more than 95 percent of the original equipment market, 77 percent of new tire replacements in manufacturers' brands, 58 percent in private brands, and only 16 percent of the retreading and recapping market. Moreover, the individual members of the Big Four had varying proportions of their output in different parts of the line. In 1952, one member of the Big Four had 53 percent of its domestic tire sales in original equipment while another had only 38 percent.[10] Even wider

[10] Information supplied by one of the major tire companies. More recent data are not available.

variation occurred among the individual companies in the division of their sales between manufacturers' brands and private brands. Some regional requirements of the major mail-order houses and the private brands sold by a few of the largest department stores are made up entirely of the production of manufacturers outside the Big Four. The market strength of a manufacturer of replacement tires accordingly varies by these regions, with greater or lesser strength depending on the character of the distributors or the presence of small manufacturers entrenched in their own market areas.

TABLE 5-4. *Concentration Ratios, Automobile and Truck Tires, by Market Segment, 1962*

Market Segment	Percent of Total Tire Production	
	Big Four	All Others
Original equipment	95.5	4.5
Replacement: new tires	70.0	30.0
Manufacturer-owned brands	76.7	23.3
Private brands	58.1	41.9
Retreads	16.0	84.0
All tires	64.2	35.8

Source: Data from a tire company and the Rubber Manufacturers Association.

The net effect of this spread of market rivalries, with varying degrees of buying power and specialized forms of distribution, appears to have carried over to the consumer in both price and quality. Tire mileage in general has, according to calculations supplied by the industry, more than doubled in the past twenty-five years. The range open to consumers may be seen in the price spreads for each of the six main types of passenger car tires. Table 5-5 suggests that even at list prices the consumer could, in 1962, satisfy his need for replacement tires at prices ranging from under $12 for retreads to more than $75 for a premium tire of the most popular size.[11] Furthermore, since the mid-1920's, wholesale prices of automobile tires have risen markedly less than has the

[11] In recent years, automobile tire prices have come to be heavily discounted from list prices. This is reflected in the lower published prices of the mail-order houses. The Sears, Roebuck fall-winter catalogue for 1962 lists prices (including federal tax) for new replacement tires ranging from $10.93 (6.70-15, tube type, rayon) to $38.95 (9.50-14, 4-ply nylon tubeless).

TABLE 5-5. *List Prices, Passenger Car Tires, by Grade, 1962*

Grade	Consumer List Prices [a] (Dollars)	
	Blackwall	Whitewall
Premium, nylon		
With blowout and puncture protection		76.75-84.35
With puncture protection and other features		67.00-80.60
Butyl		42.60-42.95
First line		
Nylon	30.70-34.65	35.30-39.85
Rayon	27.90-29.90	32.80-35.15
Second line, nylon	21.25-23.05	25.50-27.65
Third line, nylon	17.60-18.15	21.55-22.25
Retreads [b]		
First line	12.95	14.00
Second line	11.60	12.75
Mud and snow		
First line, nylon	26.70-29.90	32.75-36.50
Second line, nylon	22.60-25.90	27.75-31.75
Third line, rayon	24.70-24.80	30.25-30.40

Source: Data from a tire company.
[a] 7.50-14, 4-ply tubeless.
[b] One company only. The price in this case is for customer-supplied tire carcass.

average price for all nonfarm, nonfood products as a whole.[12]

These data on the tire industry suggest that even in the presence of a Big Four, producing the major fraction of a commodity for which there is no ready substitute, substantial elements of competitive behavior have nevertheless appeared. An underlying competitive force has come from the threat of entry posed by the economic power of large and aggressive buyers.

Floor and Wall Coverings: A Loosely Defined Industry

In each of the foregoing illustrations, competition arose from factors outside the industry in question. Aluminum is a primary

[12] Data from the *Wholesale Prices* and *Price Indexes* serials, published annually by the Bureau of Labor Statistics.

metal for which the market is largely determined by a matching of its properties and economies with those of available but physically different substitutes. Tires represent a well-defined, fabricated product for which there is no ready substitute, but which is subject to control by the potential competition of large and powerful buyers.

The floor and wall coverings industry, in contrast, will have a very high or a moderate concentration ratio, depending on the boundaries drawn for the industry. The 1958 concentration ratio for the "hard surface floor coverings" industry was 83 percent when based on value of shipments of the four largest producers. For wool carpets and rugs, concentration was lower—47 percent for the four largest companies, 66 percent for the eight largest. For "carpets and rugs except wool," the four largest producers accounted for only 32 percent of the market, and the eight largest 45 percent.[13] For floor and wall coverings as a whole, the figure would, of course, be even lower.

Although current data are not available, the Federal Trade Commission's report on concentration of productive facilities in 1947 showed that the three largest producers of linoleum held more than 90 percent of the industry's total net capital assets, the largest producer alone accounting for almost 60 percent. The Federal Trade Commission based its ratios of concentration on the net capital assets owned by the corporations listed as manufacturers of linoleum and closely related hard surface floor coverings.[14]

The first problem in the interpretation of these varying concentration figures is, of course, definition of the relevant industry. In the language of the trade, the term "hard surface" in floor coverings was originally used to distinguish linoleum and closely related products from carpets and rugs, in which wool had long been the basic material. More recently, the term "smooth surface" has been substituted for "hard surface" to take account of the fact that there are varying degrees of flexibility or rigidity in the nonwoolen products competing as hard surface floor cov-

[13] *Concentration Ratios in Manufacturing Industry, 1958, op. cit.,* Table 2, p. 15.
[14] Federal Trade Commission, *Report on the Concentration of Productive Facilities, 1947* (U.S. Government Printing Office, 1949), Table 3, p. 21; pp. 76-77.

TABLE 5-6. *Product Classes in the Floor and Wall Covering Industry, by Firm, 1964*

Industry	Asphalted Felt Base Floor and Wall Coverings — Linoleum	Floor Tiles — Asphalt	Floor Tiles — Rubber	Floor Tiles — Other: (Plastic and Cork)	Wall Tiles — Ceramic	Wall Tiles — Other: (Plastic and Metal)	Adhesives for Floor and Wall[b] Covering	Carpets and Rugs — Wool	Carpets and Rugs — Cotton	Carpets and Rugs — Synthetics
American Biltrite Rubber Co.			X	X						
American Encaustic Co.					X					
A-1 Plastics Co.						X				
Alloy Tile Corp.						X				
Armstrong Cork Co.	X	X	X	X			X			
Artloom Carpet Co. Inc.										X
Bigelow-Sanford										X
Bird & Son, Inc.	X	X								
Bonafide Mills, Inc.	X	X		X						
Cambridge Tile Co.					X					
Carey (Philip) Mfg. Co.		X		X						
Carthage Mills										
Church (C. F.) Mfg. Co.		X		X						
Congoleum-Nairn	X	X	X	X		X	X			
Danbury Rubber Co.			X	X						
Dodge Cork Co.				X						
Fremont Rubber Co.			X	X						
Goodrich (B. F.) Co.		X	X	X						
Goodyear Tire and Rubber Co.			X	X						
Guild Crest Corp.		X		X				X		X
Hachmeister, Inc.				X						

Hightstown Rug Co.
Johns-Manville
Kentile, Inc.
Lees (James) & Sons Co.
Mannington Mills
Mastic Tile Corp.
Mohasco Industries
Mosaic Tile Co.
Moultile, Inc.
Mundet Cork Co.
New London Mills
Pabco Products, Inc.
Robbins Floor Products, Inc.
Ruberoid Corp.
Sandura Co.
Sloane-Delaware Corp.
S & W Moulding Co.
Tile-Tex Co. Inc.
United Cork Co.
U.S. Rubber Co.
U.S. Stoneware
Uvalde Rock Asphalt Co.
Vikon Tile Corp.
Wilson Plastics
Wright Mfg. Co.

Source: Standard and Poor's, ed., *Industry Surveys* (Standard and Poor's Corporation, 1963, 1964).
a Classes in which companies are engaged in production are indicated by "X."
b Including tiles.

103

erings. Manufacturers of linoleum and related coverings have also come to use the term "resilient" coverings to distinguish their sheets and tiles from such rigid flooring, wall, and ceiling materials as solid wood boards and ceramic tiles (the latter included in the stone, glass, and clay industry). Thus a leading company in flooring now designates its main field of operation as the "resilient, smooth-surface floor and wall covering industry."

These products, in turn, cannot be isolated from competition with related products in the building trades, with household equipment, carpets, rugs, paints, boards, tiles, and sheet goods. More specifically, the resilient, smooth-surface coverings—of cork, wood-flour, felt, asphalt, asbestos, gypsum, and rubber, with linseed oil and various other binders—compete more or less directly with soft-surface floor coverings—rugs and carpets made from various types of natural and synthetic fibers—as well as with painted floors and walls of all types; wall covering materials such as pre-decorated panel board, plastic tile, fiberboard, paper, burlap, and plaster; wood flooring products including plywood and hardboard; ceramic material such as tile, brick, and architectural glass; and other inorganic materials including terrazzo, stone, and cement. Table 5-6 provides an indication of the diversification of the individual companies in this "industry."

Furthermore, new concepts of insulation against sound, extreme temperatures, humidity, and sensitivity to shock are continuing to extend the range of materials to meet a growing list of industrial and scientific requirements in studios, factories, and laboratories, as well as in homes. Floor covering materials have also found new uses in furniture, kitchen equipment, and transportation equipment.

Before World War II, the trend was toward relatively cheaper forms of floor covering, and the more expensive inlaid or moulded linoleums gave way rapidly to the cheaper asphalted felt base flooring. The rising consumer income of recent years has found the industry emphasizing better quality products, with a resultant redistribution of the sales volume toward tiled floors, the use of the smooth floorings as background for finer carpets and rugs, and synthetic compositions for basements, recreation rooms, and offices.

Any attempt to quantify these trends encounters the problem that the names given to the various types of more or less directly competitive coverings do not necessarily mean the same materials or processes from year to year. The shift of preferences among these materials is seen in the different rates at which their respective sales have grown. Linoleum proper, whether in standard felt back or other forms, doubled in physical volume of shipments from the late thirties to 63 million square yards in 1947, and then fell to an annual figure of approximately 37 million square yards in 1958. Shipments of woven wool carpets and rugs were almost 90 million square yards in 1935, 73 million in 1954, and only 52 million in 1958. At the same time, woven fiber carpets and rugs, a negligible item in the Census of 1935, showed shipments of about 7 million square yards in 1958. By comparison, asphalted felt base floor and wall covering—the cheapest linoleum type covering—had in 1958 only 103 million square yards of shipments, a decline of more than 50 percent from the 1947 total of 236 million square yards. Floor tile, on the other hand, which did not exceed 5 million square yards in 1939, accounted for more than 167 million square yards in 1958.[15]

Each of these fields provides borderline areas of competition for the others in spite of continuing sales effort to differentiate the lines for special use. Floor and wall materials promoted for their insulating properties are produced by manufacturers in paper and lumber, glass, clay, plastics, cork, asbestos, and gypsum, as well as asphalt and felt. Many of these companies are not ordinarily placed in the floor and wall covering industry. Nevertheless, their impact on the market makes them members of the industry so far as the consumer's range of selection is concerned, whatever may be the conventional classifications on the raw material and processing side.

Analysis of the concentration of industrial production is concerned with the vitality of competitive effort. Concentration of

[15] The figures on floor coverings are taken from: U.S. Bureau of the Census, *Census of Manufactures: 1947* (U.S. Government Printing Office, 1949), Vol. 2, Table 6, p. 526 and Table 6, pp. 189-90; and *Census of Manufactures: 1958* (U.S. Government Printing Office, 1961), Vol. 2, Pt. 1, Table 6, p. 22D-8 and Pt. 2, Table 6A, p. 32E-16 and Table 6A, p. 39D-13.

output in large-scale enterprise is characteristic of a substantial proportion of total manufacturing production. But this concentration is not necessarily, or even typically, a reflection of industrial specialization. In many instances, and floor covering is an illustration, this concentration is accompanied by wide product diversity and the creation of a number of markets where competition must be met. As a consequence, the ratios of total production ascribed to the four or eight leading firms of a narrowly defined industry may prove unrealistic for gauging the scope or vigor of the competition faced in the market as a whole.

Such statistics cannot, therefore, be expected to shed light on a number of key factors that determine the degree of market control or the range of market choice. It is probable that in floor coverings the representation of even three or four nationwide producers through distributors in local markets, with or without the presence of smaller, independent firms, in many instances provides a broader range of choice than was available in earlier periods when suppliers and consumers could not so readily be reached. The statistics of concentration leave room for more qualitative analysis of the influence and impact of competitive practice. The one pervasive factor in the body of statistics on industry and product structures, a factor which these illustrations confirm, is the number of permutations and combinations of product and use in what may formerly have been a single industry or simple market. Given the degree of product and process realignment that can occur even over short periods of time, the current holding of a high percentage of a product or industry by a few dominant firms may be indicative only of limited or short-lived power to control the disposition of the product or its competitors.

6

Concentration of Financial Power

HISTORICALLY, THE CONCENTRATION of economic power has been reflected in the increasing proportion of the nation's capital and income that has gone into incorporated as distinguished from unincorporated enterprise. Thus, the economic power of large corporations is commonly identified with their financial position. The assets and earnings of the big business sector are impressive for their magnitude alone. Robert Doane estimated that in 1870 only one-fifth of business expenditures occurred in the corporate sector, yet by the second decade of the twentieth century, corporations surpassed unincorporated enterprises in volume of business expenditures, and by 1920 they accounted for almost three-fifths of all expenditures made in private enterprise. Between 1929 and 1960, the corporate sector continued to increase from 56 percent to 65 percent of total business gross product.[1]

The present chapter discusses the way in which this financial power is manifested. It reviews the financial resources of big

[1] See Tables 6-1 and 6-2. Note that comparable figures for the entire period 1870-1960 are not available. The data prior to 1929 in Table 6-1 are based on Doane's estimate of business "expenditures," which he defines as "all expenditures for goods and services, but does not include all transactions and conveyances such as represented in purely transfers of property, bank accounts, etc." (Doane, *The Measurement of American Wealth*, Harper, 1933, p. 211.) The figures subsequent to 1929 in Table 6-2 are Department of Commerce estimates of gross business product. This is defined as the net income originating in private firms, mutual organizations, and government enterprises, plus capital consumption allowances and indirect taxes.

business in relation to the corresponding record for the economy as a whole. Growth over the past thirty years in assets and income of the small, intermediate, and big business sectors is discussed in both relative and absolute terms. The position of the nation's 100 largest industrial corporations is also examined to complete the setting for analysis in later chapters of competitive behavior at the big business level.

TABLE 6-1. *Distribution of Business Activity, 1870-1920*
(Percent)

Year	Corporate	Noncorporate
1870	21.0	79.0
1880	24.2	75.8
1890	31.0	69.9
1900	41.2	58.8
1910	41.0	59.0
1920	57.3	42.7

Source: Robert R. Doane. *The Measurement of American Wealth* (Harper, 1933), Table 18, p. 63.

In the nineteenth century, distinction between corporations and unincorporated business served fairly well to separate the large aggregation of capital from the small. Indeed, the formation of a corporation then represented the launching of an enterprise with capital requirements far beyond the capacity of an individual proprietor or a partnership. In early years, a corporation was established by special franchise under an act of the legislature.

TABLE 6-2. *Distribution of Business Gross Product, 1929-1960*
(Percent)

Year	Corporate	Noncorporate
1929	56.1	43.9
1948	60.1	39.9
1950	61.6	38.4
1960	65.2	34.8

Source: Data on business gross product: *U.S. Income and Output*, Supplement to *Survey of Current Business* (November 1958), pp. 134-35, for years 1929-50; *Survey of Current Business*, Vol. 43 (July 1963), Table 8, p. 17, for year 1960. Data on corporate gross product: 1929, from Office of Business Economics, Department of Commerce; 1948-60, from *Survey of Current Business*, Vol. 42 (November 1962), p. 20. Noncorporate gross product obtained by subtraction.

Incorporation under general state laws has since become commonplace for all sizes of business. Although it may still be said that the giants of business are corporations, most present-day corporations are small-scale, and separation of businesses by financial size categories requires a consolidation of small corporations with unincorporated enterprises.

Financial Size Categories

For the purposes of analyzing size, three broad categories of business organization are distinguished. The smallest category includes unincorporated enterprises and small corporations which tend to be managed by their owners. The second is the category of corporations of intermediate size. The third includes the major corporations that come under the heading of big business.

The small business category here includes corporations with less than a half million dollars of assets. About 90 percent of all corporations come under this heading. In 1960-61, corporations with total assets of from $1 to $50,000 reported an average net worth of only $6,500.[2] Even those corporations with assets of $50,000 to $500,000 still appear to be no larger than partnerships. Although direct comparison of these corporations with individual proprietorships and partnerships by assets size is not possible, corporations with total assets of $50,000 to $500,000 had average incomes and sales somewhat under those of partnerships as a whole. It seems safe, therefore, to include all corporations with up to a half million dollars of assets in the small-business category.[3]

The intermediate sector includes those corporations that, while

[2] U. S. Internal Revenue Service, *Statistics of Income, 1960-61: Corporation Income Tax Returns* (U.S. Government Printing Office, 1963), p. 306.

[3] *Ibid.*, Table 3, pp. 60-61. It is recognized that the lowest income classes are not made up exclusively of firms that would be in the lowest assets classes. However, cross-checks of assets and income classes by the Internal Revenue Service show that relatively few firms in the largest assets group are in the smallest income or deficit categories. See, for example, U.S. Internal Revenue Service, *Statistics of Income, 1948* (U.S. Government Printing Office, 1953), Pt. 2, pp. 14-15, and *ibid., 1960-61, op. cit.*, pp. 216-17.

relatively uncomplicated in structure and product mix, neverthe-less represent a pooling of capital by a number of individuals and separation of ownership from management. This sector is here defined to include a broad range of corporations with assets from a half million dollars up to $100 million.

The remaining corporate sector, where assets per firm exceed $100 million, is termed the big business sector. In that sector, the corporation has attained or is approaching the character of an investment pool and may include a number of business divisions, a corps of specialized and general managers, and shareowners as numerous as employees. Operations are generally on a national scale and usually extend to by-products of the original line. There were 1,333 corporations in this big business sector in 1960.[4] The big business industrials with which this study is primarily con-cerned included the 400 corporations, each with assets of $100 million or more in 1960.

Distribution of Assets

There are substantial limitations to the use of assets as a measure of the financial importance of big business. The assets of financial firms are, for example, largely duplications of the assets of others. Furthermore, total assets may vary widely in the extent to which they are offset by debt, and also in the proportion of liquid capital to fixed facilities. For example, finance and insurance together accounted in 1960-61 for nearly half (49.5 percent) of the assets of corporate enterprise, but less than 2 percent of the gross capital assets. In contrast, the public utility area, where assets consist mainly of fixed facilities, accounted for about 8 percent of assets of all corporations, but 22.5 percent of all capital assets.

The industries with which the present study is concerned—mining, manufacturing, construction, trade, and services—occupied middle ground between finance and public utilities. Total assets in trade, $92 billion (wholesale and retail), represented about

4 *Ibid.*, Table 3, pp. 60-61.

$3.36 for every $1.00 of capital assets ($27 billion). The total assets of manufacturers were about 1.4 times capital assets.

By confining the discussion to the industrial sector, some of the more serious problems of duplication are avoided. Out of the aggregate of $1,207 billion of assets reported for all corporations in 1960-61, the total assets of the industrials accounted for $407 billion. Of this total, the 400 largest reported assets of $173 billion.[5]

The assets of unincorporated business enterprises are only a small fraction of the total for corporations. The most comprehensive recent study places the value of the assets of unincorporated business enterprises at $138 billion in 1958.[6] Separate estimates for unincorporated businesses in the industrial sector are not available for 1958. For 1948, however, estimates indicate that unincorporated industrials (mining, manufacturing, construction, services, and trade) held assets amounting to roughly 82 percent of the total assets of unincorporated business.[7] In 1958, the assets of unincorporated business were about 13 percent of all corporate assets in that year.[8] If these percentages remained unchanged, the 1960 assets of unincorporated industrials amounted to approximately $128.5 billion.

This permits the 1960 distribution of industrial assets to be estimated, as in Table 6-3. Here the 400 largest industrial corporations are shown to control assets about equal to those of the approximately 65,000 corporations of intermediate size, and only slightly less than the combined total amounts of the approximately 662,000 small corporations and over 4,000,000 unincorporated industrial firms. There is little doubt, therefore, that a large fraction of the nation's industrial resources is held by the corporate industrial giants.

[5] Ibid., Table 7, pp. 118-53.

[6] Raymond W. Goldsmith, Robert E. Lipsey, Studies in the National Balance Sheet of the United States (Princeton University Press, 1963), Vol. 2, pp. 43-69.

[7] Estimates by the author based on unpublished data provided by Raymond W. Goldsmith in 1954.

[8] Goldsmith and Lipsey, op. cit., pp. 43-69, and U.S. Internal Revenue Service, Statistics of Income, 1958-59, Corporation Income Tax Returns (U. S. Government Printing Office, 1961), p. 41.

Statistics of corporate income tend, however, to overstate this conclusion. The smaller the enterprise, the greater is the amount of business transactions per dollar of assets. In 1960, the 662,000 firms with assets of less than $500,000 reported an aggregate of $176 billion of total receipts and $62 billion in assets; the 65,000 corporations of intermediate size showed $318 billion of receipts as against $172 billion of assets. The big business corporations had gross receipts of $212 billion against total assets of $173 billion.[9] In other words, the smaller businesses average more than

TABLE 6-3. *Number of Industrial Enterprises, by Size of Assets, 1960*

Assets Class	Number of Firms	Total Assets (Billions of Dollars)
Small		
Unincorporated	4,052,000[a]	128.5[b]
Corporations (under $500,000)	662,188	61.7
Total	4,714,188	190.2
Intermediate		
Corporations ($500,000 to $100,000,000)	65,270	172.0
Big business		
Corporations (over $100,000,000)	400	172.9

Source: U.S. Internal Revenue Service, *Statistics of Income, 1960-61, Corporation Income Tax Returns* (U.S. Government Printing Office, 1963), Table 4, pp. 62-96.

[a] See Table 3-1, "Civilian Employment by Industry and Class of Worker, April 1960." The figure of 4,052,000 is the total number of proprietors and self-employed (4,498,000) minus those in the finance, transportation, and communications category (446,000).

[b] Estimated. See text, p. 111.

$28 of transactions per dollar of assets, while the largest industrial enterprises had sales of less than $13 per dollar of assets. These overall comparisons are borne out in the size breakdowns within industry groups as well. It would seem that the major assets of the small entrepreneur, his training and ability to make a sale or render a service, are not of the kind listed on the balance sheet.

[9] *Statistics of Income, 1960-61, op. cit.,* Table 4, pp. 62-96.

This conclusion is also supported by the statistics of corporate profit which follow later in this chapter.

In terms of measured assets the 400 largest industrial corporations account for more than 40 percent of the total assets of all industrial corporations and almost a third of the total assets of all industrial enterprises. Control of assets of this magnitude implies the power to make decisions with significant effects on other major sectors of the economy. The following section of this chapter examines the manner in which this concentration of financial power has influenced the distribution of national income both within the corporate sector and between the corporate and non-corporate sectors of the economy.

Allocation of Corporate Gross Product

Since 1929, gross national product has increased in real terms by about 170 percent, for an average annual growth rate of roughly 3 percent. All major parts of the economy have shared in the general increase. In 1963 dollars, gross national product was $214 billion in 1929, declined to $150 billion in 1933, and rose to $585 billion by 1963.[10]

As already indicated, the share of business gross product contributed by the corporate sector during this period increased substantially. The corporate sector as a whole originated about 56 percent of total business gross product in 1929; in 1960, it originated almost two-thirds. Three representative years, 1929, 1948, and 1960, are selected for closer examination in Table 6-4.

Payrolls account for the major fraction of gross product originating in the corporate sector. Employee compensation constituted 63 percent of corporate gross product in 1929 and remained at around 64 percent throughout the period following World War II.

Profits before income taxes, which accounted for 19 percent of corporate gross product in 1929, declined sharply during the

10 Council of Economic Advisers, *Economic Report of the President, January 1964* (U.S. Government Printing Office, 1964), p. 208.

TABLE 6-4. *Distribution of Corporate Gross Product,*
1929, 1948, 1960

Charges Against Gross Product	Amount (Billions of dollars)			Percent of Total		
	1929	1948	1960	1929	1948	1960
Gross corporate product	53.2ᵃ	140.7	282.8	100.0	100.0	100.0
Indirect taxes	ᵇ	12.6	29.5	6.2	9.0	10.4
Capital consumption allowances	ᵇ	7.7	25.9	8.3	5.5	9.2
Employee compensation	33.7	90.0	183.1	63.3	64.0	64.7
Net interest	1.6	.3	.6	3.0	.2	.2
Profits before tax including inventory valuation adjustment	9.9	30.0	43.7	19.0	21.3	15.5
Profits after tax	8.0	19.7	20.1	15.0	14.0	7.1

Source: *Survey of Current Business*, Vol. 42, No. 11 (November 1962), pp. 20 and 27; No. 7 (July 1963), p. 17; *U. S. Income and Output*, Supplement to the *Survey of Current Business* (November 1958), Table 1-12, pp. 134-35.

ᵃ From Office of Business Economics, Department of Commerce.

ᵇ Not available.

1930's. They regained the 1929 percentage after World War II and, in fact, exceeded it in 1948. Since the early 1950's, corporate profits have not increased as rapidly as total product. As of 1960, corporate profits before taxes were 15.5 percent of corporate gross product. When the comparison is made on the basis of net income after taxes, the share attributable to net corporate profits declines from 15.0 percent in 1929 to 7.1 percent in 1960. Thus, of the contribution by corporations to gross product, the payroll share has remained unchanged and an increasing percentage has been transferred to government revenues.

Relative Growth of the Corporate and Noncorporate Sectors

The relative growth of the corporate and noncorporate sectors may be illustrated by the use of 1929 figures as a base for indexes of payrolls and profits, as indicated by Table 6-5.

Growth in the size as well as in the number of proprietary enterprises is reflected in the increase in noncorporate payrolls and entrepreneurial income. The relative decline in farm income is, of course, immediately apparent in the latter. Profits before tax rose relatively more in the corporate than in the noncorporate sector.[11]

TABLE 6-5. *Indexes of Payrolls, Corporate Profits, and Entrepreneurial Income, by Sector, 1929 to 1962*
(1929=100)

Type of Income	Year				
	1929	1940	1948	1960	1962
Gross national product[a]	100	96	248	482	531
Payrolls					
Corporate	100	96	267	543	589
Noncorporate	100	92	274	482	527
Government	100	172	386	1031	1186
Corporate profits[b]					
Before tax	100	90	304	431	450
After tax	100	71	206	239	262
Entrepreneurial income[c]					
Including farm	100	88	272	313	337
Excluding farm	100	96	254	389	416

Source: *U.S. Income and Output,* Supplement to *Survey of Current Business* (November 1958), pp. 134-35; *Survey of Current Business,* Vol. 43 (July 1963), Table 8, p. 17; and *Economic Report of the President, January 1963,* Table C-1.
  [a] Current dollars.
  [b] Including inventory adjustment.
  [c] Including proprietor's income of other private business.

Growth of Large and Small Corporations

This allocation of the nation's economic growth into the corporate and noncorporate sectors still leaves the question whether a disproportionate share of the growth has been gained

[11] After-tax income of unincorporated enterprises is not available, but it is clear from the data in Table 6-5 that the corporate tax cut heavily into the before-tax income of corporations.

at the top of the corporate scale. Although the comparability of data on distribution of corporate incomes leaves much to be desired, the rough breakdown according to size shown in Table 6-6 for 1929 and 1960 provides some clues.

In 1929, the largest 300 corporations in terms of before tax income representing .11 percent of all corporations with income, accounted for 42 percent of total corporate net income, excluding deficits. In 1960, the 571 largest firms, representing only .09 percent of all corporations with income, accounted for 52 percent of total corporate income, excluding deficits.

This relative growth at the upper extreme appears to have been realized at the expense of the medium-sized corporations. The second and third largest groups, representing 7 percent of all firms in 1929, earned 46 percent of total corporate profits in 1929, whereas the 8.4 percent of the firms in these categories in 1960 accounted for only 38 percent of corporate net income in that year.

The pattern fails to support the contention that the largest firms have smothered growth within the smaller size categories. Indeed, growth both in number of firms and net income is impressive in all size categories. So far as the overall picture is concerned, the evidence is that growth of the large corporations has moved along with an enlargement of economic opportunity at all levels of enterprise.[12]

Financial Position of the Industrial Giants

The concentration of financial power in American business can also be illustrated by the relative position of the nation's giant

[12] The situation varies somewhat by year. In 1948, not a recession year, the top .11 percent of all corporations with income accounted for only 40 percent of all corporate net income, excluding deficits. This lower figure lends additional support to the conclusion that growth at the top has far from excluded economic growth of the medium-sized and smaller corporations.

There is the added factor that, in 1960, probably a higher proportion of small companies was owned or controlled by large corporations or their stockholders than was true in 1929. Correction for these differences should not, however, materially alter the foregoing conclusion.

TABLE 6-6. *Distribution of Corporate Income by Income Class, 1929 and 1960*[a]

Income Class	Corporations			Corporate Net Income		
	Number	Percent of Corporations With Income	Percent of Corporations With and Without Income	Amount (Millions of dollars)	Percent of Total Net Income	
					Excluding Deficits	Including Deficits
			1929			
Over $5,000,000	300	.11	.07	4,886	42	56
$500,000-$5,000,000	2,393	.89	.52	3,049	26	35
$50,000-$500,000	16,573	6.15	3.63	2,303	20	26
$0-$50,000	250,164	92.85	54.86	1,416	12	16
Deficit	186,591		40.92	—2,914		—33
Total	456,021	100.00	100.00	8,740	100	100
			1960			
Over $10,000,000	571	.09	.05	26,061	52	60
$500,000-$10,000,000	6,903	1.03	.61	12,363	25	28
$50,000-$500,000	49,679	7.41	4.36	6,613	13	15
$0-$50,000	613,086	91.47	53.75	5,345	11	12
Deficit	470,335		41.24	—6,877		—16
Total	1,140,574	100.00	100.00[b]	43,505	100[b]	100[b]

Source: U.S. Internal Revenue Service, *Statistics of Income, 1960-61: Corporation Income Tax Returns* (U.S. Government Printing Office, 1963), Table 8, p. 154; *Statistics of Income for 1929* (U.S. Government Printing Office, 1931), pp. 23-24.

[a] Size classes by total assets are available for 1960; but for 1929 the IRS size classification was made by income only, so that a direct comparison of these groups by assets size cannot be made. The less satisfactory classification by income size is used in this table instead. Even this is not perfect. Data for 1929 exclude dividends from domestic corporations. Comparable data for 1960 are not available, and the 1960 figures in Table 6-6 include intercorporate dividends. In the table, the income categories are grouped so that about the same percentage of all corporations falls in each of the four classes for both years.

[b] Does not add to total because of rounding.

firms. In 1960, the 100 largest industrial corporations accounted for assets of some $125 billion.[13] Total assets reported by all industrial corporations in that year were $407 billion.[14] The 100 largest industrials thus accounted for nearly 31 percent of the assets of all industrial corporations. If the $128 billion estimate (Table 6-3) for assets of unincorporated industrials is included, the share of the 100 largest would amount to roughly 24 percent of all assets in the industrial sector.

In terms of profits before taxes, the 100 largest industrials in 1960 accounted for approximately $15.1 billion, or about 53 percent of the $28.7 billion in profits reported for all corporate industrials.[15] The share of the 100 largest in total business income, that is, income of industrials, other business corporations, and unincorporated enterprises, amounted to about 15 percent. This

TABLE 6-7. *Business Profits Before Tax, by Sector, 1960*
(Dollar amounts in millions)

Sector	Amount	Percent
100 largest industrial corporations[a]	15,103	14.69
Other industrial corporations	13,608	13.23
Nonindustrial corporations	15,789	15.35
Proprietors' income of all noncorporate business	46,236	44.96
Rental income of persons	12,110	11.77
Total	102,846	100.00

Source: U.S. Office of Business Economics, *Survey of Current Business*, Vol. 43 (July 1963), Table 8, p. 17; U.S. Internal Revenue Service, *Statistics of Income, 1960-61, Corporation Income Tax Returns*, Table 2, pp. 52-59.
[a] Compiled from *Moody's Industrial Manual* (Moody's Investors Service, 1963). See Table 7-7 for definition of 100 largest industrial corporations.

[13] See Table 7-7.
[14] Table 6-8.
[15] Corporate profits in Table 6-6 are from *Statistics of Income, 1960-61, op. cit.*, and include intercorporate dividends in the amount of $3.1 billion. These data match the profit figures reported for the 100 largest more closely than the alternative series available from the Office of Business Economics. However, for all corporations, 1960 "compiled net profit" (Internal Revenue Service) was very close to 1960 "profit before tax" (Office of Business Economics)—$44.5 billion as compared with $44.3 billion. Any distortion arising from these different definitions is therefore confined to the pattern shown within the corporate sector and is of minor importance in terms of the corporate-noncorporate comparison. The interpretation of these profit rates is, however, far from straightforward. See also below, note 16.

breakdown into the sectors comprising total business profits is shown in Table 6-7.

The 100 largest industrials, small in numbers of firms, thus account for a significant share of the assets and a very significant share of the before tax income of the industrial sector. Although data for the 100 largest are not entirely comparable with those for the industrial sector as a whole, this comparison suggests that the earnings ratios of the 100 largest are high compared with the average for all corporations. For the 100 largest, profits before tax were roughly one-eighth of total assets. For all industrials before tax, profits were only one-fourteenth of total assets in 1960-61. This tendency for earnings to rise with size of firm is also apparent from the standard sources of corporate statistics.[16]

Trend in Share of the 100 Largest

The growth in total assets held by the 100 largest industrials in relation to the assets of all corporations within the corresponding area of the economy is shown in Table 6-8. Any generalization from this table must recognize that these figures are not strictly comparable. Approximations are especially rough for the year 1909, which antedates regular income tax returns and modern standards for publicly issued financial statements. Nevertheless the top 100 have apparently registered about a 25 percent increase from 1948 to 1960 in their proportion of all industrial corporate assets. To what extent differences in the percentages between the earlier and later years can be attributed to changed accounting practice is unknown.

[16] See *Statistics of Income, 1960-61, op. cit.,* Table 4, pp. 62-96; and Federal Trade Commission, *Quarterly Financial Report for Manufacturing Corporations,* Fourth Quarter, 1960, Table 4, p. 11. For a detailed analysis and an indication that earnings ultimately decline with size of firm, see H. O. Stekler, *Profitability and Size of Firm* (Institute of Business and Economic Research, 1963). Stekler concludes that "while there is a positive relationship between profitability and size, the parabolic relationship (i.e., increasing and then decreasing profitability with increasing size) yields a better fit. This result is in agreement with our previous qualitative analysis where a definite tapering off and/or decline in profitability was observed in the medium and larger size classes."

TABLE 6-8. *Total Assets, All Industrial Corporations and the 100 Largest, 1909, 1929, 1948, and 1960*[a]

(Dollar amounts in billions)

Year	All Industrial Corporations	100 Largest Industrial Corporations	
		Amount	Percent of Total
1909	$ 33.4	$ 8.7	26.0
1929	114.9	28.5	24.8
1948	184.2	49.5	26.9
1960	406.7	125.5	30.8

Source: For 1909 data on all industrials, see *Report of Commissioner of Internal Revenue, 1910*, pp. 71-72; total assets equal capitalization plus bonded indebtedness. For 1929, 1948, and 1960, see U.S. Internal Revenue Service, *Statistics of Income for 1929* (U.S. Government Printing Office), Table 19, pp. 332-33; *1948*, Pt. 2, Table 4, pp. 130-45; and *1960-61*, Table 4, pp. 62-96. For 100 largest, see annual reports of the companies, *Moody's Industrial Manual* (Moody's *Investors Service*, for years 1909-63); and *Standard Corporation Descriptions* (Standard and Poor's, for years 1909-63).

[a] Total assets exclude depreciation reserves.

Comparisons by Assets, Sales, and Income

A sifting of the financial statements of the 100 largest industrials illustrates the difficulty, to which attention was drawn earlier, of deriving from any one financial yardstick applied across the business structure a definitive measure of size and market power. Some of the industrial giants, engaged in primary production, reveal their magnitude in the extent of their physical resources; others, carrying commodities already processed, reflect their commanding position in terms of sales, although they rank comparatively low in fixed capital assets. In general, a comparison of the importance of industrial corporations by their assets is feasible only for firms in the same industry, with competing product lines. In 1960, an industrial corporation was certain of a place among the 200 largest if it had as much as $170 million in total assets.[17] Yet that volume of assets could, depending on the industry, represent leadership or a minor fraction of the market. In automotive manufacture, it would

[17] Estimate from "The 500 Largest Industrial Corporations," *The Fortune Directory* (August 1961), pp. 2-19.

represent a relatively small enterprise with only a minor percentage of the national output of motor cars. But in carpet manufacture, the largest company, claiming one-fourth of the output of the industry, would not even approach a place among the 200 largest industrials. In petroleum there were 10 companies in 1960 with assets above the $1 billion figure, yet the diffusion of the industry enabled a $444 million company (Richfield Oil Corporation) to dominate an important regional market.

The ratio of assets to sales is also far from comparable among industries. In the distributive trades, the volumes of sales for the giant enterprises run anywhere from three to ten times their total assets. A grocery chain with $711 million in total assets but less than $210 million in fixed capital assets had annual sales in 1960 of more than $5 billion.[18] By contrast, a primary producer, for example in gypsum, might have assets over $150 million with sales under $150 million. Throughout manufacturing there are extreme variations in the ratio of assets to sales among industries and in the ratio of sales to net income. These variations will be reflected in different rankings of the large manufacturing corporations by assets, by sales, and by income respectively. In meatpacking, for instance, assets of $500 million may be consistent with an annual sales volume of $2 billion, while in the production of a primary metal, the same amount of assets may mean less than a half billion dollars in sales.[19]

Numerous other aspects of the large corporate enterprise have to be considered together with size, whether by total assets, invested capital, sales, employment, or net income, in order to

---

[18] *Moody's Industrial Manual* (Moody's *Investment Service*, 1963), p. 2620.

[19] For example, in 1960, the Great Atlantic and Pacific Tea Company and International Nickel of Canada, Ltd., ranking 59th and 61st among the industrials by size of assets, compared as follows in assets, sales, and income (in millions of dollars):

	Atlantic & Pacific Tea Company	International Nickel Company
Total Assets	711.22	678.74
Sales	5,246.58	502.12
Income before Taxes	123.21	162.24
Income after Taxes	59.01	80.70

Data are from *Moody's Industrial Manual* (Moody's *Investment Service*, 1963), pp. 2443, 2620.

determine the degree to which the size of the corporation is indicative of economic power concentrated therein. Here relative size, or rather growth in size, is taken as one indication of an accumulation of economic power. It is important to recognize that there are a number of "bigness" factors. Possession of one does not necessarily guarantee the possession of others.

It has been noted that the 100 largest industrial firms have shown a gradual increase in their proportion of total business assets since the 1920's. These figures, however, are for the giant group as a whole. They give no clue to the dynamics of growth and competitiveness among the separate enterprises that make up the 100 largest. The following chapter presents an analysis of change over time in the relative positions of the companies that are dominant in their particular industries and that have traditionally been taken as symbols of the entrenchment of market leadership in big business.

7

The 100 Largest Industrials

A SUBSTANTIAL PROPORTION of the nation's capital resources is under the control of the 100 largest industrial firms. This concentration could imply entrenchment and rigidity of big business leadership. It could also be consistent with the emergence of new firms, products, and industries among the ranks of giant industrials.

This chapter examines the turnover of firms among the largest 100 industrial corporations since 1909, in an attempt to learn the extent to which individual companies have maintained their positions of leadership. Its aim is to determine whether the group at the top tends to remain the same over long periods of time or whether it undergoes substantial change. There would be greater cause to suspect a decline in business rivalry and a tendency toward exclusion of competition if the membership and ranking of the largest firms remained relatively unchanged through the years than there would be if the group showed substantial turnover.

Nature of the Data

Lists of the 100 largest industrials were prepared for six selected years: 1909, 1919, 1929, 1935, 1948, and 1960. The criterion for inclusion in any one of these lists is the amount of the assets held by an individual company during the year in question.[1] The six lists include 218 companies that appeared among the 100 largest in one or more of the selected years.[2] They represent 20 industry groups. Complete lists for each of the six years appear in tables at the end of this chapter.

The total assets of the companies are based on consolidated balance sheets. Insofar as possible, accounts have been standardized to exclude depreciation reserves from the asset accounts. Where reserves for depreciation were clearly identified, these were subtracted from gross asset accounts. Particularly during the early period, these data are suspect. The very nature of these early and scanty records almost inevitably makes this the case.[3]

[1] These lists were compiled from *Standard Corporation Descriptions* (Standard and Poor's, for the years 1909-63); *Moody's Industrial Manual* (Moody's Investors' Service, for the years 1909-63); Adolf A. Berle, Jr. and Gardiner C. Means, *The Modern Corporation and Private Property* (Commerce Clearing House, 1932); The National Resources Committee, *The Structure of the American Economy* (U.S. Government Printing Office, 1939), Pt. 1; Federal Trade Commission data on the largest manufacturing corporations; and, especially for 1909, unpublished materials furnished by Rufus Tucker.

[2] If the Maxwell Motor Company and the Chrysler Corporation, Schwarzchild and Sulzberger Co. and Wilson and Co., and General Theatres Equipment, Inc. and Twentieth Century Fox Films are, in each instance, considered separate firms, 221 companies appear in the six lists. These are instances in which a name change or reorganization suggests that the same basic company remained among the 100 largest even though the tables show a new entry. In a number of other less obvious instances, companies among the 100 in early years were acquired by companies appearing on the lists in later years. See Notes to Tables 7-2 — 7-7.

[3] Cf. Norman R. Collins, Lee E. Preston, "The Size Structure of the Largest Industrial Firms, 1909-1958," *American Economic Review*, Vol. 51, December 1961. Collins and Preston present similar lists of the 100 largest for 1909, 1919, 1929, 1935, and 1948. These lists were prepared from essentially the same sources, but are not identical with Tables 7-2 — 7-7. Part of the discrepancy arises because Collins and Preston did not adjust reported asset accounts to exclude depreciation reserves. In some instances, the Collins-Preston lists include estimates based on averages for years bracketing the year of the list in question. Still other differences may reflect the ingenuity of Collins and Preston in uncovering additional sources, or, alternatively, their judgment regarding the relative reliability of these sources. For the most part, however, differences are minor in terms of the use to which these lists are put.

These lists were prepared to permit analysis of change in composition of the group of the 100 largest industrials between 1909 and 1960. Three separate aspects of the lists are discussed: change in the rank order of industries containing the individual giants; change in company membership and rank within each industry group; and change in the membership and rank order of the individual companies apart from their industry classes.

As outlined in earlier chapters, the United States economy is an amalgamation of many institutions. Private firms, public regulatory agencies, and even public opinion interact. The focus of this study is on the outcome of the system as a whole. The discussion that follows does not distinguish growth by merger from purely internal growth by individual corporate firms. The important question, in this overall view, is not what would have happened in the absence of merger, but what happened in the presence of all the factors affecting turnover, including merger.[4]

Similarly, no attempt is made to isolate change that would have occurred by merger had merger not been blocked by judicial action. Again the focus is not on what would have happened had regulatory pressure not been brought to bear, but rather on what did develop from this interplay between public and private agency during the period examined. The corollary is that judicial divestitures are regarded as changes induced by the legal framework in which big business has operated. To ignore or rule out these actions would be to ignore a major component of the operation of the United States economy.[5]

The issue, therefore, is whether corporate competition, economic growth, public attitudes, and government control have, in the last half century, stimulated a turnover among giants that continually challenges entrenchment, or whether, alternatively,

[4] For a contrary view, see George J. Stigler, "The Statistics of Monopoly and Merger," *Journal of Political Economy*, Vol. 64 (February 1956), pp. 35-37. Stigler suggests that shifts due to merger should be considered "turnunder rather than turnover."

[5] A number of reviewers of the first edition of this study noted that much of the change in the relative ranking of particular corporations could be attributed

there has been a tendency toward rigid or even increased control
in the hands of a few corporate giants.

Measures of Turnover

Chart 1 graphically presents the relative shift between 1909
and 1960 in the 20 industries represented among the 100 largest
firms. The definition and membership of the industries are of
necessity partially arbitrary. Large firms are not typically confined to single industries. For example, the chemical companies
as well as the metal companies are active in the field of metallurgy;
the rubber companies manufacture plastic chemicals; the chemical companies are producers of textile fibers; farm equipment
manufacturers are also engaged in various electrical lines, and so
on. The industrial categories assigned to individual companies
follow, insofar as is practical, their official designations in the business censuses and their usual association in popular use. Different
placement of borderline cases would not appreciably affect the
general pattern.

In 1909, the iron and steel industry dominated the big business
sector of the economy, accounting for 28.6 percent of the $8.7
billion block of assets held by the 100 largest in that year. Second
to iron and steel was the petroleum industry, accounting for

---

to mergers or to enforced dissolutions. See the following reviews of *Big Enterprise
in a Competitive System:* Jesse W. Markham, *American Economic Review,* Vol. 45
(June 1955), p. 448; Carl Kaysen, *Explorations in Entrepreneurial History,* Vol. 7
(1955), p. 237; C. D. Edwards, *University of Pennsylvania Review,* Vol. 103 (May
1955), p. 991; and Merton J. Peck, *Review of Economics and Statistics,* Vol. 38
(May 1956), p. 235. Identification of instances where merger or dissolution was
responsible for such alterations in rank is not easy. Corporations of this size are
almost continuously engaged in the acquisition or disposal of some facilities. Those
mergers that resulted in the immediate disappearance of a member firm, or dissolutions creating a new giant immediately appearing, have been indicated in the
Tables 7-2 — 7-7, but this in no way measures the true effect of either of these
activities. It is probably true that none of the 218 firms in this list was created
without substantial reliance on the acquisition at some time of substantial operating
facilities under previously independent control. Such is the way of big business.

CHART 1. *Assets of the 100 Largest Industrial Firms, by Industry, 1909 and 1960ᵃ*

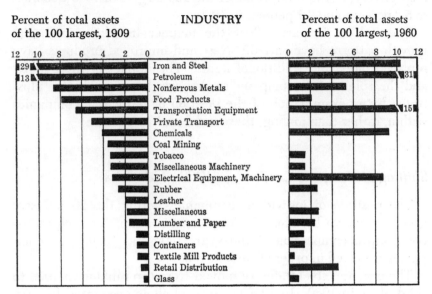

Source: Tables 7-2 through 7-7.
ᵃTotal assets, 1909, $8.7 billion; total assets, 1960, $125.5 billion.

another 12.6 percent of the 1909 total,[6] followed by the non-ferrous metals industry (consisting mainly of copper) with 8.7 percent. The 1909 rank order of these 20 groups is indicated by the left-hand side of the chart.

Against this 1909 list, Chart 1 shows a similar array of the 100 largest industrials in 1960. The 1960 industry distribution differs substantially from the 1909 distribution. Most noteworthy, per-haps, are the relative decline in the iron and steel group—from 28.6 percent of the 1909 list to 10.3 percent in 1960—and the rise in the petroleum industry—from 12.6 percent in 1909 to top ranking in 1960 with 31.3 percent of the entire block of assets

---

[6] This ordering departs from that shown by the 1954 edition of this book. Since publication of that edition, new data released by the Standard Oil Company of New Jersey indicate that the earlier estimate of $371.1 million was too low. Assets of the company for 1909 are here shown at $800.4 million. This estimate is based on a study by Ralph W. Hidy and Muriel E. Hidy, *Pioneering in Big Business, 1882-1911* (Harper, 1955), p. 636.

held by the 100 largest in that year. The nonferrous metals and the food products industries, with 8.7 percent and 7.9 percent, respectively, of the total assets of the 100 largest in 1909 declined to 5.2 percent and 2.1 percent in 1960.

These shifts in part reflect the manner in which industrial growth patterns have varied.[7] New and improved products have replaced older and traditional items. The impact of these shifts and the role of intercompany rivalry are, however, better illustrated by an examination of the position of individual companies within, rather than among, these industrial categories.

Shifting of Company Leadership Within Industries

The position of individual companies within the 20 industry groups is shown by Chart 2. This chart contains for each industry group a comparison of the years 1909 and 1960. The companies are listed in order of rank in 1909.

The iron and steel industry moved from top ranking in 1909 to third place in 1960. In 1909, U.S. Steel alone accounted for 20.6 percent of the total assets of the 100 largest and controlled more than two-thirds of the total assets of the 13 iron and steel companies on the list in that year. By 1960, the share of United States Steel was 4 percent of the total assets of the 100 largest, and only 4 of the original 13 steel companies remained among the 100 largest. Of the nine companies that disappeared from the list of 100, 3 did so by merger. Bethlehem Steel acquired Pennsylvania Steel in 1911, Lackawanna Steel in 1922, and Cambria Steel in 1923.[8] There were 5 newcomers by 1960.

[7] M. A. Adelman estimates that of 69 companies dropping from the 100 largest between 1909 and 1948, 46 can be attributed to differential rates of industry growth. See M. A. Adelman, "A Note on Corporate Concentration and Turnover," *American Economic Review*, Vol. 44 (June 1954), pp. 392-96.

[8] Mergers or consolidations are indicated only if the surviving firm appears on the 1960 list of the 100 largest and if both firms were among the 100 largest at the beginning of the time period under consideration. The 1954 merger of National Enamel and Stamping with New York Shipbuilding is not, for example, noted since even the consolidated firm was not large enough to qualify as one of the 100 largest in 1960. However, even when the consolidated firm remains among the 100 largest, there is no necessary implication that the merging firms would independently have remained among the 100 largest had the merger not taken place.

CHART 2. *The 100 Largest Industrials, by Total Assets, 1909 and 1960* [a]

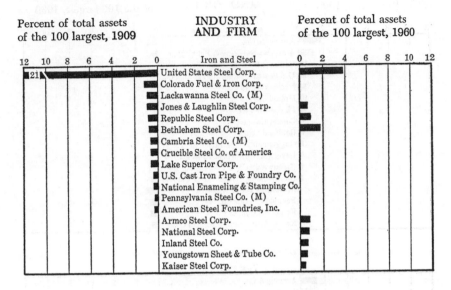

| Percent of total assets of the 100 largest, 1909 | INDUSTRY AND FIRM | Percent of total assets of the 100 largest, 1960 |

Iron and Steel

United States Steel Corp.
Colorado Fuel & Iron Corp.
Lackawanna Steel Co. (M)
Jones & Laughlin Steel Corp.
Republic Steel Corp.
Bethlehem Steel Corp.
Cambria Steel Co. (M)
Crucible Steel Co. of America
Lake Superior Corp.
U.S. Cast Iron Pipe & Foundry Co.
National Enameling & Stamping Co.
Pennsylvania Steel Co. (M)
American Steel Foundries, Inc.
Armco Steel Corp.
National Steel Corp.
Inland Steel Co.
Youngstown Sheet & Tube Co.
Kaiser Steel Corp.

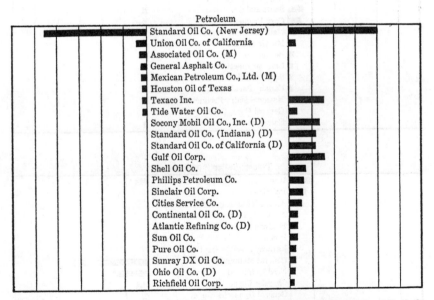

Petroleum

Standard Oil Co. (New Jersey)
Union Oil Co. of California
Associated Oil Co. (M)
General Asphalt Co.
Mexican Petroleum Co., Ltd. (M)
Houston Oil of Texas
Texaco Inc.
Tide Water Oil Co.
Socony Mobil Oil Co., Inc. (D)
Standard Oil Co. (Indiana) (D)
Standard Oil Co. of California (D)
Gulf Oil Corp.
Shell Oil Co.
Phillips Petroleum Co.
Sinclair Oil Corp.
Cities Service Co.
Continental Oil Co. (D)
Atlantic Refining Co. (D)
Sun Oil Co.
Pure Oil Co.
Sunray DX Oil Co.
Ohio Oil Co. (D)
Richfield Oil Corp.

[a] Companies on the 1909 list removed by reason of merger are indicated by (M) if the successor company to the merger appears on the 1960 list. Companies appearing on the 1960 list created by the dissolution of companies appearing on the 1909 list are indicated by (D). See also notes, pages 152-53.

CHART 2 *(Continued)*

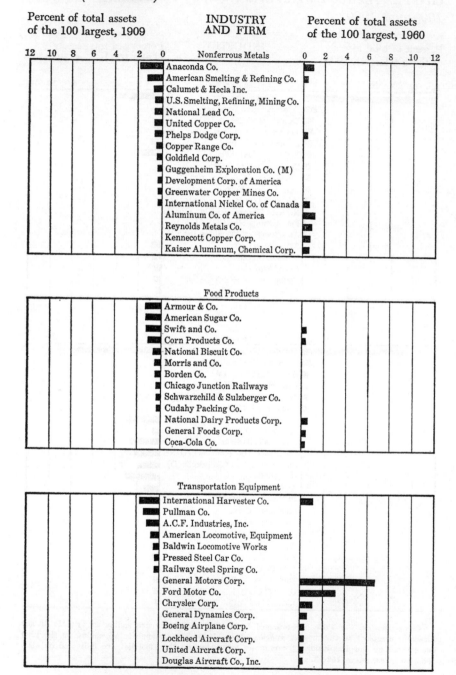

| Percent of total assets of the 100 largest, 1909 | INDUSTRY AND FIRM | Percent of total assets of the 100 largest, 1960 |

Nonferrous Metals

- Anaconda Co.
- American Smelting & Refining Co.
- Calumet & Hecla Inc.
- U.S. Smelting, Refining, Mining Co.
- National Lead Co.
- United Copper Co.
- Phelps Dodge Corp.
- Copper Range Co.
- Goldfield Corp.
- Guggenheim Exploration Co. (M)
- Development Corp. of America
- Greenwater Copper Mines Co.
- International Nickel Co. of Canada
- Aluminum Co. of America
- Reynolds Metals Co.
- Kennecott Copper Corp.
- Kaiser Aluminum, Chemical Corp.

Food Products

- Armour & Co.
- American Sugar Co.
- Swift and Co.
- Corn Products Co.
- National Biscuit Co.
- Morris and Co.
- Borden Co.
- Chicago Junction Railways
- Schwarzchild & Sulzberger Co.
- Cudahy Packing Co.
- National Dairy Products Corp.
- General Foods Corp.
- Coca-Cola Co.

Transportation Equipment

- International Harvester Co.
- Pullman Co.
- A.C.F. Industries, Inc.
- American Locomotive, Equipment
- Baldwin Locomotive Works
- Pressed Steel Car Co.
- Railway Steel Spring Co.
- General Motors Corp.
- Ford Motor Co.
- Chrysler Corp.
- General Dynamics Corp.
- Boeing Airplane Corp.
- Lockheed Aircraft Corp.
- United Aircraft Corp.
- Douglas Aircraft Co., Inc.

CHART 2 *(Continued)*

Percent of total assets of the 100 largest, 1909							INDUSTRY AND FIRM	Percent of total assets of the 100 largest, 1960					
12	10	8	6	4	2	0	Private Transport	0	2	4	6	8	10	12

Private Transport
- International Mercantile Marine
- New England Navigation Co.
- Atlantic Gulf & West Indies S.S.L.
- American Express Co.
- Wells Fargo & Co.

Chemicals
- E.I. du Pont de Nemours & Co.
- Virginia-Carolina Chemical
- American Agricultural Chemical
- American Cotton Oil Co.
- Eastman Kodak Co.
- American Linseed Co.
- International Salt Co.
- Allied Chemical & Dye Corp.
- Union Carbide Corp.
- Monsanto Chemical Co.
- Procter & Gamble Co.
- Dow Chemical Co.
- Olin Mathieson Chemical Corp.
- American Cyanamid Co.
- W. R. Grace & Co.

Coal Mining
- Pittsburgh Consolidation Coal Co.
- Consolidation Coal Co.
- Lehigh Coal & Navigation Co.
- Lehigh & Wilkes-Barre Coal Co.
- Lehigh Valley Coal Co.
- New River Co.

Tobacco
- American Tobacco Co.
- General Cigar Co., Inc.
- R.J. Reynolds Tobacco Co. (D)

Miscellaneous Machinery
- Singer Manufacturing Co.
- Deere and Co.
- International Steam Pump Co.
- United Shoe Machinery Corp.
- Union Typewriter Co.
- Caterpillar Tractor Co.

CHART 2 *(Continued)*

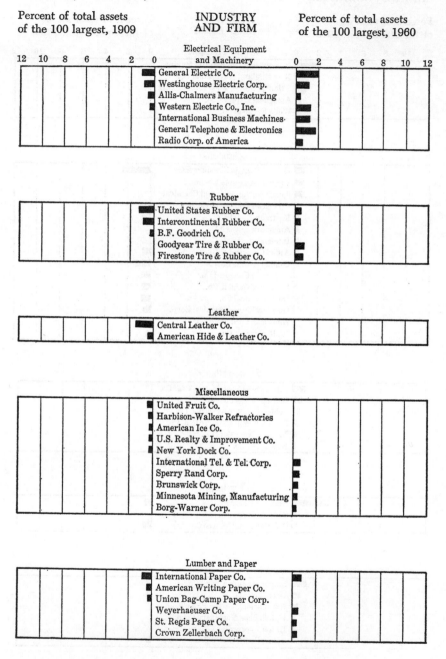

Percent of total assets
of the 100 largest, 1909

INDUSTRY
AND FIRM

Percent of total assets
of the 100 largest, 1960

Electrical Equipment
and Machinery

General Electric Co.
Westinghouse Electric Corp.
Allis-Chalmers Manufacturing
Western Electric Co., Inc.
International Business Machines·
General Telephone & Electronics
Radio Corp. of America

Rubber

·United States Rubber Co.
Intercontinental Rubber Co.
B.F. Goodrich Co.
Goodyear Tire & Rubber Co.
Firestone Tire & Rubber Co.

Leather

Central Leather Co.
American Hide & Leather Co.

Miscellaneous

United Fruit Co.
Harbison-Walker Refractories
American Ice Co.
U.S. Realty & Improvement Co.
New York Dock Co.
International Tel. & Tel. Corp.
Sperry Rand Corp.
Brunswick Corp.
Minnesota Mining, Manufacturing
Borg-Warner Corp.

Lumber and Paper

International Paper Co.
American Writing Paper Co.
Union Bag-Camp Paper Corp.
Weyerhaeuser Co.
St. Regis Paper Co.
Crown Zellerbach Corp.

CHART 2 *(Continued)*

Percent of total assets of the 100 largest, 1909	INDUSTRY AND FIRM	Percent of total assets of the 100 largest, 1960

12	10	8	6	4	2	0	Distilling	0	2	4	6	8	10	12
							National Distillers & Chemical							
							American Malting Co.							
							Schenley Industries, Inc.							
							Distiller Corp.-Seagrams, Ltd.							

Containers

American Can Co.
Continental Can Co., Inc.

Textile Mill Products

American Woolen Co.
Burlington Industries, Inc.

Retail Distribution

Sears, Roebuck & Co.
Montgomery Ward & Co., Inc.
Great Atlantic & Pacific Tea Co.
F.W. Woolworth Co.
J.C. Penny Co.
Safeway Stores, Inc.
May Department Stores Co.

Glass

Pittsburgh Plate Glass Co.
Owens-Illinois Glass Co.

In 1909 the petroleum industry was dominated by the Standard Oil Company of New Jersey. Of 7 other petroleum companies represented in 1909, 3 were still among the 100 largest in 1960. Of the 4 dropping out, 2 were merged. Standard Oil of Indiana acquired control of Pan American Petroleum and Transport (successor to Mexican Petroleum) in 1929, and Associated Oil merged with Tidewater in 1926. The oil-producing and refining properties of the other two "dropouts" were also acquired by larger companies, but not until the two firms had ceased to be among the 100 largest by virtue of their own relative decline.

By 1960, 15 new petroleum companies had appeared among the 100 largest. Six had been part of the Standard Oil organization prior to dissolution in 1911. The others were integrated companies competing with the Standard giants.

The nonferrous metals group dropped from third place in 1909 to sixth in 1960.[9] Of 13 companies on the 1909 list, 4 remained in 1960, joining 4 new companies not present in the 1909 group. The Guggenheim Exploration Company was acquired by Kennecott Copper, one of the new entrants, in 1916.

In food products, 8 companies among the 100 largest in 1909 were no longer listed in 1960. They were replaced by 3 newcomers, National Dairy Products, General Foods, and Coca-Cola. Overall, the food products group fell markedly in relative representation over the fifty-year period, much of the decline occurring in the latter part of the period.

By contrast, the transportation equipment group moved to second place in 1960, largely due to the impact of the growing automotive field. Of 7 companies among the 100 largest in 1909, only one, International Harvester, remained in 1960. The 6 "dropouts" reflect the relative decline in rail transportation in the United States. The newcomers represent the automotive, truck, and aircraft industries, as well as the shift from steam to diesel power in rail transportation. Turnover here is substantial. It also illustrates, as does the abrupt decline of the private transport group, the role which new products have in inducing major shifts in the structure of big business.

In chemicals, only 3 of the 8 corporations on the earlier list remained on the 1960 list. Seven new corporations appeared, several of which enjoyed a spectacular rise in the industry.

Coal mining was no longer represented on the 1960 list. None of the original "big six" was large enough to be listed among the 100 largest. Similarly, no leather company ranked in this category

[9] Note that the ranking of industries depends only on assets held by members of the 100 largest industrials. The pattern of shifting would be quite different if based on the assets of *all* firms in each of these major industry groups.

in 1960, despite the fact that one had been among the 10 largest in 1909.

The old American Tobacco "trust" was represented in 1960 by the successor company and R. J. Reynolds, a product of the 1911 dissolution. Significant, perhaps, is the postwar decline of Liggett and Myers, which was on the list of the 100 largest between 1919 and 1948. (See Table 7-6.)

In contrast, retailing, with only one representative in 1909, contained 7 in 1960. Here, as elsewhere among the 20 industry groups considered, the shifts in rank of individual companies may be readily attributable to the rise or fall of the industries to which they belong—plastics have replaced leathers, automobiles have outpaced trains, petroleum has displaced coal, and so on. On the other hand, some companies have had rates of growth far beyond or far below those industries with which they are or were associated. The decline of U.S. Steel does not appear to be a consequence of any long-range decline in iron and steel; by the same token, neither IBM nor duPont has merely ridden the tide of its respective industry association.

The Turnover Record in the 100 Largest

Positions of high rank as reflected by a place among the 100 largest appear, from the record, to have been relatively unsure when the full fifty-year period is examined. Table 7-1 summarizes the composition of the six lists, both for the full list of 100, and for the top 10, 25, and 50 largest corporations. Of the 100 corporations on the 1909 list, only 31 were among the 100 largest in 1960. Indeed only 59 were present in 1919, and by 1929 the number of survivors was down to 42.

For the top 10, this pattern is even more striking. Seven of the top 10 in 1909 had lost their position by 1919. Of the 3 remaining originals, however, 2 were still there forty years later, in 1960.

For the lists of intermediate length, the tendency for turnover to decline after 1929 is less evident, suggesting in turn some substantial internal shifting of position within the group of 100 largest after 1929, but in general, and for all lists, the major

TABLE 7-1. *Survivorship Among the 100 Largest Industrial Firms, Selected Years, by Year of Initial Lists*

Year of Initial List	Number of firms among the 100 largest in year of initial list remaining among the 100 largest in:					
	1909	1919	1929	1935	1948	1960
1909						
Largest 10	10	3	3	3	2	2
Largest 25	25	12	9	9	7	5
Largest 50	50	31	20	20	16	13
Largest 100	100	59	42	44	39	31
1919						
Largest 10		10	6	6	5	5
Largest 25		25	17	17	15	13
Largest 50		50	32	32	28	23
Largest 100		100	68	66	58	50
1929						
Largest 10			10	9	7	8
Largest 25			25	22	19	17
Largest 50			50	40	36	30
Largest 100			100	83	73	60
1935						
Largest 10				10	7	8
Largest 25				25	19	16
Largest 50				50	42	32
Largest 100				100	80	65
1948						
Largest 10					10	9
Largest 25					25	21
Largest 50					50	35
Largest 100					100	76

Source: Tables 7-2 through 7-7, pp. 140-51.

period of turnover is the 1909-19 interval, with 1919-29 running second.

In the most recent twelve-year period, 9 of the top 10, 21 of the top 25, 35 of the top 50, and 76 of the top 100 were in the lists in both years. This compares with 3 of the top 10, 12 of the top 25, 31 of the top 50, and 59 of the top 100 for the shorter ten-year period 1909 to 1919. Corresponding figures for 1919 to 1929 are 6, 17, 32, and 68. Especially at the top end of the scale, the tendency for increased "survivorship" is apparent.[10]

The early periods, however, were also those in which turnover resulting from merger and dissolution was greatest. If a merger is considered to create a new position among the 100 largest if both merging companies appear on the list of 100 prior to the merger *and* if the surviving firm appears on the first list following the merger, 2 new positions result from the merger of firms on the 1909 list, 11 from mergers of firms on the 1919 list, 4 from mergers among the 1929 list of 100 largest, and none from mergers among firms on either the 1935 or 1948 lists.[11] Eleven entrants in 1919 were firms that, prior to the 1911 dissolutions, had been part of the Standard Oil or American Tobacco combinations.

Even taking turnover induced by these factors into account, membership in the 100 largest is far from stable. Moreover, in addition to turnover among companies, there has been turnover

---

[10] Collins and Preston, exploring similar lists of the 100 largest, and considering turnover during the periods 1909-1919, 1919-1929, 1929-1935, 1935-1948, and 1948-1958, reach essentially similar conclusions: "The amount of movement within the size distribution . . . can be described as relatively high in the first three periods and relatively low in the last two. The rate of entry and exit among the giant firms can be described as relatively high in the first two periods and relatively low in the last two." (Collins and Preston, *op. cit.*, pp. 1000-01.) These authors conclude that ". . . The evidence of mobility *does* accord with a general assumption that large-scale corporations enjoy an increasing amount of entrenchment by virtue of their size." The conclusion, however, is a qualified one: "Whether the increasing stability of position among the largest firms is due to their dynamic management policies and the institutionalization of innovation remains an open question, and it is certainly not to be concluded from the analysis alone that there has been any net decline in the scope and vigor of competition." *Ibid.*

[11] This definition of the creation of a new position by merger is ambiguous. For example, both Bethlehem Steel and Cambria Steel appear on the 1909 list. Cambria dropped from the 1919 list as a consequence of its own relative decline, and was acquired by Bethlehem in 1923. Bethlehem continued to be among the 100 largest in all subsequent years. Thus, by these criteria, the Cambria merger did not create a new position between 1919 and 1929, but would have if the comparison had been between 1909 and 1929 (e.g. if the 1919 list had not been compiled). Similarly, there is no check that Lackawanna Steel, acquired by

within companies. Some giants with consecutive membership in the 100 largest throughout the half century bear little resemblance to their earlier namesakes. The product mix of duPont of 1909 is scarcely that of the present leader in the chemicals field. General Electric is not the electrical manufacturing company of the turn of the century.

Whatever interpretation is placed on this experience generally, the data suggest that continued economic dominance is not accomplished through any size-generated immunity to market pressure, but rather by ability to respond to that pressure, to develop with developing industries and products, to cross product lines where advantageous, and to drop activities where continued investment would fail to provide the basis for sound corporate growth.

With respect to turnover itself, mergers have, of course, played an important, if diminishing, role.[12] Antitrust dissolutions in the early period similarly increased the apparent rivalry in later

---

Bethlehem in 1922, but among the 100 largest in 1919 (hence creating a new position in the 1929 list) would have been among the 100 largest had a list been prepared for 1922 immediately prior to the Lackawanna merger. Elimination of these uncertainties is not possible without lists of the 100 largest for each of the 51 years considered.

A similar, though less serious, ambiguity arises in respect to divestitures. Standard Oil of Ohio, part of the Standard Oil empire prior to the 1911 divestiture, appears among the 100 largest only in 1948. Thus Standard of Ohio was an entrant created by the 1911 proceedings only if the comparison is between 1909 and 1948. In the above tabulation, new positions arising from mergers, and new entrants created by judicial divestiture, are counted only between the five pairs of consecutive lists. The Cambria merger is not included, nor is Standard of Ohio considered an entrant introduced by the 1911 divestiture.

[12] Note that a merger does not necessarily increase turnover among the 100. largest. For example, the merger of two smaller declining members of this group, each destined independently to drop from the 100 largest, may permit one firm to remain among that group. Thus one opening is apparently created by the merger whereas in the absence of that merger there would have been two. Few, if any, of these firms attained their present stature without, at one time or another, acquiring substantial property formerly under independent control. Indeed, one reason for the overall view here presented is the difficulty of distinguishing growth by merger from internal growth. For the giant firms, the acquisition and disposal of operating facilities has become almost a part of daily operations. The significance of this point is developed further in Chap. 10.

periods. Perhaps more than any other factor, the disparity of economic growth among different industrial sectors has introduced instability among the ranks of the 100 largest.

A standard for "sufficient" mobility does not exist. Rivalry has many meanings, and the fifty-year record can be variously interpreted. Nevertheless, it is relevant that, of the 100 largest in 1909, only 31 retained that distinction in 1960. Even between 1948 and 1960, 24 of the 100 largest dropped from the list. Oligopoly may be a feature of modern industrial markets. Among the 100 largest, however, the pattern is less than one of extreme rigidity in terms of size.

TABLE 7-2. *The 100 Largest Industrial Corporations, 1909: Assets in 1909 and Rank 1909-1960* [a]

Rank						Company	1909 Assets	
1909	1919	1929	1935	1948	1960		Million Dollars	*Percent of Total*
1	1	1	2	3	3	United States Steel Corp............	$1,804	*20.63*
2	2	2	1	1	1	Standard Oil Co. (New Jersey)[56].......	800	*9.15*
3	19	28	23	17	42	American Tobacco Co................	286	*3.27*
4	12	—	—	—	—	International Mercantile Marine Co.[26]..	192	*2.20*
5	14	8	8	19	28	Anaconda Co.[5]......................	170	*1.94*
6	13	17	14	18	22	International Harvester Co...........	166	*1.90*
7	35	—	—	—	—	Central Leather Co..................	138	*1.58*
8	26	22	24	82	—	Pullman Co.........................	131	*1.50*
9	3	14	20	30	—	Armour & Co.......................	125	*1.43*
10	34	66	72	—	—	American Sugar Co.................	124	*1.42*
11	8	24	52	39	63	United States Rubber Co............	121	*1.38*
12	17	34	45	54	90	American Smelting & Refining Co.....	119	*1.36*
13	37	51	50	79	—	Singer Manufacturing Co.[54]..........	113	*1.29*
14	4	19	19	27	77	Swift and Co.......................	113	*1.29*
15	27	54	58	93	—	Pittsburgh Consolidation Coal Co.[15] [46]..	104	*1.19*
16	11	11	13	9	11	General Electric Co................	102	*1.17*
17	38	82	85	84	—	A.C.F. Industries, Inc...............	101	*1.15*
18	76	—	—	—	—	Colorado Fuel and Iron Corp.........	101	*1.15*
19	39	77	69	—	95	Corn Products Co.[3].................	97	*1.11*
20	—	—	—	—	—	New England Navigation Co..........	93	*1.06*
21	41	49	30	60	39	American Can Co....................	90	*1.03*
22	44	86	—	—	—	American Woolen Co................	86	*.98*
23	61	—	—	—	—	Lackawanna Steel Co...............	85	*.97*
24	25	41	40	35	52	Jones & Laughlin Steel Corp.[29].......	84	*.96*
25	28	29	33	16	20	Westinghouse Electric Corp..........	84	*.96*
26	23	59	65	58	66	B. F. Goodrich Co.[23]..............	82	*.94*
27	59	—	—	—	—	Atlantic Gulf & West Indies S.S. Lines..	79	*.90*
28	75	—	92	64	71	Deere and Co.[18].....................	76	*.87*
29	67	35	56	52	58	Union Oil Co. of California[63]..........	75	*.86*
30	18	12	9	7	8	E.I. duPont de Nemours & Co........	75	*.86*
31	42	—	—	—	—	Consolidation Coal Co...............	74	*.85*
32	49	21	21	28	26	Republic Steel Corp.................	73	*.83*
33	50	—	—	—	—	Virginia-Carolina Chemical Corp.......	72	*.82*
34	73	26	26	46	32	International Paper Co..............	71	*.81*
35	64	94	—	—	—	American Locomotive & Equipment Corp.........................	69	*.79*
36	6	5	7	12	12	Bethlehem Steel Corp.[31]..............	68	*.78*
37	82	73	64	99	—	National Biscuit Co..................	65	*.74*
38	—	—	—	—	—	Cambria Steel Co.[11]..................	60	*.69*
39	88	—	—	—	—	Associated Oil Co...................	59	*.67*
40	—	—	—	77	79	National Distillers & Chemical Corp.[42].	59	*.67*
41	58	—	—	—	—	Calumet & Hecla, Inc.[10].............	58	*.66*
42	52	—	—	—	—	American Agricultural Chemical Co....	55	*.63*
43	47	79	75	—	—	Crucible Steel Co. of America.........	54	*.62*
44	—	—	—	—	—	Lake Superior Corp.[32]................	54	*.62*
45	96	—	100	65	85	Allis-Chalmers Manufacturing Co......	53	*.61*
46	29	30	27	13	14	Sears, Roebuck & Co................	53	*.61*
47	78	—	—	—	—	U. S. Smelting, Refining & Mining Co...	50	*.57*
48	—	—	—	—	—	United Copper Co.[65].................	50	*.57*
49	72	92	77	86	—	National Lead Co....................	50	*.57*
50	21	78	39	61	97	Phelps Dodge Corp.................	49	*.56*

TABLE 7-2. *(Continued)*

1909	1919	1929	1935	1948	1960	Company	Million Dollars	Percent of Total
			Rank				1909 Assets	
51	74	—	90	—	—	Lehigh Coal & Navigation Co.........	47	.54
52	—	—	—	—	—	International Steam Pump Co.[28]......	47	.54
53	—	—	—	—	—	American Express Co..[70]............	46	.53
54	56	—	—	—	—	Morris and Co.[41]....................	44	.50
55	55	23	32	20	17	Western Electric Co., Inc............	43	.49
56	—	—	—	—	—	American Writing Paper Co...........	42	.48
57	84	99	—	—	—	Baldwin Locomotive Works[8].........	42	.48
58	—	—	—	—	—	Copper Range Co....................	41	.47
59	33	39	41	47	—	United Fruit Co.....................	41	.47
60	—	—	—	—	—	General Asphalt Co..................	40	.46
61	81	—	81	—	—	United Shoe Machinery Corp.........	40	.46
62	—	53	67	66	—	Borden Co.[9].......................	40	.46
63	83	—	—	—	—	Mexican Petroleum Co.[38]............	40	.46
64	—	—	—	—	—	Goldfield Corp......................	39	.45
65	94	—	—	—	—	American Cotton Oil Co..............	38	.43
66	—	—	—	—	—	Wells Fargo & Co.[70].................	38	.43
67	—	—	—	—	—	American Hide & Leather Co........	38	.43
68	—	—	—	—	—	Lehigh Valley Coal Co..............	37	.42
69	—	—	—	—	—	Houston Oil of Texas................	37	.42
70	—	—	—	—	—	Guggenheim Exploration Co.[24]........	37	.42
71	—	—	—	—	—	Lehigh and Wilkes-Barre Coal Co.[33]....	36	.41
72	69	60	49	33	33	Eastman Kodak Co..................	35	.40
73	—	—	—	—	—	Pressed Steel Car Co.[49]..............	35	.40
74	—	—	—	—	—	Railway Steel Spring Co.[50]...........	35	.40
75	—	—	—	—	—	Harbison-Walker Refractories Co......	34	.39
76	—	—	—	—	—	Development Corp. of America.......	34	.39
77	—	—	—	—	—	American Malting Co...............	34	.39
78	—	—	—	—	—	Greenwater Copper Mines & Smelter Co.	34	.39
79	—	—	—	—	—	American Linseed Co................	34	.39
80	—	—	—	—	—	Intercontinental Rubber Co.[25]........	34	.39
81	—	—	—	—	—	Union Bag-Camp Paper Corp........	33	.38
82	—	—	—	—	—	New River Co......................	33	.38
83	92	52	29	45	61	International Nickel Co. of Canada, Ltd.	32	.37
84	—	—	—	—	—	U. S. Cast Iron Pipe & Foundry Co....	32	.37
85	—	—	—	—	—	Chicago Junction Railways & Union Stock Yards Co....................	31	.35
86	—	—	—	—	—	American Ice Co.....................	31	.35
87	—	—	—	—	—	U. S. Realty & Improvement Co.......	31	.35
88	—	—	—	—	—	New York Dock Railway.............	31	.35
89	—	—	—	—	—	National Enameling & Stamping Co....	30	.34
90	—	97	74	70	65	Pittsburgh Plate Glass Co...........	29	.33
91	—	—	—	—	—	Schwarzchild and Sulzberger Co.[52].....	28	.32
92	—	—	—	—	—	Pennsylvania Steel Co.[43]..............	27	.31
93	98	31	42	55	38	Tide Water Oil Co.[6].................	26	.30
94	—	—	—	—	—	International Salt Co.[27]..............	26	.30
95	16	9	11	6	6	Texaco Inc..........................	26	.30
96	—	—	—	—	—	General Cigar Co., Inc..............	26	.30
97	65	—	97	—	—	Cudahy Packing Co..................	25	.29
98	—	—	—	—	—	Union Typewriter Co.[64].............	25	.29
99	100	27	25	44	51	Allied Chemical & Dye Corp.[1]........	25	.29
100	—	—	—	—	—	American Steel Foundries, Inc........	25	.29
							$8,746	

[a] See "Notes to Tables," pp. 152-53.

TABLE 7-3. *The 100 Largest Industrial Corporations, 1919: Assets in 1919 and Rank 1909-1960* [a]

Rank						Company	1919 Assets	
1909	1919	1929	1935	1948	1960		Million Dollars	Percent of Total
1	1	1	2	3	3	United States Steel Corp............	$2,366	13.81
2	2	2	1	1	1	Standard Oil Co. (New Jersey)........	853	4.98
9	3	14	20	30	—	Armour & Co........................	491	2.86
14	4	19	19	27	77	Swift and Co........................	490	2.86
—	5	3	3	2	2	General Motors Corp................	447	2.61
36	6	5	7	12	12	Bethlehem Steel Corp.[31]............	357	2.08
—	7	6	6	10	4	Ford Motor Co......................	333	1.94
11	8	24	52	39	63	United States Rubber Co............	305	1.78
—	9	7	4	5	7	Socony Mobil Oil Co., Inc.[55]........	300	1.75
—	10	—	—	—	—	Midvale Steel and Ordnance[39]........	280	1.63
16	11	11	13	9	11	General Electric Co.................	277	1.62
4	12	—	—	—	—	International Mercantile Marine Co.[26]..	269	1.57
6	13	17	14	18	22	International Harvester Co..........	267	1.56
5	14	8	8	19	28	Anaconda Co.......................	237	1.38
—	15	16	16	15	21	Sinclair Oil Corp....................	232	1.35
95	16	9	11	6	6	Texaco Inc.........................	224	1.31
12	17	34	45	54	90	American Smelting & Refining Co......	215	1.25
30	18	12	9	7	8	E.I. duPont de Nemours & Co.........	214	1.25
3	19	28	23	17	42	American Tobacco Co...............	206	1.20
—	20	25	22	14	16	Union Carbide Corp.[62]...............	200	1.17
50	21	78	39	61	97	Phelps Dodge Corp.................	186	1.09
—	22	—	—	—	—	Magnolia Petroleum Co.[36]...........	182	1.06
26	23	59	65	58	66	B. F. Goodrich Co..................	176	1.03
—	24	10	10	11	10	Standard Oil Co. of California[57].......	174	1.02
24	25	41	40	35	52	Jones & Laughlin Steel Corp.[29]........	169	.99
8	26	22	24	82	—	Pullman Co.........................	169	.99
15	27	54	58	93	—	Pittsburgh Consolidation Coal Co.[15][46]..	161	.94
25	28	29	33	16	20	Westinghouse Electric Corp..........	160	.93
46	29	30	27	13	14	Sears, Roebuck & Co...............	155	.90
—	30	4	5	4	9	Standard Oil Co. (Indiana)[58]........	155	.90
—	31	67	46	32	—	Liggett and Myers Tobacco Co.[34]......	151	.88
—	32	—	—	—	—	Chile Copper Co.[12]..................	149	.87
59	33	39	41	47	—	United Fruit Co.....................	148	.86
10	34	66	72	—	—	American Sugar Co..................	147	.86
7	35	—	—	—	—	Central Leather Co.................	147	.86
—	36	15	12	8	5	Gulf Oil Corp.......................	143	.83
13	37	51	50	79	—	Singer Manufacturing Co.[54]..........	140	.82
17	38	82	85	84	—	A.C.F. Industries, Inc................	139	.81
19	39	77	69	—	95	Corn Products Co.[3].................	138	.81
—	40	20	18	25	49	Kennecott Copper Corp.[24]...........	136	.79
21	41	49	30	60	39	American Can Co...................	135	.79
31	42	—	—	—	—	Consolidation Coal Co...............	135	.79
—	43	38	28	29	23	Aluminum Co. of America[2]..........	133	.78
22	44	86	—	—	—	American Woolen Co................	133	.78
—	45	43	54	57	73	Pure Oil Co........................	132	.77
—	46	44	—	—	—	Prairie Oil and Gas Co.[48].............	130	.76
43	47	79	75	—	—	Crucible Steel Co. of America........	127	.74
—	48	—	93	—	—	Wilson and Co., Inc.[71]...............	127	.74
32	49	21	21	28	26	Republic Steel Corp.................	126	.74
33	50	—	—	—	—	Virginia-Carolina Chemical Corp.......	121	.71

TABLE 7-3. *(Continued)*

1909	1919	1929	1935	1948	1960	Company	Million Dollars	Percent of Total
—	51	33	36	31	30	Goodyear Tire & Rubber Co.........	113	.66
42	52	—	—	—	—	American Agricultural Chemical Co....	111	.65
—	53	98	—	—	—	Cuba Cane Sugar Corp.............	110	.64
—	54	37	31	50	56	Youngstown Sheet and Tube Co.[72]....	109	.64
55	55	23	32	20	17	Western Electric Co., Inc............	108	.63
54	56	—	—	—	—	Morris and Co.[41]..................	103	.60
—	57	61	55	26	34	R. J. Reynolds Tobacco Co.[51]........	103	.60
41	58	—	—	—	—	Calumet & Hecla, Inc.[10].............	100	.58
27	59	—	—	—	—	Atlantic Gulf & West Indies S. S. Lines.	99	.58
—	60	—	—	—	—	Great Northern Iron Ore Properties....	99	.58
23	61	—	—	—	—	Lackawanna Steel Co...............	95	.55
—	62	55	51	34	47	Atlantic Refining Co.[7]..............	95	.55
—	63	91	63	38	36	Proctor & Gamble Co...............	94	.55
35	64	94	—	—	—	American Locomotive & Equipment Corp...........................	93	.54
97	65	—	97	—	—	Cudahy Packing Co..................	92	.54
—	66	—	—	—	—	Steel and Tube Co. of America[60].......	92	.54
29	67	35	56	52	58	Union Oil Co. of California...........	90	.53
—	68	58	35	42	60	F. W. Woolworth & Co..............	89	.52
72	69	60	49	33	33	Eastman Kodak Co.................	89	.52
—	70	93	—	—	—	P. Lorillard Co.[35]..................	88	.51
—	71	72	—	—	—	Studebaker Corp....................	88	.51
49	72	92	77	86	—	National Lead Co...................	88	.51
34	73	26	26	46	32	International Paper Co...............	86	.50
51	74	—	90	—	—	Lehigh Coal & Navigation Co.........	85	.50
28	75	—	92	64	71	Deere and Co......................	84	.49
18	76	—	—	—	—	Colorado Fuel and Iron Corp.........	83	.48
—	77	89	59	80	87	Ohio Oil Co.......................	82	.48
47	78	—	—	—	—	U. S. Smelting, Refining & Mining Co...	80	.47
—	79	46	—	—	—	Vacuum Oil Co.[69]..................	80	.47
—	80	—	—	—	—	Utah Copper Co.[68]..................	79	.46
61	81	—	81	—	—	United Shoe Machinery Corp.........	79	.46
37	82	73	64	99	—	National Biscuit Co.................	78	.46
63	83	—	—	—	—	Mexican Petroleum Co.[38]............	77	.45
57	84	99	—	—	—	Baldwin Locomotive Works..........	76	.44
—	85	62	60	41	43	Firestone Tire & Rubber Co.........	74	.43
—	86	—	—	—	—	Midwest Refining Co.[40].............	73	.43
—	87	50	47	24	57	Montgomery Ward & Co., Inc........	71	.41
39	88	—	—	—	—	Associated Oil Co..................	69	.40
—	89	—	—	—	—	Libby, McNeill & Libby.............	68	.40
—	90	—	—	—	—	Maxwell Motor Co., Inc.[37]..........	67	.39
—	91	85	83	—	—	Crane Co..........................	66	.39
83	92	52	29	45	61	International Nickel Co. of Canada, Ltd.	65	.38
—	93	—	—	—	—	Packard Motor Car Co..............	63	.37
65	94	—	—	—	—	American Cotton Oil Co.............	63	.37
—	95	—	—	—	—	Greene Cananea Copper Co..........	61	.36
45	96	—	100	65	85	Allis-Chalmers Manufacturing Co.....	61	.36
—	97	—	—	—	—	Pierce Oil Corp.[45]..................	60	.35
93	98	31	42	55	38	Tide Water Oil Co.[6].................	60	.35
—	99	96	71	51	50	Inland Steel Co....................	59	.34
99	100	27	25	44	51	Allied Chemical & Dye Corp.[1]........	54	.32

Multi-row header (for reference):

Rank						Company	1919 Assets	
1909	1919	1929	1935	1948	1960		Million Dollars	Percent of Total

$17,138

[a] See "Notes to Tables," pp. 152-53.

TABLE 7-4. *The 100 Largest Industrial Corporations, 1929:*
Assets in 1929 and Rank 1909-1960 [a]

Rank						Company	1929 Assets	
1909	1919	1929	1935	1948	1960		Million Dollars	Percent of Total
1	1	1	2	3	3	United States Steel Corp............	$2,286	8.02
2	2	2	1	1	1	Standard Oil Co. (New Jersey)........	1,767	6.20
—	5	3	3	2	2	General Motors Corp.................	1,131	3.97
—	30	4	5	4	9	Standard Oil Co. (Indiana)[53].........	850	2.98
36	6	5	7	12	12	Bethlehem Steel Corp.[31].............	802	2.82
—	7	6	6	10	4	Ford Motor Co......................	761	2.67
—	9	7	4	5	7	Socony Mobil Oil Co., Inc.[55]........	708	2.49
5	14	8	8	19	28	Anaconda Co.......................	681	2.39
95	16	9	11	6	6	Texaco Inc.........................	610	2.14
—	24	10	10	11	10	Standard Oil Co. of California[57]......	605	2.12
16	11	11	13	9	11	General Electric Co.................	516	1.81
30	18	12	9	7	8	E.I. duPont de Nemours & Co........	497	1.74
—	—	13	15	21	15	Shell Oil Co.......................	486	1.71
9	3	14	20	30	—	Armour & Co.......................	452	1.59
—	36	15	12	8	5	Gulf Oil Corp......................	431	1.51
—	15	16	16	15	21	Sinclair Oil Corp...................	401	1.41
6	13	17	14	18	22	International Harvester Co...........	384	1.35
—	—	18	—	—	—	General Theatres Equipment, Inc.[21]....	360	1.26
14	4	19	19	27	77	Swift and Co.......................	351	1.23
—	40	20	18	25	49	Kennecott Copper Corp.............	338	1.19
32	49	21	21	28	26	Republic Steel Corp.................	332	1.17
8	26	22	24	82	—	Pullman Co.........................	316	1.11
55	55	23	32	20	17	Western Electric Co., Inc............	309	1.08
11	8	24	52	39	63	United States Rubber Co............	308	1.08
—	20	25	22	14	16	Union Carbide Corp.................	307	1.08
34	73	26	26	46	32	International Paper Co..............	283	.99
99	100	27	25	44	51	Allied Chemical & Dye Corp.........	277	.97
3	19	28	23	17	42	American Tobacco Co................	265	.93
25	28	29	33	16	20	Westinghouse Electric Corp..........	254	.89
46	29	30	27	13	14	Sears, Roebuck & Co................	252	.88
93	98	31	42	55	38	Tide Water Oil Co..................	251	.88
—	—	32	17	—	—	Koppers Co.[30]......................	250	.88
—	51	33	36	31	30	Goodyear Tire & Rubber Co.........	243	.85
12	17	34	45	54	90	American Smelting & Refining Co.....	241	.85
29	67	35	56	52	58	Union Oil Co. of California..........	241	.85
—	—	36	68	89	—	Paramount Pictures Corp............	237	.83
—	54	37	31	50	56	Youngstown Sheet and Tube Co.......	236	.83
—	43	38	28	29	23	Aluminum Co. of America............	235	.82
59	33	39	41	47	—	United Fruit Co.....................	226	.79
—	—	40	37	48	62	National Dairy Products Corp........	225	.79
24	25	41	40	35	52	Jones & Laughlin Steel Corp.........	222	.78
—	—	42	—	—	—	International Match Corp............	218	.77
—	45	43	54	57	73	Pure Oil Co........................	215	.75
—	46	44	—	—	—	Prairie Oil and Gas Co.[48]..............	210	.74
—	—	45	34	22	24	Chrysler Corp.[13]....................	210	.74
—	79	46	—	—	—	Vacuum Oil Co.[69]....................	206	.72
—	—	47	53	94	—	American Radiator & Standard Sanitary Corp........................	199	.70
—	—	48	87	63	46	Continental Oil Co.[16]................	198	.70
21	41	49	30	60	39	American Can Co....................	191	.67
—	87	50	47	24	57	Montgomery Ward & Co., Inc.........	188	.66

TABLE 7-4. *(Continued)*

Rank						Company	1929 Assets	
1909	1919	1929	1935	1948	1960		Million Dollars	*Percent of Total*
13	37	51	50	79	—	Singer Manufacturing Co.[54]...........	183	.64
83	92	52	29	45	61	International Nickel Co. of Canada, Ltd.	182	.64
62	—	53	67	66	—	Borden Co.........................	174	.61
15	27	54	58	93	—	Pittsburgh Consolidation Coal Co.[15][46]..	172	.60
—	62	55	51	34	47	Atlantic Refining Co...............	167	.59
—	—	56	48	91	—	Warner Brothers Pictures, Inc........	167	.59
—	—	57	57	—	—	Glen Alden Corp.[22][33].................	167	.59
—	68	58	35	42	60	F. W. Woolworth & Co..............	165	.58
26	23	59	65	58	66	B. F. Goodrich Co..................	164	.58
72	69	60	49	33	33	Eastman Kodak Co.................	163	.57
—	57	61	55	26	34	R. J. Reynolds Tobacco Co.[51]........	163	.57
—	85	62	60	41	43	Firestone Tire & Rubber Co..........	162	.57
—	—	63	—	—	—	United Stores Co.[67]..................	162	.57
—	—	64	78	67	48	Radio Corp. of America..............	159	.56
—	—	65	—	—	—	United Drug Co., Inc.[66]..............	158	.55
10	34	66	72	—	—	American Sugar Co.................	157	.55
—	31	67	46	32	—	Liggett and Myers Tobacco Co.[34]......	150	.53
—	—	68	38	37	59	Great Atlantic & Pacific Tea Co., Inc..	147	.52
—	—	69	44	23	18	Phillips Petroleum Co., Inc..........	145	.51
—	—	70	—	—	—	Prairie Pipe Line Co.[47]..............	140	.49
—	—	71	80	—	—	Marshall Field and Co..............	137	.48
—	71	72	—	—	—	Studebaker Corp...................	134	.47
37	82	73	64	99	—	National Biscuit Co.................	133	.47
—	—	74	—	—	93	Richfield Oil Corp..................	132	.46
—	—	75	86	—	—	Philadelphia and Reading Corp.......	129	.45
—	—	76	73	88	—	Wheeling Steel Corp................	128	.45
19	39	77	69	—	95	Corn Products Co..................	127	.45
50	21	78	39	61	97	Phelps Dodge Corp.[44]...............	125	.44
43	47	79	75	—	—	Crucible Steel Co. of America........	124	.44
—	—	80	61	73	—	Loew's, Inc.......................	124	.44
—	—	81	43	36	40	National Steel Corp................	121	.42
17	38	82	85	84	—	A.C.F. Industries, Inc..............	119	.42
—	—	83	79	—	72	Crown Zellerbach Corp.............	118	.41
—	—	84	—	—	—	Long-Bell Lumber Co...............	116	.41
—	91	85	83	—	—	Crane Co.........................	116	.41
22	44	86	—	—	—	American Woolen Co...............	114	.40
—	—	87	—	—	—	Sinclair Crude Oil Purchasing Co.[53]....	112	.39
—	—	88	89	—	—	International Shoe Co...............	111	.39
—	77	89	59	80	87	Ohio Oil Co.......................	111	.39
—	—	90	70	85	—	S. S. Kresge Co...................	110	.39
—	63	91	63	38	36	Proctor & Gamble Co..............	109	.38
49	72	92	77	86	—	National Lead Co..................	108	.38
—	70	93	—	—	—	P. Lorillard Co.[35]..................	107	.38
35	64	94	—	—	—	American Locomotive & Equipment Corp............................	106	.37
	—	95	66	49	31	Armco Steel Corp..................	104	.36
—	99	96	71	51	50	Inland Steel Co....................	103	.36
90	—	97	74	70	65	Pittsburgh Plate Glass Co...........	102	.36
—	53	98	—	—	—	Cuba Cane Sugar Corp..............	101	.35
57	84	99	—	—	—	Baldwin Locomotive Works...........	99	.35
—	—	100	—	—	—	Cleveland-Cliffs Iron Co.............	98	.34
							$28,487	

ᵃ See "Notes to Tables," pp. 152-53.

TABLE 7-5. *The 100 Largest Industrial Corporations, 1935: Assets in 1935 and Rank 1909-1960* [a]

Rank						Company	1935 Assets	
1909	1919	1929	1935	1948	1960		Million Dollars	*Percent of Total*
2	2	2	1	1	1	Standard Oil Co. (New Jersey)........	$1,895	*7.55*
1	1	1	2	3	3	United States Steel Corp..............	1,822	*7.26*
—	5	3	3	2	2	General Motors Corp.[19].............	1,492	*5.95*
—	9	7	4	5	7	Socony Mobil Oil Co., Inc.[55].........	790	*3.15*
—	30	4	5	4	9	Standard Oil Co. (Indiana)[58].........	693	*2.76*
—	7	6	6	10	4	Ford Motor Co.....................	682	*2.72*
36	6	5	7	12	12	Bethlehem Steel Corp................	673	*2.68*
5	14	8	8	19	28	Anaconda Co.......................	582	*2.32*
30	18	12	9	7	8	E.I. duPont de Nemours & Co.......	581	*2.32*
—	24	10	10	11	10	Standard Oil Co. of California[57].......	580	*2.31*
95	16	9	11	6	6	Texaco Inc.......................	474	*1.89*
—	36	15	12	8	5	Gulf Oil Corp.....................	430	*1.71*
16	11	11	13	9	11	General Electric Co.................	398	*1.59*
6	13	17	14	18	22	International Harvester Co..........	365	*1.45*
—	—	13	15	21	15	Shell Oil Co......................	358	*1.43*
—	15	16	16	15	21	Sinclair Oil Corp..................	331	*1.32*
—	—	32	17	—	—	Koppers Co.[30]....................	331	*1.32*
—	40	20	18	25	49	Kennecott Copper Corp.............	324	*1.29*
14	4	19	19	27	77	Swift and Co......................	321	*1.28*
9	3	14	20	30	—	Armour & Co......................	317	*1.26*
32	49	21	21	28	26	Republic Steel Corp.................	297	*1.18*
—	20	25	22	14	16	Union Carbide Corp................	271	*1.08*
3	19	28	23	17	42	American Tobacco Co...............	264	*1.05*
8	26	22	24	82	—	Pullman Co........................	259	*1.03*
99	100	27	25	44	51	Allied Chemical & Dye Corp.........	252	*1.00*
34	73	26	26	46	32	International Paper Co..............	248	*.99*
46	29	30	27	13	14	Sears, Roebuck & Co................	234	*.93*
—	43	38	28	29	23	Aluminum Co. of America...........	223	*.89*
83	92	52	29	45	61	International Nickel Co. of Canada, Ltd.	211	*.84*
21	41	49	30	60	39	American Can Co...................	209	*.83*
—	54	37	31	50	56	Youngstown Sheet and Tube Co.......	207	*.83*
55	55	23	32	20	17	Western Electric Co.................	199	*.79*
25	28	29	33	16	20	Westinghouse Electric Corp..........	194	*.77*
—	—	45	34	22	24	Chrysler Corp.[13]...................	193	*.77*
—	68	58	35	42	60	F. W. Woolworth & Co..............	192	*.77*
—	51	33	36	31	30	Goodyear Tire & Rubber Co.........	192	*.77*
—	—	40	37	48	62	National Dairy Products Corp.......	192	*.77*
—	—	68	38	37	59	Great Atlantic & Pacific Tea Co., Inc...	191	*.76*
50	21	78	39	61	97	Phelps Dodge Corp..................	185	*.74*
24	25	41	40	35	52	Jones & Laughlin Steel Corp.........	185	*.74*
59	33	39	41	47	—	United Fruit Co....................	185	*.74*
93	98	31	42	55	38	Tide Water Oil Co.[6]..................	183	*.73*
—	—	81	43	36	40	National Steel Corp.................	181	*.72*
—	—	69	44	23	18	Phillips Petroleum Co., Inc...........	174	*.69*
12	17	34	45	54	90	American Smelting & Refining Co.[4]....	172	*.69*
—	31	67	46	32	—	Liggett and Myers Tobacco Co.[34]......	171	*.68*
—	87	50	47	24	57	Montgomery Ward & Co., Inc.......	169	*.67*
—	—	56	48	91	—	Warner Brothers Pictures, Inc.........	168	*.67*
72	69	60	49	33	33	Eastman Kodak Co.................	168	*.67*
13	37	51	50	79	—	Singer Manufacturing Co...........	163	*.65*

TABLE 7-5. *(Continued)*

Rank						Company	1935 Assets	
1909	1919	1929	1935	1948	1960		Million Dollars	Percent of Total
—	62	55	51	34	47	Atlantic Refining Co................	163	.65
11	8	24	52	39	63	United States Rubber Co............	159	.63
—	—	47	53	94	—	American Radiator & Standard Sanitary Corp......................	159	.63
—	45	43	54	57	73	Pure Oil Co........................	157	.63
—	57	61	55	26	34	R. J. Reynolds Tobacco Co.[51]........	154	.61
29	67	35	56	52	58	Union Oil Co. of California..........	152	.61
—	—	57	57	—	—	Glen Alden Corp....................	151	.60
15	27	54	58	93	—	Pittsburgh Consolidation Coal Co.[15][46]..	142	.57
—	77	89	59	80	87	Ohio Oil Co........................	140	.56
—	85	62	60	41	43	Firestone Tire & Rubber Co..........	139	.55
—	—	80	61	73	—	Loew's, Inc........................	129	.51
—	—	—	62	98	—	Hearst Consolidated Publications, Inc..	129	.51
—	63	91	63	38	36	Proctor & Gamble Co...............	127	.51
37	82	73	64	99	—	National Biscuit Co.................	125	.50
26	23	59	65	58	66	B. F. Goodrich Co..................	124	.49
—	—	95	66	49	31	Armco Steel Corp...................	123	.49
62	—	53	67	66	—	Borden Co.........................	120	.48
—	—	36	68	89	—	Paramount Pictures Corp............	119	.47
19	39	77	69	—	95	Corn Products Co..................	119	.47
—	—	90	70	85	—	S. S. Kresge Co....................	119	.47
—	99	96	71	51	50	Inland Steel Co.....................	118	.47
10	34	66	72	—	—	American Sugar Co.................	118	.47
—	—	76	73	88	—	Wheeling Steel Corp................	113	.45
90	—	97	74	70	65	Pittsburgh Plate Glass Co...........	110	.44
43	47	79	75	—	—	Crucible Steel Co. of America........	109	.43
—	—	—	76	56	55	Sun Oil Co.........................	107	.43
49	72	92	77	86	—	National Lead Co...................	104	.41
—	—	64	78	67	48	Radio Corp. of America.............	103	.41
—	—	83	79	—	72	Crown Zellerbach Corp..............	101	.40
—	—	71	80	—	—	Marshall Field and Co..............	97	.39
61	81	—	81	—	—	United Shoe Machinery Corp........	96	.38
—	—	—	82	—	—	General American Transportation Corp.	96	.38
—	91	85	83	—	—	Crane Co..........................	95	.38
—	—	—	84	75	54	Continental Can Co., Inc...........	95	.38
17	38	82	85	84	—	A.C.F. Industries, Inc..............	95	.38
—	—	75	86	—	—	Philadelphia and Reading Corp........	93	.37
—	—	48	87	63	46	Continental Oil Co.[16]...............	92	.37
—	—	—	88	—	—	R. H. Macy and Co., Inc...........	91	.36
—	—	88	89	—	—	International Shoe Co..............	83	.33
51	74	—	90	—	—	Lehigh Coal & Navigation Co........	82	.33
—	—	—	91	—	—	Gimbel Brothers, Inc................	80	.32
28	75	—	92	64	71	Deere and Co......................	80	.32
—	48	—	93	—	—	Wilson and Co., Inc.[71].............	79	.31
—	—	—	94	—	—	American Metal Climax, Inc.........	79	.31
—	—	—	95	—	—	Minnesota and Ontario Paper Co......	78	.31
—	—	—	96	—	—	Brown Co..........................	76	.30
97	65	—	97	—	—	Cudahy Packing Co.................	76	.30
—	—	—	98	62	91	J. C. Penney Co....................	74	.29
—	—	—	99	100	78	St. Regis Paper Co.................	74	.29
45	96	—	100	65	85	Allis-Chalmers Manufacturing Co......	73	.29
							$25,088	

[a] See "Notes to Tables," pp. 152-53.

TABLE 7-6. *The 100 Largest Industrial Corporations, 1948: Assets in 1948 and Rank 1909-1960* [a]

Rank						Company	1948 Assets	
1909	1919	1929	1935	1948	1960		Million Dollars	Percent of Total
2	2	2	1	1	1	Standard Oil Co. (New Jersey)........	$3,526	7.12
—	5	3	3	2	2	General Motors Corp.................	2,958	5.97
1	1	1	2	3	3	United States Steel Corp............	2,535	5.12
—	30	4	5	4	9	Standard Oil Co. (Indiana)[58]........	1,500	3.03
—	9	7	4	5	7	Socony Mobil Oil Co., Inc.[55].........	1,443	2.91
95	16	9	11	6	6	Texaco Inc.........................	1,322	2.67
30	18	12	9	7	8	E.I. duPont de Nemours & Co........	1,304	2.63
—	36	15	12	8	5	Gulf Oil Corp......................	1,191	2.40
16	11	11	13	9	11	General Electric Co.................	1,177	2.38
—	7	6	6	10	4	Ford Motor Co.....................	1,149	2.32
—	24	10	10	11	10	Standard Oil Co. of California[57]......	1,075	2.17
36	6	5	7	12	12	Bethlehem Steel Corp...............	1,029	2.08
46	29	30	27	13	14	Sears, Roebuck & Co...............	789	1.59
—	20	25	22	14	16	Union Carbide Corp.................	723	1.46
—	15	16	16	15	21	Sinclair Oil Corp...................	710	1.43
25	28	29	33	16	20	Westinghouse Electric Corp..........	694	1.40
3	19	28	23	17	42	American Tobacco Co...............	687	1.39
6	13	17	14	18	22	International Harvester Co..........	672	1.36
5	14	8	8	19	28	Anaconda Co.......................	660	1.33
55	55	23	32	20	17	Western Electric Co.................	650	1.31
—	—	13	15	21	15	Shell Oil Co.......................	641	1.29
—	—	45	34	22	24	Chrysler Corp.[13]....................	597	1.21
—	—	69	44	23	18	Phillips Petroleum Co., Inc..........	579	1.17
—	87	50	47	24	57	Montgomery Ward & Co., Inc.........	579	1.17
—	40	20	18	25	49	Kennecott Copper Corp.............	575	1.16
—	57	61	55	26	34	R. J. Reynolds Tobacco Co.[51]........	531	1.07
14	4	19	19	27	77	Swift and Co.......................	522	1.05
32	49	21	21	28	26	Republic Steel Corp.................	508	1.03
—	43	38	28	29	23	Aluminum Co. of America...........	504	1.02
9	3	14	20	30	—	Armour & Co......................	448	.90
—	51	33	36	31	30	Goodyear Tire & Rubber Co.........	445	.90
—	31	67	46	32	—	Liggett and Myers Tobacco Co.[34].....	425	.86
72	69	60	49	33	33	Eastman Kodak Co..................	412	.83
—	62	55	51	34	47	Atlantic Refining Co................	383	.77
24	25	41	40	35	52	Jones & Laughlin Steel Corp.........	379	.77
—	—	81	43	36	40	National Steel Corp.................	360	.73
—	—	68	38	37	59	Great Atlantic & Pacific Tea Co., Inc...	359	.72
—	63	91	63	38	36	Proctor & Gamble Co...............	356	.72
11	8	24	52	39	63	United States Rubber Co............	348	.70
—	—	—	—	40	75	Distillers Corporation—Seagrams, Ltd..	346	.70
—	85	62	60	41	43	Firestone Tire & Rubber Co..........	344	.69
—	68	58	35	42	60	F. W. Woolworth & Co..............	342	.69
—	—	—	—	43	89	Schenley Industries, Inc.............	342	.69
99	100	27	25	44	51	Allied Chemical & Dye Corp.........	339	.68
83	92	52	29	45	61	International Nickel Co. of Canada, Ltd.	323	.65
34	73	26	26	46	32	International Paper Co...............	323	.65
59	33	39	41	47	—	United Fruit Co....................	320	.65
—	—	40	37	48	62	National Dairy Products Corp........	318	.64
—	—	95	66	49	31	Armco Steel Corp...................	316	.64
—	54	37	31	50	56	Youngstown Sheet and Tube Co.......	312	.63

TABLE 7-6. *(Continued)*

Rank						Company	1948 Assets	
1909	1919	1929	1935	1948	1960		Million Dollars	*Percent of Total*
—	99	96	71	51	50	Inland Steel Co......................	311	*.63*
29	67	35	56	52	58	Union Oil Co. of California...........	298	*.60*
—	—	—	—	53	29	Dow Chemical Co.[17].................	294	*.59*
12	17	34	45	54	90	American Smelting & Refining Co.....	290	*.59*
93	98	31	42	55	38	Tide Water Oil Co.[6].................	288	*.58*
—	—	—	76	56	55	Sun Oil Co..........................	285	*.58*
—	45	43	54	57	73	Pure Oil Co.........................	285	*.58*
26	23	59	65	58	66	B. F. Goodrich Co...................	283	*.57*
—	—	—	—	59	—	Celanese Corp. of America...........	283	*.57*
21	41	49	30	60	39	American Can Co....................	276	*.56*
50	21	78	39	61	97	Phelps Dodge Corp..................	274	*.55*
—	—	—	98	62	91	J. C. Penney Co.....................	265	*.54*
—	—	48	87	63	46	Continental Oil Co.[16]................	262	*.53*
28	75	—	92	64	71	Deere and Co.......................	258	*.52*
45	96	—	100	65	85	Allis-Chalmers Manufacturing Co......	254	*.51*
62	—	53	67	66	—	Borden Co..........................	252	*.51*
—	—	64	78	67	48	Radio Corp. of America..............	248	*.50*
—	—	—	—	68	—	Standard Oil Co. (Ohio)[59]...........	242	*.49*
—	—	—	—	69	19	International Business Machines Corp..	242	*.49*
90	—	97	74	70	65	Pittsburgh Plate Glass Co...........	227	*.46*
—	—	—	—	71	67	Weyerhaeuser Co....................	227	*.46*
—	—	—	—	72	—	American Viscose Corp...............	227	*.46*
—	—	80	61	73	—	Loew's, Inc.........................	223	*.45*
—	—	—	—	74	84	General Foods Corp..................	222	*.45*
—	—	—	84	75	54	Continental Can Company, Inc........	222	*.45*
—	—	—	—	76	98	Coca-Cola Co.......................	222	*.45*
40	—	—	—	77	79	National Distillers & Chemical Corp.[42].	215	*.43*
—	—	—	—	78	64	American Cyanamid Co..............	212	*.43*
13	37	51	50	79	—	Singer Manufacturing Co.............	209	*.42*
—	77	89	59	80	87	Ohio Oil Co.........................	203	*.41*
—	—	—	—	81	99	May Department Stores Co...........	199	*.40*
8	26	22	24	82	—	Pullman Co.........................	195	*.39*
—	—	—	—	83	68	Burlington Industries, Inc...........	194	*.39*
17	38	82	85	84	—	A.C.F. Industries, Inc...............	190	*.38*
—	—	90	70	85	—	S. S. Kresge Co.....................	189	*.38*
49	72	92	77	86	—	National Lead Co....................	183	*.37*
—	—	—	—	87	27	Monsanto Chemical Co..............	183	*.37*
—	—	76	73	88	—	Wheeling Steel Corp.................	182	*.37*
—	—	36	68	89	—	Paramount Pictures Corp............	182	*.37*
—	—	—	—	90	86	Owens-Illinois Glass Co.............	180	*.36*
—	—	56	48	91	—	Warner Brothers Pictures, Inc........	176	*.36*
—	—	—	—	92	—	J. P. Stevens and Co., Inc...........	176	*.36*
15	27	54	58	93	—	Pittsburgh Consolidation Coal Co.[15 46]..	173	*.35*
—	—	47	53	94	—	American Radiator & Standard Sanitary Corp.......................	171	*.35*
—	—	—	—	95	—	Skelly Oil Co.......................	169	*.34*
—	—	—	—	96	—	Twentieth Century-Fox Film Corp.[61]...	169	*.34*
—	—	—	—	97	—	Allied Stores Corp..................	165	*.33*
—	—	—	62	98	—	Hearst Consolidated Publications, Inc..	163	*.33*
37	82	73	64	99	—	National Biscuit Co.................	162	*.33*
—	—	—	99	100	78	St. Regis Paper Co..................	158	*.32*
							$49,528	

[a] See "Notes to Tables," pp. 152-53.

TABLE 7-7. *The 100 Largest Industrial Corporations, 1960: Assets in 1960 and Rank 1909-1960* [a]

Rank						Company	1960 Assets	
1909	1919	1929	1935	1948	1960		Million Dollars	Percent of Total
2	2	2	1	1	1	Standard Oil Co. (New Jersey)........	$10,090	8.04
—	5	3	3	2	2	General Motors Corp................	8,553	6.81
1	1	1	2	3	3	United States Steel Corp............	4,781	3.81
—	7	6	6	10	4	Ford Motor Co.....................	4,032	3.21
—	36	15	12	8	5	Gulf Oil Corp......................	3,843	3.06
95	16	9	11	6	6	Texaco Inc........................	3,647	2.91
—	9	7	4	5	7	Socony Mobil Oil Co., Inc.[55].........	3,455	2.75
30	18	12	9	7	8	E.I. duPont de Nemours & Co......	3,134	2.50
—	30	4	5	4	9	Standard Oil Co. (Indiana)[58].........	2,926	2.33
—	24	10	10	11	10	Standard Oil Co. of California[57].......	2,782	2.22
16	11	11	13	9	11	General Electric Co.................	2,551	2.03
36	6	5	7	12	12	Bethlehem Steel Corp..............	2,275	1.81
—	—	—	—	—	13	General Telephone & Electronics[20].....	2,205	1.76
46	29	30	27	13	14	Sears, Roebuck & Co...............	2,204	1.76
—	—	13	15	21	15	Shell Oil Co........................	1,885	1.50
—	20	25	22	14	16	Union Carbide Corp.................	1,713	1.36
55	55	23	32	20	17	Western Electric Co...............	1,665	1.33
—	—	69	44	23	18	Phillips Petroleum Co., Inc..........	1,647	1.31
—	—	—	—	69	19	International Business Machines Corp..	1,624	1.29
25	28	29	33	16	20	Westinghouse Electric Corp..........	1,521	1.21
—	15	16	16	15	21	Sinclair Oil Corp...................	1,487	1.18
6	13	17	14	18	22	International Harvester Co..........	1,457	1.16
—	43	38	28	29	23	Aluminum Co. of America...........	1,374	1.09
—	—	45	34	22	24	Chrysler Corp.[13]....................	1,369	1.09
—	—	—	—	—	25	Cities Service Co.[14].................	1,343	1.07
32	49	21	21	28	26	Republic Steel Corp.................	1,139	.91
—	—	—	—	87	27	Monsanto Chemical Co..............	1,090	.87
5	14	8	8	19	28	Anaconda Co......................	1,086	.87
—	—	—	—	53	29	Dow Chemical Co.[17].................	1,040	.83
—	51	33	36	31	30	Goodyear Tire & Rubber Co.........	1,037	.83
—	—	95	66	49	31	Armco Steel Corp...................	1,004	.80
34	73	26	26	46	32	International Paper Co..............	977	.78
72	69	60	49	33	33	Eastman Kodak Co.................	959	.76
—	57	61	55	26	34	R. J. Reynolds Tobacco Co.[51]........	947	.75
—	—	—	—	—	35	Reynolds Metals Co.................	941	.75
—	63	91	63	38	36	Proctor & Gamble Co...............	931	.74
—	—	—	—	—	37	International Telephone & Telegraph Corp............................	924	.74
93	98	31	42	55	38	Tide Water Oil Co.[6].................	898	.72
21	41	49	30	60	39	American Can Co...................	891	.71
—	—	81	43	36	40	National Steel Corp................	866	.69
—	—	—	—	—	41	Olin Mathieson Chemical Corp........	860	.69
3	19	28	23	17	42	American Tobacco Co...............	851	.68
—	85	62	60	41	43	Firestone Tire & Rubber Co..........	850	.68
—	—	—	—	—	44	Sperry Rand Corp.[64]................	849	.68
—	—	—	—	—	45	General Dynamics Corp.............	842	.67
—	—	48	87	63	46	Continental Oil Co.[16]................	833	.66
—	62	55	51	34	47	Atlantic Refining Co...............	820	.65
—	—	64	78	67	48	Radio Corp. of America.............	816	.65
—	40	20	18	25	49	Kennecott Copper Corp.............	808	.64
—	99	96	71	51	50	Inland Steel Co....................	804	.64

TABLE 7-7. *(Continued)*

Rank						Company	1960 Assets	
1909	1919	1929	1935	1948	1960		Million Dollars	*Percent of Total*
99	100	27	25	44	51	Allied Chemical & Dye Corp.........	801	.64
24	25	41	40	35	52	Jones & Laughlin Steel Corp.........	794	.63
—	—	—	—	—	53	Kaiser Aluminum & Chemical Corp....	786	.63
—	—	—	84	75	54	Continental Can Co., Inc............	767	.61
—	—	—	76	56	55	Sun Oil Co.........................	766	.61
—	54	37	31	50	56	Youngstown Sheet and Tube Co.......	755	.60
—	87	50	47	24	57	Montgomery Ward & Co., Inc........	740	.59
29	67	35	56	52	58	Union Oil Co. of California...........	734	.58
—	—	68	38	37	59	Great Atlantic & Pacific Tea Co., Inc...	711	.57
—	68	58	35	42	60	F. W. Woolworth & Co..............	693	.55
83	92	52	29	45	61	International Nickel Co. of Canada, Ltd.	679	.54
—	—	40	37	48	62	National Dairy Products Corp.......	670	.53
11	8	24	52	39	63	United States Rubber Co.............	645	.51
—	—	—	—	78	64	American Cyanamid Co..............	641	.51
90	—	97	74	70	65	Pittsburgh Plate Glass Co...........	625	.50
26	23	59	65	58	66	B. F. Goodrich Co..................	613	.49
—	—	—	—	71	67	Weyerhaeuser Co....................	612	.49
—	—	—	—	83	68	Burlington Industries, Inc...........	606	.48
—	—	—	—	—	69	W. R. Grace and Co................	606	.48
—	—	—	—	—	70	Caterpillar Tractor Co..............	598	.48
28	75	—	92	64	71	Deere and Co......................	597	.48
—	—	83	79	—	72	Crown Zellerbach Corp..............	594	.47
—	45	43	54	57	73	Pure Oil Co.......................	592	.47
—	—	—	—	—	74	Sunray DX Oil Co..................	589	.47
—	—	—	—	40	75	Distillers Corporation—Seagrams, Ltd.	589	.47
13	37	51	50	79	76	Singer Manufacturing Co............	582	.46
14	4	19	19	27	77	Swift and Co.......................	573	.46
—	—	—	99	100	78	St. Regis Paper Co.................	564	.45
40	—	—	—	77	79	National Distillers & Chemical Corp.[42].	540	.43
—	—	—	—	—	80	Boeing Airplane Co.................	537	.43
—	—	—	—	—	81	Lockheed Aircraft Corp.............	534	.43
—	—	—	—	—	82	Brunswick Corp....................	530	.42
—	—	—	—	—	83	United Aircraft Corp................	523	.42
—	—	—	—	74	84	General Foods Corp.................	513	.41
45	96	—	100	65	85	Allis-Chalmers Manufacturing Co......	499	.40
—	—	—	—	90	86	Owens-Illinois Glass Co.............	492	.39
—	77	89	59	80	87	Ohio Oil Co.......................	470	.37
—	—	—	—	—	88	Kaiser Steel Corp..................	467	.37
—	—	—	—	43	89	Schenley Industries, Inc.............	464	.37
12	17	34	45	54	90	American Smelting & Refining Co......	458	.36
—	—	—	98	62	91	J. C. Penney Co....................	455	.36
—	—	—	—	—	92	Minnesota Mining & Manufacturing Co.	447	.36
—	—	74	—	—	93	Richfield Oil Corp..................	444	.35
—	—	—	—	—	94	Safeway Stores, Inc.................	442	.35
19	39	77	69	—	95	Corn Products Co..................	440	.35
—	—	—	—	—	96	Borg-Warner Corp..................	427	.34
50	21	78	39	61	97	Phelps Dodge Corp.................	427	.34
—	—	—	—	76	98	Coca-Cola Co.......................	424	.34
—	—	—	—	81	99	May Department Stores Co...........	420	.33
—	—	—	—	—	100	Douglas Aircraft Co., Inc............	417	.33
							$125,518	

[a] See "Notes to Tables," pp. 152- 53.

Notes to Tables 7-2 through 7-7

Sources: Assets shown in these tables are from Moody's *Industrial Manual* (New York: Moody's Investors Service) and Moody's *Public Utility Manual* (New York: Moody's Investors Service) unless otherwise noted. In the preparation of these lists, depreciation reserves, if clearly identified, were deducted from gross asset accounts. Reserves in the liabilities accounts which may have been for depreciation but were not so specified were not deducted. U.S. Treasury tax notes, if deducted from liabilities, were added to the asset accounts. In most instances (see note 74 below) eligibility was confined to United States firms with major operations in the nonregulated industrial (mining, manufacturing, trade, and service) field. Exceptions to these procedures and other irregularities are noted below.

These notes also indicate a number of instances of name change or change in ownership among the 100 largest that may be of help in the interpretation of the lists and the tables derived from them. Companies are arranged alphabetically; for the most part, the present name of each company has been used to identify the corporations on each of the lists.

1 Allied Chemical and Dye Corp. was General Chemical Corp. in 1909 and 1919.

2 Aluminum Co. of America: assets for 1919 provided by the company, July 1964.

3 The American Cotton Oil Co., after a series of reorganizations beginning in the early 1920's, ultimately reappears as part of the Corn Products Co., successor to Corn Products Refining, in 1960.

4 American Smelting and Refining Co.: assets for 1935 are from *The Structure of the American Economy*, Pt. 1, Basic Characteristics, a report prepared by the National Resources Committee under the direction of Gardiner C. Means, June 1939, p. 274.

5 The Anaconda Copper Co. was the Amalgamated Copper Co. in 1909.

6 The Associated Oil Co. merged with the Tide Water Oil Co. in 1926 to form the Tide Water Associated Oil Co. In 1956, this became the Tide Water Oil Co.

7 The Atlantic Refining Co. was part of the Standard Oil organization prior to 1911.

8 Baldwin Locomotive Works: assets shown in 1909 are for Dec. 31, 1910.

9 Borden Co.: assets for 1909 estimated by the author from capital stock shown by Moody's and additional information furnished by the company.

10 Calumet and Hecla, Inc.: assets for 1909 estimated by the company, July 1964. Assets for 1919 estimated in Adolf A. Berle, Jr. and Gardiner C. Means, *The Modern Corporation and Private Property* (New York: The Macmillan Company, 1932), p. 336.

11 The Cambria Steel Co. was acquired by Bethlehem Steel in 1923. Cambria was not among the 100 largest in 1919.

12 A majority interest in the Chile Copper Co. was acquired by the Anaconda Co. in 1923.

13 The Chrysler Corp. is the successor company to the Maxwell Motor Co.

14 The Cities Service Co. completed disposition of its domestic utility holdings in 1954, enabling it to be classified as an industrial in 1960.

15 The Consolidation Coal Co. was acquired by the Pittsburgh Coal Co. in 1945. Pittsburgh Coal did not appear among the 100 largest in 1948.

16 The Continental Oil Co. was part of the Standard Oil organization prior to 1911.

17 The production facilities of the Cleveland-Cliffs Iron Co. were acquired by Dow Chemical Co. in 1935. Dow Chemical does not appear among the 100 largest in 1935.

18 Deere and Co.: assets shown in 1909 are for October 31, 1912.

19 General Motors Corp.: assets for 1935 are from *The Structure of the American Economy, op. cit.*, p. 274.

20 General Telephone and Electronics changed from a predominantly telephone operating concern to one engaged substantially in manufacturing, enabling it to be classified in the 1960 list.

21 General Theatres Equipment, Inc. in 1929 includes Fox Films and Fox Theatres, acquired in 1929. Assets for 1929 are from Berle and Means, *op. cit.*, p. 19.

22 Glen Alden Corp.: assets for 1929 estimated by the company, July 1964.

23 B. F. Goodrich Co.: assets shown in 1909 are the Moody's figure for December 31, 1912, less the assets of the Diamond Rubber Co. given as $16.4 million in 1911.

24 The Guggenheim Exploration Co. was acquired by the Kennecott Corp. in 1916.

25 The Intercontinental Rubber Co., Inc. was acquired by Texas Instruments, Inc. in 1953. Texas Instruments was not among the 100 largest in 1960.

26 International Mercantile Marine Co. adopted present name, U.S. Lines Co., in 1943.

27 International Salt Co.: assets for 1909 estimated from capital stock and long-term debt.

28 International Steam Pump Co. was reorganized, following receivership proceedings, as Worthington Pump and Machinery Corp. in 1916.

29 Jones and Laughlin Steel Corp.: assets for 1909 and 1919 estimated by the company, July 1964.

30 Koppers Co.: assets for 1929 from Berle and Means, *op. cit.*, p. 20. Assets for 1935 estimated in *The Structure of the American Economy, op. cit.*, p. 274.

31 The Lackawanna Steel Co. was acquired by Bethlehem Steel in 1922.

32 The Lake Superior Corp. was acquired by Algoma Steel Corp., Ltd. (Ontario) in 1935. The consolidated assets of Lake Superior and Algoma Steel were less than those of the 100 largest in 1935.

33 The physical properties of the Lehigh and Wilkes-Barre Coal Co. were acquired by Glen Alden Corp. in 1929. Lehigh and Wilkes-Barre Coal was not among the 100 largest in 1919.

34 The Liggett and Myers Tobacco Co. was created in the dissolution of American Tobacco Co. in 1911.

35 P. Lorillard and Co. was created in the dissolution of American Tobacco Co. in 1911.

Notes to Tables (Continued)

[36] The Magnolia Petroleum Co. was acquired by Socony Mobil (Standard Oil Co. of New York) in 1925.

[37] The Maxwell Motor Co. was the predecessor of Chrysler Corp.

[38] The Mexican Petroleum Co. was gradually acquired by Standard Oil Co. (Indiana) between 1925 and 1929.

[39] Midvale Steel and Ordnance was acquired by Bethlehem Steel Corp. in 1923.

[40] The Midwest Refining Co. was acquired by Standard Oil Co. (Indiana) in 1923. Midwest Refining was not among the 100 largest in 1919.

[41] Morris and Co.: assets shown in 1909 are for October 1, 1910. Acquired by Armour and Co. in 1923.

[42] The National Distillers & Chemical Corp. was Distillers Securities, Inc. in 1909.

[43] The Pennsylvania Steel Co. was acquired by Bethlehem Steel Corp. in 1916.

[44] Phelps Dodge Corp.: assets for 1929 are from Berle and Means, *op. cit.*, p. 21.

[45] The Pierce Oil Corp. was part of the Standard Oil organization prior to 1911, and was dissolved in liquidation proceedings, 1939–40.

[46] The Pittsburgh Consolidation Coal Co. was the Pittsburgh Coal Co. prior to 1958.

[47] The Prairie Pipe Line Co., created in 1915 to take over the transportation business of Prairie Oil and Gas, was acquired by Sinclair Oil in 1932. Prairie Pipe Line was not among the 100 largest in 1919.

[48] The Prairie Oil and Gas Co. was part of the Standard Oil organization prior to 1911, and was acquired by Sinclair Oil Corp. in 1932.

[49] Pressed Steel Car Co. was reorganized under the Federal Bankruptcy Act in 1936 and 1951. The present name, U.S. Industries, Inc., was adopted 1960.

[50] Railway Steel Spring Co. was acquired by American Locomotive and Equipment Corp. in 1926. Railway Steel Spring was not among the 100 largest in 1919.

[51] The R. J. Reynolds Tobacco Co. was controlled by the American Tobacco Co. prior to divestiture in 1911. Assets shown in 1919 are for December 31, 1920.

[52] Schwarzchild and Sulzberger was the predecessor of Wilson and Co.

[53] The Sinclair Crude Oil Purchasing Co. was acquired by Standard Oil Co. (Indiana) in 1930.

[54] Singer Manufacturing Co.: assets for 1909 estimated by the author and appraised as acceptable by company, July 1964. Assets for 1919 provided by the company, July 1964. Assets for 1929 estimated by Berle and Means, *op. cit.*, p. 21.

[55] The Socony Mobil Oil Co., Inc. (Standard Oil of New York) was part of the Standard Oil organization prior to 1911.

[56] Standard Oil Co. (New Jersey): assets for 1909 are from Ralph W. Hidy and Muriel E. Hidy, *Pioneering in Big Business 1882–1911* (New York: Harper Brothers, 1955), p. 637. The Standard Oil Co. (New Jersey) is considered after 1911 as the successor company to the original Standard Oil Co. (New Jersey).

[57] Standard Oil Co. of California was part of the Standard Oil organization prior to 1911.

[58] Standard Oil Co. (Indiana) was part of the Standard Oil organization prior to 1911. Assets for 1929 estimated by Berle and Means, *op. cit.*, p. 20.

[59] The Standard Oil Co. (Ohio) was part of the Standard Oil organization prior to 1911.

[60] The Steel and Tube Co. of America was acquired by the Youngstown Sheet and Tube Co. in 1923.

[61] The Twentieth Century Fox Film Corp. is considered the successor company to General Theaters Equipment.

[62] Union Carbide Corp.: assets for 1919 are considered by the company to be the best approximation of total assets.

[63] Union Oil Co. of California: assets shown in 1909 are for December 31, 1911.

[64] Union Typewriter Co. is the predecessor company to Remington Typewriter and Remington Rand. In 1956 the merger of the Sperry Corp. and Remington Rand created Sperry Rand Corp.

[65] United Copper Co.: assets for 1909 are estimated from the par value of capital stock outstanding; see John Moody, *The Truth About the Trusts* (New York: Moody Publishing Company, 1904), pp. 40–41.

[66] The United Drug Co. was acquired by the Rexall Drug Co., 1933. Rexall does not appear among the 100 largest.

[67] United Stores Co.: assets for 1929 are from Berle and Means, *op. cit.*, p. 21.

[68] The Utah Copper Co. was acquired by Kennecott Copper Corp. during the period 1915–1923.

[69] The Vacuum Oil Co. was part of the Standard Oil organization prior to 1911, and was acquired by Socony Mobil Oil Co. (Standard Oil of New York) in 1931.

[70] Wells Fargo & Co., after transfer of its domestic express business to American Railway Express in 1918, was acquired by the American Express Co. in 1925. In 1919, neither American Express, then largely a financial organization, nor American Railway Express, a public utility, appears among the 100 largest industrials. In terms only of assets, however, each would have qualified. American Express reported 1919 assets of $63 million and American Railway Express of $108 million. By 1929, neither of these two firms had assets as large as the 100th largest industrial.

[71] Wilson and Co., Inc. is the successor company to Schwarzchild and Sulzberger.

[72] Youngstown Sheet and Tube Co.: assets for 1919 provided by the company, July 1964.

[73] The Greene Cananea Copper Co. was controlled by Anaconda Copper by 1929.

[74] The lists of the 100 largest include two Canadian firms: International Nickel and Distillers Corp. —Seagrams Ltd. In each case, American operations were judged sufficiently predominant to justify inclusion. Assets shown are from consolidated accounts.

153

8

Price Competition in Big Business

ANALYSIS OF BIG BUSINESS pricing practices must begin with the question of the degree to which large corporations, particularly those dominating their respective industries, have the power to determine market prices. "Price," however, is not a simple, unambiguous term in modern business practice. It has come to represent the value, not just of the product itself, but of the whole bundle of services associated with the seller and his product. In such circumstances, price can and will reflect such factors as the availability of repair parts and servicing facilities, promotional aids afforded to distributors, product design, and any number of other differentiating qualities. Spreading or narrowing of observed price differentials can result not only from changes in the market valuations of the commodities themselves, but also from changes in these other aspects of the product to which the quoted price applies. This chapter is devoted to a discussion of these and other factors influencing the price policy of large firms.

Pricing for Large-Scale Operation

The model of pure competition implies that the competitor must accept the prevailing market price. For most industrial commodities, however, this model is unduly restrictive. It excludes the wide range of effort that typically accompanies aggressive large-scale selling. For day-to-day operations, it would be more realistic to say that the large firms generally put a price on what they offer, and then apply nonprice measures of persuasion to move goods at this figure.

The price policy of a firm reckoning with the probable actions of its competitors may nevertheless result in an identical price quotation. This situation is most probable where the commodity lacks characteristics enabling buyers to distinguish the product of one seller from that of another. In these circumstances, market advantage may then be sought through price concessions in the form of special allowances or in other accommodations to the customer's interests. On the other hand, price differentials among firms may be expected when knowledge about the goods is imperfect, when products are perishable or styles are "dated," when there is local shortage or surplus, where there are special advantages of location, or where sharp differences in product sponsorship or appeal are present. The market itself will, of course, eventually determine in what respects the policy of a particular firm is tenable, and in what respects it must be modified.

What is the effect of firm size on the sensitivity of price to market influences? One common generalization is frequently supported by experience: as size of firm increases, price policy tends to put relatively less emphasis on the short tem; it becomes fitted to the longer-term objectives of fostering continuity and growth of production and earnings. Price decisions are likely to be built on a long-term projection of total demand and the share of the market the firm sets as its target. They are also influenced by rates of return on investment, which, in turn, reflect both past experience and current state of business. The price decision also represents a policy determination in which the known elements in the firm's operations are considered simultaneously with what can be learned about the offerings of competitors and the price resistance of buyers. The adoption of a price policy does not mean that a firm escapes from the need to adapt this policy to changes in the market. There are, in fact, significant differences in methods and timing of price adjustments among the nation's large firms.[1]

[1] For a more detailed discussion and a series of case illustrations, see A. D. H. Kaplan, Joel B. Dirlam, and Robert F. Lanzillotti, *Pricing in Big Business* (Brookings Institution, 1958), esp. pp. 251-90.

Types of Administered Prices

Administered pricing—the predetermination of a quoted price based on a firm's calculation of long-term prospects and costs—is a concomitant of large-scale operation. Firms with significant shares of their respective markets will, for reasons indicated above, normally "administer" their prices and announce them to the trade. The spread between cost and selling price will be determined in part by whether the company is one of the low-cost producers or one that must meet a low-cost competitor's price. The corporation with a large share of its industry's output will probably exert a noticeable impact on the market when it announces a general price decision, but that fact in itself does not indicate that the decision has been immune from, or responsive to, outside pressure for cost reduction, product improvement, or price change.

The character and market effect of the policies behind administered pricing are far from uniform among large corporations. Neither the size of the business nor its share of the total output is necessarily the determining factor. Far more influential are the character of the commodity and the ease with which substitutes may be obtained from alternative sources of supply. The point of this observation may be sharpened by a brief description and comparison of selected market situations in which the price policy of big business has had wide influence.

Market Leadership in Price Cutting

Testimony in the suit of the government against the Great Atlantic and Pacific Tea Company [2] revealed that the company policy was to build a scale of prices designed to produce and hold a volume of business that the company set as its target. On occasion, the price scale did not yield a profit until consumer response neared target volume. When the desired sales level was

[2] *United States v. New York Great Atlantic & Pacific Tea Co.*, 173 F 2d 79 (C.C.A.–7th 1949).

attained, increased volume reduced unit costs to yield the expected profit.[3]

This behavior, however, reflects the structural characteristics of the industry. The retail food business is one where price competition is influenced by the presence of many small competitors and low fixed capital requirements. This business is one of the easiest for entry and exit. Levels of efficiency in buying, selling, and operating are varied. The large companies have achieved substantial economies both in purchasing and operation. Although the aggregate demand for food at any given time appears relatively inelastic, the variety of grades and the large percentage of merchandise in which quality is more important than brand name tend to create a high degree of cross-elasticity of demand between the products of competitors.[4] Consumers readily move from one to another for a better buy. The tendency to shop for bargains in price and quality, favored by modern transportation and packaging for self-service, is not severely limited by such factors as proximity, special services of the neighborhood grocer, or fixed consumer habits of ordering. The large chains have been able to attain the high volume consistent in these circumstances with a low margin policy, and if necessary, to maintain this pricing policy through a temporary period of loss.

Market Leadership in Price Maintenance

A quite different approach to the strengthening of market position is illustrated by the hold-the-line price policy of a primary producer of copper in meeting the market for scrap. Copper recovered from scrap by the custom smelter competes directly with newly mined copper in the final market, and the historic volatility of the copper market is intensified by fluctuations in the supply of scrap. When a large surplus of copper scrap accumu-

---

[3] See Robert R. Bowie, *Government Regulation of Business* (The Foundation Press, 1955), p. 1300.

[4] The private brand names of the chains have themselves become a selling feature, challenging the premium value of standard brand names.

lated in the stocks of the custom smelting companies in the spring of 1949, the market price fell in a few weeks from 18 cents to 12 cents. Spot prices were not only below the cost of newly mined copper, but were also substantially below the average cost of inventories held by fabricators. Under the price leadership of the largest producer, newly mined copper continued to be quoted at the "normal price," even though at that figure little or none moved into the current market. Under this policy of maintained prices for new copper, a policy followed by the three chief mining companies, the stocks of the custom smelters were rapidly cleared from the market. At this point, the leading producers of primary copper edged down from their hold-the-line price to a figure at which new copper would again sell and yield investment returns.[5]

The leading copper mining corporations do not deal directly with hundreds of thousands of consumers, nor is their basic output disturbed for long by direct competition with a host of small competitors. About 90 percent of the output of primary copper is produced by four large companies.[6] Copper demand, in the short run and apart from inventory speculation, is rather unresponsive to price. The market share of each company is well established. This stability of relative position and market outlet is reinforced by ownership of fabricating subsidiaries. The high investment involved in profitable exploitation of the large ore beds serves as a practical barrier to the entry of newcomers. Nevertheless, the industry as a whole has a history of extreme price fluctuations resulting from international developments, wars, construction, and inventory cycles. As a result, stabilization ranks high among the objectives of the industry. The role of the dominant firm in holding an umbrella over the industry has apparently become a custom in the trade in which companies at each stage of operation, from raw material to finished product, acquiese. The most powerful long-run impact of competition on the copper producers has occurred when substitute metals and alloys have

[5] See A. D. H. Kaplan, Joel B. Dirlam and Robert F. Lanzillotti, *op. cit.*, pp. 176-181.

[6] *Concentration Ratios in Manufacturing Industry, 1958*, Report prepared by the U.S. Bureau of the Census for the Subcommittee on Antitrust and Monopoly of the Senate Judiciary Committee, 87 Cong. 2 sess. (1962), p. 141.

invaded the industry at the fabricating end and reacted on the final demand for primary copper.[7] The vigor of overall competition is further intensified by the continuing introduction of new products by the chemical companies and others that create a diffuse spectrum of better buys that the copper producers, for survival, must ultimately meet.

Market Leadership in Standard Pricing

A third example will illustrate what is often regarded as the typical approach in big business. The General Motors Corporation, producing motor cars for a nationwide market, must annually review its models and their price structure. Price-making starts from a base of past experience in terms of average or standard costs for various levels of output. Estimates are made of the number of units the market will absorb within an assumed price range and the share that the company and its distributors expect or hope to attain. This estimate of salable output is then converted into unit costs. Expected return on the investment is added to set standard prices to the distributors. The further addition of distributor's margins provides a provisional retail price. The final determination of price also takes into account the current competitive climate—stocks in the hands of dealers, the vigor of the secondhand market, the general willingness of the public to enter into the market for postponable durable goods, the current popularity of competitive lines and a best guess as to the price at which they will be offered. The quotation being made, any basic price changes are postponed to the next model year, and the competitive efforts of the manufacturers meanwhile are directed to sales promotion and to operating efficiency.[8]

Price changes undoubtedly evoke some shifting of demand in

[7] More aluminum than copper wire has been used by the telephone companies since about 1949. One peculiar twist to this development is that Anaconda Copper has produced aluminum ingot since 1955 and by 1958 accounted for three percent of the ingot capacity. See Merton J. Peck, *Competition in the Aluminum Industry: 1945-1958* (Harvard University Press, 1961), pp. 18, 175.

[8] For a more detailed discussion, see Kaplan, Dirlam, Lanzillotti, *op. cit.*, pp. 48-55.

major consumer durables. Automobile dealers point out that for many customers without a definite company allegiance, a price differential of as little as $25 can shift sales from one model to another. Nevertheless, price competition is governed by the characteristic features of durable consumer goods. Durable goods are not purchased frequently, and replacement is postponable. Model changes require extensive retooling and testing, different materials, and new promotion. The present members of the industry are survivors of two generations of drastic elimination of the inefficient. Industry experience permits shrewd estimating of competitors' costs and at least informed judgment of the appeal of competing lines.[9] The relatively few sellers, with output fitting into familiar price lines, may be expected to take their cue from the firm with the strongest market position and the lowest costs. Under these conditions, a cost method building up to an announced price appears to the corporation to be a sound basis for maximum sales consistent with continuity of operation.

New Product Pricing

The most dynamic pricing in big business occurs when new products, with uncertain market dimensions, are introduced. The first price is often that of a high-cost, low-volume specialty seeking out new uses and demands. This phase may be long or short, depending on the novelty of the product and the imagination of the seller or potential user. With the uncovering of latent demand, it becomes possible to shift from experimental to volume output, with declining costs and prices. With little regard for general market conditions, the appearance of this "maturity" phase is the signal for a policy of stable pricing, providing that the sellers remain few and demand conditions undergo no major shift.

Ammonia furnishes an outstanding illustration of a product with a history of initial radical price changes followed by price

[9] Sometimes this judgment is not too accurate. See Thomas P. Murphy, "How Edsel Lured Those Dealers," *Fortune*, Vol. 57, No. 3 (September 1957), pp. 242-55, and Robert Sheenan, "It's a New Kind of Ford Motor Co.," *Fortune*, Vol. 65, No. 2 (February 1962), pp. 116-17.

stability. The commercial synthesis of anhydrous ammonia began in 1921. During the next three years, five companies adopted the new process and offered the potent anhydrous product at 30 cents a pound [10] as against 7 cents for the older aqueous ammonia. In 1925, one of the new processors captured the refrigeration business of a leading packing house by quoting a substantial reduction in price in return for a volume order. The ensuing market struggle brought down the price of anhydrous ammonia from 30 cents to 16.5 cents within a fortnight. The price of aqueous ammonia was likewise cut in half, but failed to recapture more than a fraction of the refrigeration market from the purer electrolytic product. The new process rapidly established itself, and new capacity brought down the price to an average of 14 cents in 1929. With expanding demand for refrigerators, the price was relatively unaffected by the depression of the 1930's, but seemed to lag behind the upward trend thereafter. The price averaged 14.5 cents in 1946 and 18.5 cents in 1955.[11]

The case of synthetic methanol provides another example. The average price for 1926, the year this product was introduced, was 63 cents a gallon. By 1929, the average price was down to 56.9 cents; in 1933, it was 35.5 cents; by 1946, it had dropped to 24 cents, rising again with the general price level to 30 cents in 1960.[12] Ethylene glycol, a totally new product, was sold to its first commercial users for $1.00 a pound in the early 1920's. Between then and the beginning of World War II, the price fell to 25 cents. In

[10] All prices quoted are wholesale prices. See footnote below.

[11] In August 1955, the Bureau of Labor Statistics discontinued quoting the price per pound and began quoting it on a tonnage basis, because of the fact that ammonia was by then sold almost exclusively in bulk. Since that time, there has been no standard wholesale price per pound. However, there was an increase in the average price per ton between 1955 ($87.50) and 1960 ($91.83), reflecting the general rise in costs during that period.

Prices cited above for years prior to 1929 are from William Haynes, *American Chemical Industry* (Van Nostrand, 1948), pp. 85, 453-54. Prices for 1929, 1946, 1955, and 1960 are from the following serial published by the U.S. Bureau of Labor Statistics: *Wholesale Prices, 1929*, No. 521 (1930), p. 33; *Wholesale Prices, 1946*, No. 920 (1948), p. 108; *Wholesale Prices and Indexes, 1954-56*, No. 1214 (1957), p. 211; *Wholesale Prices, 1960*, No. 1376 (1963), p. 172.

[12] Figures are from *Wholesale Prices* serial, *op. cit.: 1913 to 1927*, p. 212; *1929*, p. 33; *December and Year 1933*, p. 26; *1946*, p. 108; *1960*, p. 172.

1952, it averaged 17 cents, and by 1960 the price had declined still further to 13.5 cents. Triethanolamine, used in cosmetics, waxes, lacquers, and detergents, became available in commercial quantities at 55 cents a pound in 1928. By 1939, with progressively increasing volume, its price had fallen to 18 cents. It remained stable during the war at 20 cents, increasing in response to higher costs to 24 cents in 1950 and 24.5 in 1952, and declined to 22 cents in 1960.[13]

The apparently rigid prices since 1929 of certain basic industrial chemicals deserve special notice. These products are produced by the chemical industry in which product and technology are constantly changing. Typically, however, the basic chemicals are "old" products produced in enormous volume with low margins. For example, sulphuric acid is a widely used raw material, yet in almost no use does it appreciably affect the cost of the end product. Large chemical companies buy huge quantities and also manufacture huge quantities for themselves. Whether they make or buy is determined by considerations of convenience as well as price. The bulk of the product, the large transportation cost, and the necessity of reactivating large quantities of the diluted acid for reuse, make it essential that the supplier be near at hand. Where an outside supplier is conveniently near and will make the necessary accommodations to the requirements of the user, a customer may buy without regard to price shading. Where these conditions are not present, even an offer to sell below cost may not sufficiently offset transportation and handling costs, and the large commercial user will typically manufacture for himself. Overall, then, the consumption of sulphuric acid is not very responsive to price. Much of the output itself is a by-product of other processes. The industry has reached the mature phase. Stability, not volatility of price, is the rule.[14]

---

[13] Figure for years prior to 1952 are from annual data supplied by Union Carbide and Carbon Corporation, Chemicals Group. Figures for 1952 and 1960 are from *Oil, Paint and Drug Reporter,* special annual issue, *1961 Hi-Lo Chemical Price Issue,* February 27, 1961, pp. 154, 323.

[14] Industrial users and suppliers in the industry would point out that the rigidity in the officially quoted price of the standard product—the 66° Baumé strength in eastern works—does not apply in all markets. Insofar as it is a by-

Price Policy and Costs

It is difficult, if not impossible, to discuss price policy without reference to costs. This does not mean that costs are the decisive determinant of price. The multiproduct firm typically discriminates among its many products, selling at different margins over costs for different products. Profits on individual items will be varied as competition is encountered in individual markets.

The costs considered in big business pricing are largely long-run costs. In cases of new product pricing, the producer may look ahead to external economies from which major cost savings will ensue, or he may visualize a succession of cost-output relationships resulting from expected changes in the production methods with increasing demand and higher sales volume. The producer who anticipates such savings, and adopts a price policy to stimulate demand and simultaneously to accelerate cost reduction, is engaged in a policy that is not easily followed by small producers.

In cases where a firm adopts a long-run price policy, the line between the firm's choosing and the market's dictating frequently appears blurred. Benefits apparently volunteered by firms are often not gestures of generous impulse, but rather reflect long-run planning to increase profitability. Such planning, in turn, is based on careful calculation of potential market response and pressure. Once it is recognized that large producers think in terms of long-run costs and demand, the influence of market forces on them becomes more evident. Frequently, a member of an oligopoly

---

product, pricing reflects the possibilities of use or disposal in particular markets. If average prices over the past fifty years are examined, a more dynamic picture emerges. For the 66° Bé product itself, the average price moved between $11 and $21 per ton. In the boom year of 1929, it was $14, well below the average of the 1920's. Meanwhile, the production of other grades for new uses was reflected in a decline of the average price for the oleum from $27.20 in 1904 to $13.25 in 1929. The 50° acid, at the other extreme, ranged from $5.31 in 1911 to $13.89 in 1917, with a steady decline after World War I to a level between $7.50 and $8.00 in the late 1920's. In the early thirties, the price of 66° Bé averaged $15.50; it went to $16.50 in 1938, down to $15.53 in 1948, and up to $22.35 in 1960. Prices for years before 1938 are from Theodore J. Kreps, *The Economics of the Sulfuric Acid Industry* (Stanford University Press, 1938), p. 40. Figures for succeeding years are from *Wholesale Prices* serial, *op. cit.: December and Year 1938*, p. 40; *1948*, p. 39; *1960*, p. 172.

industry recognizes that the lack of competitors at a particular point in time is transitory, that the pressure of potential competition is as real as that of actual competition, and that price policy cannot ignore the ability of outsiders to enter and compete.

Influence of Size on Flexibility of Prices

How has large-scale production affected the relative flexibility of prices? With price policy in big business typically directed toward the longer-term considerations of standard costs, average return on investment, and continuing growth, few price adjustments would be expected in response to short-run fluctuations in demand or costs. Large deviations from the general market price must be weighed carefully against future as well as present impact. The members of an industry with a few giant competitors often have almost instant knowledge of what the other members are doing. Each has resources to match the other's price or merchandising tactics. A selling advantage created by price alone is destined to be short-lived among large competitors. In contrast, the small firm may reach far out to make a single transaction. By continuous sharp pricing, the small firm may replace a fringe competitor. But to supplant a large-scale competitor by extended price war involves great cost and the hazard of mutual injury without change in the relative market positions. Accordingly, the big corporation will, as a rule, move ahead on the price front only if it sees a chance of holding a new position.

The large company has to think, therefore, of the total market and the possibilities of a price move affecting its share in it. When new customers can be attracted into the market, the large corporation may elect to cut prices even though it knows its competitors will immediately follow. This has happened with refrigerators, radios, and other items moving from select to mass trade. Such opportunities are likely to be landmarks in an industry, involving the introduction and imitation of new techniques in production and merchandising.

At the same time, corporate management is aware of its responsibility for the overall stability of its operations. There is the equally sobering influence of the vulnerability of the large corporation to government action should its market superiority be exploited to the injury of established competitors. That factor, as well as respect for habitual market shares, may explain why prices of the low-cost leader sometimes serve as an umbrella over less favorably situated members of the industry.

Conditions for De-emphasis of Price

The above considerations suggest a combination of circumstances in which the de-emphasis of price rivalry could become an established industry policy. Let us assume that three or four large companies divide the bulk of the output in an industry. The product is a staple that offers no advantage to one producer over another. Total demand appears inelastic, and capacity is adequate to support it. A few stockholders hold the majority of the equity of the industry and have come to understand each other. Average returns are stable, but not high enough to attract the large capital required for an outsider to enter. Given these conditions, the attitude might be: Why raid each other's customers and risk retaliation? In these circumstances, the three or four might settle into a common policy of not disturbing the status quo.

Where price competition is static, other forms of competition may also lack vigor. The cigarette industry has been cited as a case in point. The dominant producers have avoided price rivalry. Technology and even the product itself remained relatively unchanged for almost twenty-five years prior to 1950. Since the 1930's, when unusually high profits attracted a number of competitive low-priced brands, profit margins have been low.[15] These low margins, together with the high cost of national promotion characteristic of the major brands, served to minimize the threat

---

[15] See Richard B. Tennant, "The Cigarette Industry," in *The Structure of American Industry*, Walter Adams, ed. (Macmillan Company, 1950), pp. 344-47.

of new competition. Imminent substitutes did not appear to threaten the established position of the major producers.

Between 1925 and 1950, the cigarette industry apparently was content to rest on the achievement of simple mechanization. Since the dissolution of the consolidated American Tobacco Company in 1911, the large corporations in cigarette manufacture have kept closely to their own original field of manufacture. In general, they have not produced their own leaf tobacco or cigarette paper, nor have they moved into by-products of tobacco production. Except for a flurry of price changes in the late 1920's and early 1930's, the industry, in terms of price, has displayed remarkable stability.[16] The product itself has been subject to little change. The market struggle to offset the fickleness of the consumer has placed increasing emphasis on advertising to keep the various brands alive.

Since 1950, the health scare in smoking and the resultant change in consumer taste have induced a series of new brands and new products with substantial shifts in market share. This is an interesting illustration of the de-stabilizing influence that external factors can have on the behavior of an otherwise stable situation.

Evidence on Price Rigidity

During the 1929-33 depression, many prices, especially those of agricultural commodities, dropped precipitously while others remained relatively impervious to the decline in demand. This experience appeared to reinforce a long-standing belief that the rise of big business had robbed the price system of its flexibility and that the severity of the depression was thereby increased. In a report to Congress, Gardiner C. Means drew the conclusion, from a comparison of price movements in industries of many small firms with those of industries dominated by a few large companies, that "administrative coordination—the very thing that has

---

[16] Tennant describes the price activity of 1928 and 1929 as "one of the few cases in which price policy seems to have been used as a competitive weapon among the major firms," and concludes that "price policy in this industry has normally been non-competitive in character." See Richard B. Tennant, "The Cigarette Industry," in Walter Adams, *The Structure of American Industry*, rev. ed. (Macmillan, 1954), p. 343.

made modern technology and a high standard of living possible—
has destroyed the effectiveness of the market as an overall coordi-
nator by the inflexible administered prices which are inherent in
the reduction of competing units it has produced." [17]

A statistical elaboration of this thesis appeared a few years later
in a study by the National Resources Committee:

> The main conclusion to be reached from this analysis is that, while
> many factors influence price sensitivity, the dominant factor in mak-
> ing for depression insensitivity of prices is the administrative control
> over prices which results from the relatively small number of con-
> cerns dominating particular markets.[18]

Subsequent re-examination of price trends has cast doubt on the
validity of the thesis. The statistics over the period 1890 to 1933,
the period associated with the rise of big business, reveal no substantial change in the flexibility of the quoted wholesale prices of
representative commodities. Throughout the last fifty years, and
for traceable commodities much longer, the prices of finished
goods have always changed much less frequently and have proved
much less sensitive to depression than the prices of raw materials.[19]
At the raw materials level, the bulk of nondurable goods originates
from agriculture where concentration remains relatively low.
Materials basic to the manufacture of durables are generally produced in larger organizations and in more concentrated industries.
The relative volatility of agricultural prices is not, however, to
be attributed entirely, if in part, to lesser concentration.[20] More-

[17] *Industrial Prices and Their Relative Inflexibility*, S. Doc. 13, 74 Cong.
1 sess. (1935), p. 12.

[18] U.S. National Resources Committee, *The Structure of the American Economy*,
Pt. 1 (1939), p. 143.

[19] See Don D. Humphrey, "The Nature and Meaning of Rigid Prices, 1890-
1933," *Journal of Political Economy*, Vol. 45 (1937), p. 651. Humphrey argues
(p. 658) that: "The view that increasing price rigidities have been the product
of industrial concentration and technology . . . has not been proved by statistics."
See also Edward S. Mason, "Price Inflexibility," *Review of Economic Statistics*,
Vol. 20 (1938), pp. 58-63.

[20] For an interesting and clear discussion of factors underlying price volatility
in agriculture, see Theodore W. Schultz, *Production and Welfare of Agriculture*
(Macmillan, 1950), pp. 64-82.

over, the correlation between concentration of output and price over the business cycle is inconclusive.[21]

In a more recent study of the association between industrial concentration and price increases during the 1950's, Richard T. Selden and Horace J. DePodwin found that the level of concentration in 1954 explained at most 10 percent of the size of industrial price changes during the 1953 to 1959 period.[22] Selden and DePodwin summarize their main conclusions as follows:

> The investigation reported in this paper was undertaken to test one simple hypothesis—that inflation since 1953 can be traced to industries with the power to "administer" their prices. Using concentration as our measure of degree of administration and BLS wholesale price data to measure price increases, we found the following:
>
> 1. The relationship between price change and concentration for 322 five-digit SIC product classes is extremely low. Of eight possible tests made on these data, the best one can do is to explain 9 percent of price variation by referring to economic concentration.
>
> 2. When the data on five-digit product classes are combined and analyzed by major industry groups, only one group yields a significant coefficient of correlation, and more than half of the groups yield negative coefficients.
>
> 3. On a four-digit industry class basis the best that one can do is to explain 10 percent of price variation in terms of economic concentration.

These authors further conclude that "the principal ground on which the administrative inflation hypothesis has gained widespread reputation is its repeated assertion. . . . In the light of the findings presented in this article, we suggest that it is time to put the administrative inflation hypothesis to rest."

[21] See, for example, John M. Blair, "Economic Concentration and Depression Price Rigidity," and "Comment" by Gideon Rosenbluth, *American Economic Review, Papers and Proceedings,* May 1955, pp. 566, 598; and Jules Backman, "Economic Concentration and Price Inflexibility," with "Rejoinder" by John M. Blair, *Review of Economics and Statistics,* Vol. 40 (November 1958), p. 399.

[22] "Business Pricing Policies and Inflation," *Journal of Political Economy,* Vol. 71 (April 1963), pp. 116-27.

These essentially negative findings, which are consistent with an earlier TNEC work,[23] are not surprising. The major determinants of price and output behavior, in this broad sense, are to be found in the nature of the product itself—its durability, stage of fabrication, and final market. Price behavior inevitably reflects costs, regardless of market structure, and, in particular, the relative importance of fixed overhead costs and fluctuations in costs of raw materials. For agricultural products, the total supply may be relatively fixed and independent of price for periods of as long as one year. The labor costs of agriculture are in large part residual, stemming mainly from self-employed and family labor. The same is true of many small unincorporated partnerships and family-owned establishments. Industrial wages, on the other hand, are generally sticky and place a floor under pricing policy. It would require extreme price reductions which, in the presence of relatively fixed labor costs, would be unprofitable ones to break through the resistance of buyers to the purchase of major durable goods during recessions. To be sure, sellers will try to take advantage of opportunities for mutually beneficial price control, especially when costs do not decline with increasing volume. The evidence, however, suggests that factors other than concentration account for the bulk of differences in the flexibility of prices in these different industries.

[23] Temporary National Economic Committee, *Investigation of Concentration of Economic Power*, Monograph 27, *The Structure of Industry*, 76 Cong. 3 sess. (1941), pp. 312-13.

9

Competitive Pressures
on Big Business

BIG BUSINESS is subject to competitive pressure from many sources. In some instances, the pressure to compete stems from institutional forces within the corporate organization itself. Corresponding external pressure comes not only from the actions of competitors and customers but also from the influence of governmental agencies. Increasingly, at the big business level, forces of innovation compel a response either to totally new processes or to product applications that had previously been unknown. These and other factors influencing the basic behavior of the large industrial firm are discussed in this chapter.

Internal Pressures

Whether a large firm is regarded as a corporate individual with unified purpose, or as a complex federation of workers, managers, stockholders, and distributors, there is generally an internal drive to improve the position of the company and those who share the income it produces.

In contrast to the early consolidations, in which business units were at times bought in order to be scrapped, big business today is an investment in massive capacity for productive and profitable use. That capacity consists not only of fixed capital, but also of a collection of management and professional talent, highly developed organization, and a community of trained workers with job tenure. To maintain position, the various departments and divisions of the large firm each must make a maximum contribution to the effectiveness of the total enterprise. It is out of the rivalries of departments and divisions, whose special functions and particular products compete for consideration, that an effective corporate policy unfolds.

Intracompany Rivalries

Sales, research, purchasing, production, finance, and public relations divisions have viewpoints that influence company policy. Similarly, each product division of the multiplant corporation competes with the rest for a larger claim on the corporation's interest and financial resources. Sales organizations are kept alive by the prospect of higher sales at terms that appear more attractive than those of competitors. Regardless of the size already attained by the business, sales management will chafe at limitations placed on promotional effort. If a line appears to be reaching a saturation point, the sales force must be supplied with new products to avoid the risk of deterioration of the company's marketing arm. The research group is in the business of creating additional sales and profit opportunities in old and new products, and the creators need the incentive of seeing their creations competing for the customer's dollar.

The influence toward expansion exerted by sales and research departments is met by the cost consciousness of other functional groups within the corporation. The controllers—whether in the purchase of raw materials and equipment, testing of products, or weighing of outlays against expected returns—help to determine the product mix, the stability of employment and inventories, and, in general, the terms on which service and product can best be offered.[1]

---

[1] In soap manufacture, for example, the use of animal or vegetable fat at a given time may depend on market availability and price, rather than on a purely technical preference for one or the other in the manufacturing process. Similarly,

The business of most giant corporations is, as a rule, so diversified that changes in the market that adversely affect some of their product line or sales areas are not fatal. Any lethargy that might result from this relative unimportance of any one product is likely to be countered by intracompany competitive forces. Such rivalry is conspicuous where the corporation is large enough to have a number of autonomous divisions organized along regional or product lines. The production costs or earnings of one division will be compared with another with regard to sales and product mix. Relating departmental or individual plant performance to a system of standard costs or average sales stimulates alertness on the part of the various divisions. Each division, in preparing its budget for current operations or growth, must justify to the central policy group its demands on the corporation.[2]

Interdivisional competition is found especially in firms having a full line of rival products intended to serve a wide range of customer preferences. In the automotive industry, a manufacturer may produce different models in separate autonomous divisions, each of which may overlap the market for the model priced immediately below or above. Similar competitive situations have developed in building materials and in synthetic fibers, where there is a choice of substitutes manufactured by the same company but frequently developed by different research and production teams and produced in separate plants or sold through rival sales organizations.

Another aspect of intracompany competition develops where one assembling or fabricating division within an integrated company is expected to "buy" materials or parts from the division that makes them, but can demand terms from its brother division no

---

the production schedules of an assembly line operation may be determined by consideration of the economies of evening out employment and inventory accumulations, rather than by pressure from the sales force to meet orders at their peak.

[2] The use of standard costs—based on several years of operation—as the basis for comparing the showings of competing departments avoids giving too much weight to a windfall or an unusual situation because of war or weather (for example, crop excess or shortage) which may produce abnormal profits or losses not related to comparative efficiency.

less favorable than those it could obtain from outside suppliers. Meatpacking on a national scale has introduced competition among district managers of the corporation as meat products are "exported" from those regional branches located in surplus areas. Scope is thus given to the exercise of the profit motive by district managers within a framework of requirements for balanced operation of the corporation as a whole.

Companies differ in the degree to which they exploit these intracompany drives, but it would be unwise management to eliminate such incentives to corporate progress and efficiency. The larger the corporation becomes, the greater is the need for a decentralization of operations, and the more vital it is that competitive incentives be maintained in the various segments. Rivalries within the company, and the manner in which they are reconciled, serve in large part to determine the effectiveness of the large firm as market competitor.

Vying for position by divisions may still leave some anti-competitive practices intact. One operating division may seek price leadership, market quotas, or price agreements with outside competitors as a means to a profitable record. Personnel may seek to cultivate their superiors with emphasis on amicable personal relations rather than on more effective performance in cutting costs, improving service, or increasing sales. But the more complex the company, the greater is the compulsion that objective standards be set to appraise accomplishment, and the greater the probability that intracompany rivalry will promote effective use of the corporation's resources.

The trend in recent years toward more professionalized and more decentralized direction of corporations is also of significance in shaping the market outlook of big business management. It will be recalled that the large corporations of the early 1900's were frequently regarded as captive organizations manipulated by banking interests. Men who sat on the board of any one company often had interests in the financial interlocking of which the company was a part. The objectives of the allied group, rather than primary concern with the operation and growth opportunities of the individual company, governed board decisions and permeated company practice. In contrast, where the majority of the directing board consists of officers who have risen in the corporation, the board may be expected to concentrate on the position of that individual firm. The logical basis for selection of board members outside the employee fold is only to secure the benefit of disinterested and mature judgment on company problems.

Moreover, the expressed opinion of top officers in representative corporations, and the policies apparent in corporate operation, appear to indicate that the advantages expected from building a position competitively in the market outweigh those achieved through understandings to avoid competition. This may still leave to the firm the decision, suggested in the previous chapter, to resort to price competition only when that form of competition offers a market advantage that can be held.

The corporation may also be spurred by the competing claims of its participating groups for shares of the company's revenues. Impinging on management are the pressures of organized labor for wage increases and fringe benefits, of expanding areas of the business for development funds, and of the stockholders for higher dividends and capital gains. Pressure for satisfying these demands, and for improved productivity and market performance, is continually applied to the management of the large firm.

The Stockholder's Share in Company Policy

The role of the stockholder in the large corporation has been variously interpreted. The number of stockholders now equals or exceeds the number of employees in many large American corporations.[3] The effect of prevailing tax rates on inheritance and

[3] The 1962 Census of Share Owners of the New York Stock Exchange recorded 7,856,000 shareowners for the 50 largest industrial NYSE companies. This total, of course, includes duplication. The largest NYSE industrial, General Motors, is shown with 842,000 shareowners; the 50th, Corn Products Refining, is shown with 70,000. The most recent data available show that of some 18 million shareholdings for 2,930 leading corporations (as of 1951), 70 percent were holdings of less than 100 shares. See Lewis H. Kimmel, *Share Ownership in the United States* (Brookings Institution, 1952), p. 42. However, it should be noted that despite the wide distribution of share ownership, this ownership is highly concentrated. According to a 1960 survey, 4 percent of all families—those with

income is toward greater diffusion of the personal capital holdings in American corporations. Nevertheless, a few large stockholders ordinarily run the company, while the thousands of smaller holders have little voice and little inclination to influence its major de-cisions.

However, a number of developments in recent decades have made corporate managers more responsive to their stockholders. The financial reports of the large corporation with publicly distributed shares have become subject to supervision by the Securities and Exchange Commission and other public agencies. Almost any unusual gathering of proxies, or submission of major proposals for increase of officers' compensation, today receives attention as public information with public implications. Furthermore, the growing participation of investment trusts, large and small, in corporate investment provides professional examination of the quality of professional corporate managements and their objectives.

The publicity required of the operations of large companies subjects them to still another pressure. The annual report of the large corporation has become a newsworthy public document. It is reviewed both in the public press and in the financial journals. Increasingly, annual reports reflect the awareness of management to the competitive problems that confront the large firm. The typical annual report not only indicates the outlook for improvement in earnings, but is also used to explain broad policy modifications designed to prevent the erosion of earnings. Few large corporations escape the need to vindicate management policy.

In addition to this annual (or quarterly) review, the trading of shares on the stock exchange constitutes a day-to-day test of the corporation's public standing. The securities market reflects the judgment not only of individual stockholders, but of experts trained to evaluate company operations. Such an appraisal provides the stimulus for change where there are signs of weakness in the position of the company. Corporate giants are also monitored

---

incomes above $15,000 per year—owned 42 percent of all individually held stock. See University of Michigan Survey Research Center, *1960 Survey of Consumer Finances,* p. 101.

by official agencies to which their business practices must be acceptable. The very size of the giant corporation makes it the more subject to public scrutiny and criticism.

Thus, as a result of the growth in the number of stockholders, government regulations, and public opinion, the large corporation operates in a goldfish bowl. The quality of management is continually probed by the large institutional investors, the investment trusts, the mutual funds as well as by individual investors. Management is sensitive to the need for demonstrating to the stockholders that the company in which they invest is winning market favor and showing results in profitable expansion.

External Pressures

The prevalence of market forces ample to ensure competitive performance might well be assumed in an economy of atomized business.

In big business, long-run policy based in part on estimates of a company's costs and expectations seems to imply relative independence of the forces of market determination. Reference has already been made to the difference between small business and big business competition so far as short-run market pricing is concerned. At this point, attention is directed to forms of market pressure imposed on big business by the very necessity of supporting the massive scale of operations characteristic of this group of giant firms.

Big Business in the Consumer Market

Mass communication, the accompaniment of mass production, has created a consumer who expects continuous product improvement and at least the appearance of greater value per dollar. The frequent model changes characteristic of consumer durables are induced by the need to stimulate additional or replacement buying from year to year. Furthermore, competition has led the consumer to expect or to look for additional services even where the product itself has not been changed. The motorist, for example, has come to assume that the nearest corner will have a gasoline service station, that he will not be kept waiting, and that he may demand free tire inflation, water, check of oil and battery, and a host of other services.

This form of market behavior frequently forces promotion of "improvements" that are more illusory than real. It has been argued that too much emphasis has been placed on gadgets and too little on price reductions as a means of increasing sales.[4] But producers of durable equipment have apparently discovered that the largest mass market is not always in the very lowest price line, and growing demand can bring to the mass market products that had previously been available only to buyers for whom cost was of relatively little concern.

Even where advertising appears to be the major form of rivalry, and where alleged product differences may be of doubtful authenticity, product improvement eventually tends to supplement the diminishing returns of repetitive commercials or of advertisements lacking substance. To be sure, there are luxury items where advertising plays a special role and where the uninitiated observer is ill-equipped to identify the nuances of product differentiation. But the product improvement is pervasive in more common items—new soaps and detergents, some new drugs, television, phonograph records, a succession of plastic fibers, cloths, draperies, and a myriad of similar items to which the chemicals industry has contributed.

Relations Between Large Buyers and Suppliers

Large-scale buyers are a potent stimulant to cost reduction and quality improvement, especially in those industries where big business caters to other producers rather than to the final consumer.

---

[4] This emphasis on nonprice techniques of competition stems from the price rigidity or stability noted earlier. Though there is some tendency to avoid the use of short-run price changes as techniques of aggressive competition, no such rigidity extends to the use of product design, advertising, or service facilities. The observed abundance of these competitive devices is, of course, a direct implication of modern oligopoly theory. It is precisely in this way that the pressure of competition among the few develops. It is also in this way that the choice of lower prices and less "improvement" may be denied the consuming public.

This situation occurs, for example, where basic chemicals are required for further processing, or in the relation between primary metal producers and large metal-using manufacturers and assemblers. Of great importance in the maintenance of quality and the quest for low-cost methods of production is the role of the producer-buyers who develop their own specifications. A steel company may have a long-standing arrangement with a can manufacturer using large quantities of tin plate. To develop a new line, the can manufacturer may require plate coated with an alloy that will prevent deterioration of the product to be packaged. The readiness of a steel company to meet or improve on the specifications and the availability of the resultant special-purpose product takes precedence over the maintenance of a traditional relationship. Other steel companies stand ready and willing to meet specifications to gain a new account.

The large buyer confronting the large seller has a number of choices. He can seek a smaller manufacturer to take the contract. The smaller supplier may then be able to specialize or provide a degree of attention not available from a larger general line supplier. Such special orders from big business account for a large part of the business of relatively small suppliers, and of the manufacturers who supply distributors with private brands. These relationships present a continual market challenge to the large supplier seeking adequate employment for his full-line capacity.

Another threat to the supplier who relies on large contracts is the ability of the large-scale firm to manufacture for itself. Large buyers are in a position to create their own productive facilities and frequently do so when the quoted delivered price of the product in question is not low enough to offset the convenience of having the raw material available on the spot. The buyer who can become a direct competitor-producer exerts an influence similar to that of actual competitors. Here the supplier is under pressure to prove to the buyer the advantage of his continuing as a customer—receiving advantages in the form of service, product improvement, and cost reduction the independent supplier may be able to provide.[5]

[5] These options available to the large buyer frequently force the big supplier to offer special concessions. For example, automobile tire and spark plug com-

Shifts in Population and Resources

Since large companies have the resources to reach out to new sources of raw materials and power, they can also stimulate large and abrupt shifts in the location of markets. These new locations, in turn, make it necessary for established firms to meet the competition of more favorably situated competitors. Branch plants may be located or relocated to give added convenience and lower delivered prices to customers. New points of origin from which to set base prices will also emerge as policies are realigned to attract or to hold customers distant from traditional sources of supply. Trucks may be used instead of railroad freight cars, pipelines instead of trucks. New sources of labor as well tend to shake up the fixed relationships between companies.[6]

Innovation in Large-Scale Enterprise

Among all competitive factors and external pressures to which big business must respond, the most far-reaching is innovation. The search for increasing returns on investment is continuous in American enterprise. Even the little drug or hardware store is often not content to limit its merchandise to fixed-price staples, but tries to supplement returns from standard low-margin items with special purchases and auxiliary lines. Similarly, large com-

---

panies supply their products at lower prices on orders for original equipment than for replacement use. Such price concessions are often passed on to the ultimate consumer. Ideally, the Robinson-Patman Act would guarantee that such price advantages are made equally available (except for cost differences) to smaller purchasers. Acceptance of the "functional" discount is an undesirable aspect of the interpretation of this statute. For illustrations, see *Simmons Co.*, 29 FTC 727 (1939), and *Champion Spark Plug Co.*, Docket 3977, dismissed 1953.

[6] Established companies, of course, try to prevent disruptions and loss of income threatened by these regional shifts and may be successful to a degree in maintaining the traditional pattern of industry structure and behavior. The basing point system, under which competitors quoted uniform delivered prices, represented an effort, often quite unsuccessful, to prevent the outbreak of short-term price rivalries resulting from changed locations of plants and markets and new methods of transport. Such systems have for a time denied to certain customers the price advantages that the erection of newer and nearer plants, or the emergence of cheaper methods of transportation, ultimately provided.

panies try to increase their profits through a degree of product differentiation that will justify promotion of the products as brand name specialties. In time, the successful specialty will be matched by other firms and the supply so multiplied as to erode the initial advantage. What starts out as the magic detergent soon becomes just another cleaner. The fully automatic home launderer is now just another washing machine. The patent on an antifreeze runs out, and new names challenge the original brand and lower the returns to the innovator. The discovery and introduction of new profit builders have become a central focus in the efforts of most large firms.

Organizing for Innovation

In this regard, big business has rendered the development of new products and processes, even those of major importance, progressively less dependent on individual genius. Many past developments—McCormick's reaper, Morse's telegraph, Edison's incandescent bulb, Bell's telephone—may be conceived as fortuitous turning points in economic history, each creating from scratch a new industry in a society that was in the process of being industrialized. Great as these achievements were, and despite the fact that they probably would have been forthcoming even had their progenitors never lived, they were probably not induced by the competitive situation at the time.

In the present industrial age, there is a more visible interaction between economic need and product development. To keep abreast of its market, the large corporation with a diversified line has a product development organization embodying a full range of specialists, including experts in engineering design, production methods, cost analysis, market research, and sales promotion. Such groups identify product opportunities. The new development usually requires new investment, and at this point there is financial scrutiny of expectations and risks. En route from exploration to exploitation of a new product, contacts are made with customers and others with a knowledge of the possible ways in which the properties of the new product may be useful. Interested customers may themselves pursue research to see whether the product can be serviceable to them. Not infrequently, an area of an industry not previously served by a given firm may emerge as the best potential user—as when a drug company proved a profitable outlet for an industrial chemical.

The stream of innovations seldom seems to destroy existing industries. The large corporation may be shaken by the advent of new products, but instead of being destroyed, it is more likely to fight back with its own research, capital resources, and know-how, and to secure a place in the industrial realignment.

Du Pont, for example, in 1949 reported 60 percent of total sales in products unknown to the market 20 years earlier.[7] These included nylon, other synthetic fibers, cellulose plastics, lacquers, heavy chemicals, and a host of other new products which together accounted for the employment of more than half of the company's labor force. Nevertheless, the product history of this company has been matched by corresponding innovations by its chief rivals in the industry.

Similarly, the emergence of the automobile industry provided the great growth example for its time. In the fifteen short years prior to World War I, annual output expanded from a few thousand units to a half million, with sales value of $414 million. Yet a new division of a single automobile manufacturer following World War II attained dollar sales for diesel engines comparable to those of the entire automobile industry at the end of its first 15 years of existence. At the outbreak of World War II, there were some 43,000 steam locomotives on railroad lines, and less than 500 diesels. By 1961, diesels outnumbered steam locomotives 30,123 to 210.[8]

[7] E. I. du Pont de Nemours & Co., *Annual Report, 1949*, p. 13.

[8] U.S. Bureau of the Census, *Statistical Abstract of the United States, 1963* (U.S. Government Printing Office, 1963), p. 577. See Edwin Mansfield, "Intra-firm Rates of Diffusion of an Innovation," *Review of Economics and Statistics*, Vol. 45 (November 1963), pp. 348-59, for additional detail and a model of innovative activity applied to the introduction of the diesel locomotive.

Varying Pace of Innovation

The pace of innovation in the chemical industry does not represent an average for big business, and the case of the diesel engine may be regarded as at least outstanding. To obtain a more general perspective of innovation in large-scale industry, one would need to consider the less spectacular innovations that improve without uprooting industrial structures. Among them may be cited the technological advances in packaging and in the marketing of canned and frozen foods. Their impact on buying habits over the last twenty-five years, with paper, metals, and plastics frequently replacing glass and wood containers, amounts to what an earlier generation might well have called an industrial revolution. Concomitant changes in the merchandising of common retail lines can be sensed when the modern supermarket is compared with the general or grocery store of a generation ago.

In durable goods, standardization and interchangeability of parts have taken place in a succession of small steps, but their cumulative effect is seen in the ability of small assemblers to produce a variety of new electric devices and of consumers to become users of a growing list of mechanized appliances. Contributing to such diffusion of mechanized products are the smaller general purpose tools, with which heavier materials could not be handled, but which serve well for the more easily machined plastics and lighter metals.[9]

Unobtrusive yet important innovations have even altered the product mix of the relatively staid meat packing industry. Here the rise in big business is associated with the advent of the refrigerator car in the 1870's. Little appears to have happened since then in the basic process of converting livestock into edible meats, apart from the fuller use of by-products. But the industry has not been immune to the lively competition between meat fats and vegetable oils, and between organic and synthetic oils. Moreover, the original marketing basis for bigness in the packing industry—nationwide distribution from a great center (Chicago)—has been

[9] John M. Blair, "Technology and Size," American Economic Association, *Papers and Proceedings*, Vol. 38 (May 1948), pp. 130-32.

upset by the ease of trucking. A larger percentage of sales by livestock producers goes directly to branch house areas and other local markets. There has been a reorientation of the packing industry in relation to other food lines, and meat packers now compete at the laboratory level and in the market with soap, pharmaceutical, and chemical companies.

Innovation usually emerges as a logical development of the innovator's established process or product either because of technological similarities that carry over from the old to the new or because of the necessity of making use of by-products. It is not suggested that the drive for market advantage through innovation is inevitable. The pressure to innovate differs from industry to industry. Innovation may be lacking for substantial periods of time in some areas of big business. In the cigarette industry, the period of major experimentation with different blends apparently ended a quarter century ago, although recently there has been a resurgence of experimentation with various filters and with efforts to offset the reported harmful effects of cigarette smoking. A common outlook on the problem or potential of innovation is neither to be expected nor desired in an economy as large and diverse as that of the United States.[10]

However, the development of organized research facilities in big business, marking time over an extended period, is becoming less common. Top-ranking scientists and experienced engineers

---

[10] In a recent article, Edwin Mansfield examines the innovating activities of the four largest firms in several selected industries. He finds that in petroleum refining and bituminous coal the largest four firms accounted for a larger share of the innovations than of their respective markets during the 1919-58 period, but that in the steel industry they accounted for less. He suggests further that "the largest four firms seemed to account for a relatively large share of the innovating in cases where (1) the investment required to innovate was large relative to the size of the potential users; (2) the minimum size of firm required to use the innovations profitably was relatively large; and (3) the average size of the largest four firms was much greater than the average size of all potential users of the innovations." With heavy qualification, Mansfield suggests that "during 1919-1958, the sixth largest firms in the petroleum and coal industries were of about optimal size from the point of view of maximizing the rate of innovation. In the steel industry much smaller firms seem to have been optimal in this respect." See Edwin Mansfield, "Size of Firm, Market Structure, and Innovation," *Journal of Political Economy,* Vol. 7 (December 1963), p. 573.

are being attracted to company laboratories by the wealth of research facilities as well as by high personal remuneration. Research from pure science to development is supported by the administrative and financial power of the corporation. Funds devoted to industrial research and development by all companies
with such programs in 1960 were estimated by the National
Science Foundation at approximately $10.5 billion, representing
4.3 percent of their net sales. This volume of research engaged
some 307,300 (professional) research engineers and scientists.

The postwar situation has been greatly influenced by the major
role of the federal government in using the facilities of large industrial corporations in the conduct of research related to the atomic
energy and space programs and military requirements for aircraft
and electrical machinery. Over half (58 percent) of this $10.5
billion total in 1960 was government-financed. One effect of the
federal government's requirements has been to concentrate research in aircraft and electrical and other machinery industries.
The government's share of the research cost ranged from a high
of 88 percent in the aircraft and missiles industry to a low of
2.1 percent in primary ferrous products.

While about 79 percent of the research engineers and scientists
were employed by companies with 5,000 or more employees
(11,800 firms in the National Science Foundation sample), an
important part of the total industrial research program—both for
the government and private industry—was conducted in commercial consulting firms and nonprofit research agencies in which
the groups were predominantly smaller (fewer than 500 employees). Such firms and others not directly engaged in manufacturing employed about 10.6 percent of the research personnel.

Industrial expenditures on research increased from $510 million
to $4.5 billion between 1941 and 1960. The total cost of research
performed by industry increased between the two years from
$660 million to $10.5 billion, the difference between expenditure
and cost representing research financed by the government.[11]

[11] National Science Foundation, *Research and Development in Industry, 1960:
Final Report on a Survey of R&D Funds and R&D Scientists and Engineers*,
Survey of Science Resources Series, NSF 63-7 (U.S. Government Printing Office,
January 1963), p. 89.

The laboratory, traditionally the testing ground for products, is also the starting point for the more revolutionary realignments in American enterprise. In a relatively static economy, the fact that a single firm or a few firms dominate the market for particular products may indicate monopolistic control. Under the impact of innovation, the power of a monopoly to sit back and enjoy high profit margins is weakened considerably. The threat of innovation is continuous and ubiquitous. As suggested in an analysis of the 100 largest industrials, the monopoly that is merely coasting along today may tomorrow find itself unable to catch up with innovators or to regain its former position.[12]

The Blurring of Industry Boundaries

Innovation further undermines monopoly positions by blurring traditional boundaries. The process may begin as a new monopoly under patent protection, but as the new product is thrown into the struggle for new customers, that monopoly power may be limited by the competition of broader markets. For example, one company supplied all the rayon produced in the United States for eleven years, and took full advantage of that position. Its profits before taxes averaged over 70 percent on sales. Between 1915 and 1920, they ranged from 26 to 109 percent of investment. Yet rayon, a synthetic product, is today just another textile fiber with particular and by no means unvarying characteristics. The introduction of rayon increased the competition and range of alternatives in textile fiber markets. The subsequent introduction of cellulose acetate ("Celanese"), nylon, acrilan, saran, vinylites, and a number of other competing fibers created new "monopo-

---

[12] Michael Gort, in a study of the structure of 111 large companies, reports that these 111 selected companies (1) maintained establishments in an average of 9.7 four-digit industries, (2) produced goods and services in an average of 15.6 manufacturing industries (20.4 if nonmanufacturing activities are included), and (3) displayed a substantially higher rate of product addition in the 1950-54 period (107.8 per year for the 111 companies) as compared with 1939-50 (43.1 per year) or 1920-39 (48.4 per year). Gort also finds that of the 111 companies, those with the highest proportion of engineers showed the most widespread and frequent addition of new products. See Michael Gort, *Diversification and Integration in American Industry* (Princeton University Press, 1962), pp. 27-64.

lists," and at the same time extended competition in the textile fiber market and in the market for fabricated goods.

Reference was made earlier to the product substitutions stimulated by the Aluminum Corporation of America during the half century when it was the sole producer of virgin aluminum. In this connection, it may be noted, that in past wartime emergencies, shortages of strategic metals have speeded up the process of interchanging components. An alloy containing 90 percent of aluminum is replaced by one containing one percent which may not give way to the original when the shortage is past. With counter developments in technology, the substitution may run the other way. Constant alertness to innovation and potential market shifts is generally a prerequisite to maintaining a big business position. The ultimate consumer, buying competing metals in hundreds of end-product forms, similarly has his range of choice extended among suppliers who frequently change their raw material components in the hope of winning new market favor. The significance of the monopoly can, over the long run, no longer be stated realistically solely in terms of the number of sellers in narrowly defined industries. Indeed, the widening of product lines, not only through innovation but also by direct acquisition and diversification, is one of the major developments of industrial organization in the United States. In many instances industrial definitions that were once meaningful are now obsolete. Innovation has been a major factor in this development.

10

Integration, Size, and Competition

A BIG FIRM is typically an integrated firm. As such, it combines operations that would otherwise be carried on by separate small firms. The big firm may extend its range of activities by building new plants, or by creating new marketing facilities. It may integrate by merging with businesses, formerly independent, to acquire a new process or product, raw materials, or marketing facilities. In either case, the result is an increase in the size of the firm, and, where it succeeds, an increase in its power. The diverse resources of the giant can be brought to bear on markets in which smaller firms have all their limited resources at stake.

During the era of consolidation at the turn of the century, major integrations were frequently mergers of direct competitors, with the prime objective of market control. In succeeding decades, the character and objectives of integration have been modified. The government stands ready to challenge integration that seems primarily a device to eliminate competitors.

Whatever the motives behind integration, the process does involve market disturbances. The less integrated and smaller business enterprises frequently suffer, and these competitors often regard such injuries to their established markets as destructive of competition generally. The pervasiveness of this attitude has been reflected in state laws relating to chain stores and price-maintenance laws, in the McGuire-Keogh amendment [1] to the Federal Trade Commission Act, and in the Robinson-Patman

[1] 15 U.S.C. 45.

187

amendment [2] to the Clayton Act. These are defensive measures designed to reduce the differential advantages of integrated over nonintegrated enterprises.

The net effect of the processes of integration on the economy can be analyzed in two ways: first, from the standpoint of the individual firm—the motivations for integrating and advantages or disadvantages accruing to the firm from integration; and secondly, from the standpoint of markets—whether the integration of large companies into more complex organizations tends to extend or curtail the range of competition.

Integration and the Firm

Integration has many forms, frequently classified as vertical, horizontal, or conglomerate.

Vertical integration is present when a firm operates at more than one stage of production. A familiar example is the integrated flow of production from raw materials to finished goods in the iron and steel industry. The fully integrated corporation mines the ore; it transports ore to its smelters and rolling mills by company-owned rail lines and cargo vessels; through its fabricating facilities, it converts the primary metal and alloys into castings and forgings, bars, wire, sheets, rails, and various structural shapes; and it builds ships, bridges, and other steel structures using these fabricated products.

Horizontal integration occurs when a firm expands across markets at the same level of production or distribution. This type of integration may involve a merger of competing manufacturers, distributors, or plants in adjoining market areas; or it may involve an expansion from the original base over a wide area as in the case of retail chains and mail-order houses.

Conglomerate integration results when a firm diversifies to unite unrelated activities. Typical illustrations can be found in many large firms with separate operating divisions—Armstrong Cork with its production of both floor covering and glass containers, or

[2] 15 U.S.C. 21.

Sperry Rand's manufacture of electronic data processing machines and electric razors.

In practice, however, integration is seldom exclusively vertical, horizontal, or conglomerate. A firm rarely takes on a new product or line without some movement upstream toward the raw materials or downstream into promotion and distribution of end products. As the large retailer expands into new market areas, he almost inevitably takes over some wholesale functions. As volume increases, he may share or assume responsibility for the manufacture of some products. Similarly, a manufacturer may diversify to strengthen distributive outlets or to acquire new sources of raw material. The forms or combination of forms of integration may emerge both as a result of windfall opportunities and in the implementation of a long-range company policy. A tire manufacturer may run a chain of retail stores as the result of having lost dealers in the depression of the thirties. An automobile manufacturer may deliberately leave retailing to independent dealers. The motivations are many and no easier to delineate than are the forms of integration. Some of the varied motives are, however, discussed in the sections that follow.

Cost Reduction

Cost reductions can, of course, result without benefit of integration. Increased volume may produce economies of management or may facilitate improved methods of production and merchandising. Integration enters as a means of cost reduction when a fuller use of existing capacity is made possible, or when waste can be avoided by adding to product lines and markets. To take an elementary case, the delivery of milk may be made more profitable for a dairy company by the simple expedient of leaving more goods at each customer's door. The milk line is therefore rounded out with cream, butter, cheese, and ice cream. Pickup facilities, moreover, may be such that with little increase in overhead, eggs and poultry may also be included.

A similar approach to cost reduction is illustrated by the manufacturer of products with market areas limited by high transportation costs—tin cans, for example, which are bulky though light, or liquid oxygen, which must be carried in heavy containers. The spread of relatively small plants into different localities of the national market brings the manufacturer nearer to his customers. The shortened haul makes possible lower delivered prices and higher net receipts. Branching out enables the company to cultivate strategic locations more intensively through resident sales and service organizations, and the presence of local selling agencies in turn opens up possibilities of rounding out the line with supplementary products and services.

In practice, however, it is often difficult to separate the cost-reducing from the anticompetitive motives of integration. A company may have good reason, for the sake of efficiency, to make full possible use of its brand name and its selling staff by developing a complete product line. On the other hand, the broadening of the line may simultaneously have the effect of "full-line forcing" —urging, if not compelling, dealers or customers to take the whole line as the price of getting any part of it—with the result that nonintegrated competitors, carrying only selected components of the whole line, may be crowded out of the market.[3] Similarly, the desire to avoid expensive cross-hauling in reaching for customers may lead to the merger of business units in different locations.[4]

Full utilization of fixed capital is, of course, one of the most pervasive objectives leading to integration. The search for new ways of spreading overhead expense may lead to additional fields of production. As its know-how develops, the firm may find itself involved in the design and construction of the equipment with which its products are to be made, or it may move on to demonstrate end uses to which basic commodities may be put.

The urge toward fuller use of equipment and service facilities is also related to the development of uses for by-products. The

[3] The incentive to force, of course, stems from some degree of monopoly control over one or more products of the full line and some opportunity for improved exploitation of that control through the use of a tie rather than direct monopoly pricing.

[4] Note that the presence of cross-hauling in the first place implies some price rigidity and an absence of price competition. Integration therefore may reduce waste, but will not necessarily stimulate price reductions.

outstanding example, perhaps, is that of the meat packing companies, where a variety of uses has been found for fat, hides, and other animal parts not salable as meat. This development of the by-product has not been confined to routine salvaging of what would otherwise have been waste, but has led these firms into the markets of adhesives, drugs, detergents, fertilizers, and other chemicals. What to do with that something "left over" in mass production is a continual challenge to which competitors will make varying responses. Insofar as the ingenuity and pace of one cost-reducer must be met by the others in the industry, the effect is to reduce the special advantage of the innovator after the specialty or special process has become general. A new round of integration may then begin in an attempt to win differential advantages of still lower costs. Thus, integration undertaken in the first place to reduce costs may lead a firm to markets unrelated to those in which it ordinarily sells.

Security Motives

Much integration in the form of acquisition by fabricators of a dependable supply of raw materials is clearly protective in motivation. This has led the petroleum refiners to search for oil and to build pipelines. It has led automobile manufacturers to build glass factories, publishers to own pulp mills, and metal fabricators to acquire their own sources of ore, fuel, and power.[5]

This urge for security can also be reflected in vertical integration downstream and the acquisition of fabrication and distribution facilities related to the more basic products of the firm. When an aluminum producer, for example, encounters a reluctance by established manufacturers of window sash to shift from wood or steel to the lighter metals, the first thought may be to find others who can be encouraged to manufacture aluminum sash. Failing that, the primary producer may more effectively demonstrate the

---

[5] The price of such security occasionally proves to be out of proportion to the protection received. In the case of automobile glass, for example, the leading glass manufacturers have proved their ability to meet the requirements of the car makers, with a resulting decline in glass making by automotive firms.

possibilities of the new product by directly undertaking its fabrication and promotion.

If the experiment proves profitable, and it may not, the primary producer may elect to stay with it. But once the demonstration has been made, and the doubters are convinced, it may be more profitable to let the experienced fabricating companies take over. In other cases, the primary producer may continue to manufacture the specialty largely as a means of testing and promoting it, yet rely mainly on fabricating customers to carry the line.[6] A partial integration of distribution with manufacture "to see how the line goes" can be illustrated by the photographic industry. The leading manufacturer of cameras and film maintains one or two model stores in a large city without substantially entering into the retailing of photographic supplies.

Again, when tire manufacturers lost retail outlets in important centers during the great depression, at least two manufacturers defended their market position by entering the retail field. They learned, among other things, the difficulty of doing a successful retail business with tires alone. One developed a line of hard goods, including automobile accessories, home appliances, garden tools, and toys, to help the tire retailer who did not have a filling station, garage, or other service agency to supplement the sales of tires. Other tire manufacturers continued to leave retailing entirely to their customers; some elected to maintain a few demonstration outlets, while others chose to subsidize retail advertising and offer training to their retail outlets in the servicing of tires.

Partly for defensive reasons, retail stores have integrated in the opposite direction. The large retailing corporation that develops a profitable vogue for its own brand, whether in tires, apparel, food, or home equipment, frequently seeks to protect its source of supply. This may involve merely supervision of specifications, or it may extend to manufacture of the commodity.

Horizontal and conglomerate integration are defensive measures to the extent that the object is diversification to avoid risking the total capital of the corporation in one product line or in one market area. The uncertainty of any one market may make it

---

6 Aluminum chairs were initially made by Alcoa, but discontinued when the seating equipment firms enlarged their aluminum lines.

desirable to integrate to include a market area broad enough or a product line round enough to let the company realize more average situations. The company that supplies containers to canners across the continent can offset losses from drought in some areas if good crops maintain demand in others. It is pertinent, however, to note that security objectives do not stand alone. The record of big business growth has not been made by seeking merely to "sew up" existing sources and outlets. Measures of defensive integration prove successful only if they are also positive efforts to create or promote new and profitable business, either by increasing the volume of established products or by adding new products to those that already exist.

Creation of New Business

The business integration with the most powerful competitive impact is that which implements innovation. The foregoing chapter noted pressures that encourage the established big business to carry its skill, facilities, and know-how into the development of new operations. But why should innovation result in integration? Why should innovations not be exploited in separate, independent enterprises?

A business might spread the benefits of innovation without integration if, let us say, it auctioned the products of its research laboratory to other companies. In a limited way, this is done. There are occasions when the inventor immediately licenses the use of his patents. Innovators introducing a new basic product may leave it to others to find and fabricate ensuing finished products. But product innovation without product development directly by the innovator is the exception, not the rule.

To begin with, if integration to develop innovations were precluded, many innovations would not be forthcoming. The incentive to innovate rests in large measure on the company's prospect for developing successfully what it helps to discover.[7] It is difficult to envisage big business annually spending millions of dollars of

---

[7] This argument is more formally developed in R. R. Nelson, "The Simple Economics of Basic Scientific Research," *Journal of Political Economy*, Vol. 67 (June 1959), pp. 297-306.

company funds for the discovery and perfection of new processes and products that they could not recoup through their own development.

Innovation begets integration also because of a human factor in the organization of large enterprise. The personnel of the large enterprise have the normal ambition to prove the worth of their achievements. Research or product development is often carried on in separate and autonomous divisions. The test of their respective contributions comes in their relative expansion or contraction. As indicated in Chapter 9, growth and the prospect of growth are indispensable to the continuance of any enterprise as a vital competitor, large or small.

Integration, then, is the logical outcome of innovation in a company possessing the necessary resources and technical know-how. The limit for the succession of integrative steps emerging from an innovation is roughly set by the market. It comes at the point where further branching out would be less rewarding than the sale of the product in a less advanced stage to those prepared to develop its further use in connection with their own special lines. Presumably, it was neither desirable nor necessary for the company that introduced nylon to enter into the production of hosiery or shirts. The fabrication of the apparel calls for know-how and facilities in which the giant corporation has no apparent advantage once the idea of the usefulness of the fiber is established. But the producer of the fiber may profitably continue to test its properties for expanded uses. Similar considerations would stop a fabricating firm from undertaking raw material extraction. This is a matter of judgment in which a corporation has occasionally overestimated its powers or underestimated the difficulties of breaking into a strange market. In such situations, the firm will find the market to be a disciplinarian as well as a guide.

Countermeasures of Competitors

Business competition is a continuous process. Rarely can one tell where the moves and countermoves in a market shift begin or end. Integration to meet competition is frequently, in turn, the means of generating new competition. Whether defensive or innovative, it is a response as well as a stimulus to countermeasures by others. The countermoves to integration range from imitation to deliberate variations in production or marketing techniques that may eventually offset the differential advantage of the integrator.

Standardization of Integrative Patterns

A frequent reason for imitative integration is the development of a technological advance in which major economies of production are achieved by tying together in a single process what were formerly separate processes of an industry. For example, the American Rolling Mill Company developed the continuous rolling process to minimize the cooling and reworking of molten metal in transportation from one processor to the next. This step was copied by practically every other large iron and steel corporation, creating a standard pattern for the industry.

Consolidation of units representing successive stages of production has occasionally been met by imitative counteralliances. The control of ore supplied by the United States Steel consolidation was followed by similar ore integration in Bethlehem, Republic, and National Steel.[8] In copper, it was the downstream integration by one of the three great copper producing companies to ensure a fabricating outlet for part of its primary metal that eventually set a pattern for its two major rivals. Each brought at least one important fabricating subsidiary into its corporate organization. In retail distribution, demonstrations by the mail-order houses of the value of their private brand affiliations have led to extended affiliations of the distributor with the manufacturer. Recently, publishers of periodicals have followed the newspapers in acquiring pulp and paper facilities as well as engraving and art work units.

[8] There is no implication here that it was superior *efficiency* conferred on U.S. Steel by its vertical integration that led others to imitate it. The strategic advantages of owning an assured supply of ore may be sufficient to explain the imitation.

Defenses of Nonintegrating Competitors

Imitation is not always the best response to all cases of integration. When a big firm devises its own machinery to fabricate parts it formerly bought, its suppliers and competitors may find various ways of meeting the new situation. Makers of machine tools or suppliers of parts may well cooperate with the remaining nonintegrated customers to offset or surpass the differential advantage temporarily conferred on the integrated customer. But followers can usually match the innovator only by capitalizing on their distinctive resources and know-how, rather than by imitation.

The inroads of grocery chains, with their small stores spread over the community, were not met by any general move of neighborhood grocers to give up their proprietorship status and merge into similar chains. Rather, some retail grocers matched the buying power of the chains by forming their own purchasing associations. Some established wholesalers, equally hit by the retail chains, agreed to serve as mass-buying agents for independent retailers, arranging for distinctive nonchain brands and increased quantity discounts. Alert grocers turned to the development of supermarket stores. Indeed, the diversified food markets—selling meat, bakery goods, fruits, and vegetables under one roof—were largely an innovation by independent retailers under the pressure of chain competition. Under the impact of this competition, plus the spur of progressive chain store taxes, the chains, in turn, have moved to close down their less profitable smaller stores and concentrate their sales in supermarkets.

Yet the process of integration does not run solely in terms of adding new products and processes. There is a subtraction process, too, for integrated firms sometimes drop products that fail to fit in with their main operations. These "abandoned" lines provide opportunities for competitors—particularly the smaller and newer ones—to adapt themselves to the impact of integration. Special parts in vehicles and other assembled hard goods, special cleansers, waxes, detergents, special containers, specialized precision instruments, continue to be supplied in great variety by small firms to major corporations.

Creation and Elimination of Markets

Integration can be viewed as a two-pronged process—both creating and eliminating markets. Clearly the market creation effect is of major significance. In describing the mobility of the largest industrial corporations during a fifty-year period, the most intensive and extensive integrators of American business were included. Companies with the longest history of integration do not necessarily consolidate their positions nor progressively increase the gap between themselves and companies that start later. United States Steel is a prime example. Some of the factors in this fluid situation represent the effects of integration, broadly diffused across the economy.

As the development of the large integrated corporation shifted from emphasis on the absorption of existing competitors to a more discriminating quest for greater market opportunity, the integrative type of business expansion became an instrument of market dispersion. Even where companies apparently merged as a measure for mutual survival, final justification had to be a product line more attractive to the market as a whole. Otherwise, the combining firms and the more complex problems of management would only reduce their chances of survival. The firm that successfully integrates for more efficient use of its resources and knowhow, in the process will compel others in similar lines to reorganize their talents and resources. In some areas, of which plastics are a striking example, integrators have swamped the market with many alternatives from which consumers could choose. As the choice was made, there were both gainers and losers.

All firms are not equally quick to see the potential threat to their established positions by firms that move into new lines, nor have they equally responded with successful counterofferings or with retreat to more promising fields. Firms that once undertook to supply themselves with accessories or components of their main line have on occasion had to "de-integrate," finding it cheaper and more profitable to buy what had earlier been taken on as part of an integrated operation. A bed manufacturer who produced his own steel for springs later found it desirable to buy foam rubber and other newer materials for fabrication. A chemical firm, after manufacturing plastic shower curtains, found it more profitable to supply the vinyl and let others make the household furnishings. A fabricator of furniture and office supplies, who bought up forests, found his growing lines of business required plastics and metals rather than the output of his sawmills.

The record is filled with similar illustrations of interaction between formerly isolated firms. A glycerine monopoly, or even a close oligopoly in that previously monopolized line, is made more difficult by the output of glycerine or substitutable by-products of integrated meat packers, petroleum refiners, soap makers, and other producers of drugs and detergents. Metal producers cannot, by mere integration, win a monopoly of the alloy field, where chemical firms have led the way. Chemical firms, on the other hand, cannot insulate the field of plastics and synthetic fibers against experimentation by companies originally connected with the petroleum, natural gas, photographic film, glass, and coal industries. Manufacturers of glass containers, tin cans, fiber boxes, and paper bags have entered into the manufacture of plastic wrappings. For the most part, these products are the original or adapted developments emanating from combinations of circular and vertical integration. Integration, like any other form of striving for market position, is one in which the chain of countermoves and results can seldom be predicted.

Integration as Stimulant to Other Enterprise

Integration can be a potent influence in the realignment of market position, not only at the level of the integrator's direct activities, but also among the users of new products and processes. Consuming industries may take advantage of new products and processes at several levels. They may find it easy to produce a new product themselves if it can be made by a simpler process than the old. Dairies and packers can now fashion their paper containers from flat sheets; formerly they could purchase only finished containers made from more rigid materials. Industrial users create fabricated products with blends of raw materials which they can process more readily than was possible with older traditional materials requiring both machining skills and expensive heavy equipment.

This diffusion of market power has also been induced by some forms of horizontal integration. As large retailers have branched out for mass distribution, chains of dress shops, groceries, and hardware, and branches of mail-order houses have tended to take the place of small, locally established businesses. But the large clientele and the buying power of these geographically integrated distributors have also offered to small manufacturers an increasing number of large dependable outlets for their products. From such volume orders, successful smaller manufacturers have developed into large-scale manufacturers of household appliances, radio and television equipment, drugs and cosmetics, tires, farm equipment, and processed foods.

The case of petroleum illustrates still another way in which integration may infuse new vigor into the market. When the original Standard Oil Company was broken up in 1911, the New Jersey component was left primarily in refining, without marketing facilities or adequate supplies of crude oil. Standard of New York was in marketing only, without its own sources of crude or refined products. Others were similarly thrown on intermediate markets for supplies or outlets. For a time, the successor companies as independents continued to collaborate. Eventually, however, each integrated and became a full-fledged competitor. Standard of New York acquired refineries and crude oil resources to support its retail outlets. Standard of New Jersey acquired new sources of crude oil and new retail outlets for its refineries. The western components filled the gaps with crude oil pipelines, refineries, and retail stations, and further stimulated independent companies to do the same. The result has not been complete, self-contained, or uniform vertical integration in the industry, but there have been strong tendencies in that direction.

This process of integration, paralleling the vast expansion of the automotive industry, has produced a number of large, strong firms vying in individual markets, any one of which might otherwise have remained the almost exclusive preserve of one of the earlier Standard Oil subsidiaries. Integration on the scale of the petroleum industry since the Standard Oil dissolution has progressed with intensification of technological rivalry.

The question may be raised whether such integrations have not resulted in wasteful duplication of facilities. At the retail level, there has been a proliferation of service stations as each refiner increased his outlets in the hope of attracting patronage to his name. Gasoline retailing could undoubtedly be handled with fewer stations. To many motorists, however, a station eliminated would mean an increase in the amount of waiting time at the pump or oil rack. Though motorists who might prefer less "service" in return for lower prices are not provided everywhere with that choice, this opportunity is not lacking. Multipump stations handling large volume at lower margins are a challenge to the standard filling stations. Many towns have their maverick outlets offering less free service and a lower price for the gasoline. Thus, the big vertically integrated companies concentrate on product improvement and other nonprice market techniques, while the independents try out new merchandising methods stressing price.

The Equivocal Case of Integration by Merger

Merger has been historically associated with the absorption of competitors. The most obvious implication of a merger is, therefore, that it moderates conflict. This moderation of conflict takes extreme form when parallel competitors are merged to eliminate competition. Yet merger may also avoid wasteful duplication of existing facilities; speed the pooling of services, physical resources, and talents; improve efficiency through the use of centralized services, less cross-hauling, and better use of administrative skills.

Vertical integration by merger to forestall developing competition between Carnegie and rival interests was apparently one of the objectives in the formation of United States Steel. A pertinent lesson of that historic merger is that not only did the merger eliminate competition among former suppliers and customers, but also that the consolidation, once formed, was obsessed by a fear of realizing its full potential. Exposed to the scrutiny of hostile public opinion, the company, for a quarter century after consolidation, consciously refrained from the vigorous competition and more imaginative integration that might have permitted it to keep abreast of economic progress. Smaller steel makers took advantage of this preoccupation of the giant with the traditional iron and steel business, and obtained a running start in the lighter and more profitable types of steel in demand by the automotive and other growing industries.

Firms may merge, however, to pool skills and facilities or to exploit some new market or technology. Uniting companies that are complementary may result in increased efficiency and new products. Some notable cases include the merging of petroleum and chemical firms to exploit the chemistry of petroleum derivatives. The roster of such mergers is growing; their products are purchased in virtually all industries.

Every combination of formerly independent suppliers and fabricators realigns markets in greater or lesser degree. Every association of functions in integration circumvents established customers or suppliers and, if successful, creates a competitive advantage. If prohibited from exercising that advantage, integrated firms may be forced merely to hold a price umbrella over nonintegrated firms, and a public policy originally aimed at maintaining competition will end by suppressing its most dynamic manifestations. The American economy has as much to fear from well-intentioned efforts to protect uniformity in pricing and marketing methods through public laws—the vain attempt under the slogan of fair trade to make competition "riskless"—as from the unfair tactics of integrated big business.[9]

Merger, then, cannot be judged by form alone. One can weigh the result only after seeing whether entry remains essentially open, whether the merger increases or diminishes the alternatives open to consumers, whether, in short, the nation ultimately benefits through lower costs and prices and improved products.

[9] For a careful and sweeping analysis in this regard, see Robert Bork, "Vertical Integration and the Sherman Act: The Legal History of an Economic Misconception," *The University of Chicago Law Review* (Autumn 1954), pp. 154-201.

The Public Interest in Limiting Integration

Neither Congress nor the courts have prevented large-scale enterprise from expanding and becoming more integrated as it expands. Periodic attacks on specific business organizations have not effectively challenged the proposition that some of the largest American businesses fit into a national design for a vigorous and productive economy. But the public will continue to be alerted to the danger that further integration, already coupled with great size, may threaten as well as stimulate competition.

Integration and Balance of Power

In the formulation of public policy, account has been taken of situations in which the breaking up of a large integrated company may result in an imbalance of market power. The courts explicitly recognized in the Alcoa and National Lead cases [10] the possibility that the splitting up of an integrated company would diminish rather than increase the vigor of competition.[11]

Whether the court's appraisals of those particular situations in aluminum and titanium were correct, the opinions rested on the principle that certain areas of the competitive system require the strength of "well-integrated organizations" to compete effectively.[12] The judicial pronouncements recognize that in a progressive private enterprise system, where the channels of business opportunity must be kept open, the costly way to keep them open is to split up the efficient because the less efficient could not otherwise compete successfully.

Integration and Excessive Size

While integration is recognized in specific cases as a means of promoting competition, the involvement of integration in the

[10] *United States v. Aluminum Co. of America,* 91 F. Supp. 333 (S.D.N.Y. 1950). *United States v. National Lead Co. et al.,* 334 U.S. 319 (1947).

[11] This reasoning did not, however, prevent the divestiture of Aluminium Ltd. in the Alcoa case.

[12] *United States v. Aluminum Co. of America,* 91 F. Supp. 416 (S.D.N.Y. 1950).

related issue of excessive size and attendant monopoly power remains. The permissiveness of further integration when size and market share are already large was the issue that divided the Supreme Court in passing on the United States Steel Corporation's acquisition of a new plant in California. The corporation, having purchased the huge Geneva plant in Utah, which it built for the government in World War II, arranged to acquire the Consolidated Steel plant as a Pacific Coast fabricating outlet for the Geneva output. The majority of the United States Supreme Court condoned the acquisition of the fabricating facilities by the steel company as essential to its West Coast operations. Justice Reed, speaking for the majority, interpreted the general principle involved in the contemplated integration as follows:

It seems clear to us that vertical integration, as such without more, cannot be held violative of the Sherman Act. It is an indefinite term without explicit meaning. Even in the iron industry, where could a line be drawn—at the end of mining the ore, production of pig iron or steel ingots, when the rolling mill operation is completed, fabrication on order, or at some stage of manufacture into standard merchandise? No answer would be possible and therefore the extent of permissible integration must be governed, as other factors in Sherman Act violations, by the circumstances of individual cases. Technological advances may easily require a basic industry plant to expand its processes into semi-finished or finished goods so as to produce its iron articles in greater volume and with less expense.

It is not for the courts to determine the course of the nation's economic development.[13]

However, the minority opinion, as delivered by Justice Douglas, is revealing for the present discussion. The four justices of the minority agreed with the majority that to enter effectively into the development of the Pacific steel industry, the company would have to integrate. What they feared, however, was that as United States Steel added to its already huge size, it would be that much closer to monopoly power over steel. Thus:

[13] *United States v. Columbia Steel*, 334 U.S. 495, 525-26 (1948). Columbia Steel is the U.S. Steel subsidiary through which the Consolidated Steel plant was purchased.

The result might well be different if Consolidated were merging with or being acquired by an independent West Coast producer for the purpose of developing an integrated practical plan to put together an independent western unit of the industry with sufficient resources and strength to compete with the giants of the industry. Approval of this acquisition [that is, the acquisition by United States Steel] works in precisely the opposite direction. It makes dim the prospects that the western steel industry will be free from the control of the eastern giants. . . . Its serious impact on competition and the economy is emphasized when it is recalled that U.S. Steel has one third of the whole steel production of the entire country. The least I can say is that a company that has that tremendous leverage on our economy is big enough.[14]

More recently, in the Brown Shoe case, it is significant that the court argued that one factor bearing on its decision was "the history of tendency toward concentration in the industry." [15] In his decision, Chief Justice Warren asserted that "we cannot avoid the mandate of Congress that tendencies toward concentration in industry are to be curbed in their incipiency, particularly when those tendencies are being accelerated through giant steps striding across a hundred cities at a time." [16]

Methods of Government Intervention

When economic power is greater than is necessary for technological advancement, and when it impairs competition, it becomes a matter for public concern. This amounts to a maxim in the American conception of an enterprise economy. The basic problem is to relate this maxim to reality. It is revealing to see how the government's attempts to resolve the problem of excessive size and integration in the cases of oil, steel, and the lighter metals furnish a clue to the relative significance of public and private activities in the shaping of economic policies. In petroleum, the government splintered the integrated corporation in the hope that its pieces would become effectively competitive. In steel, it was

---

[14] *Ibid.*, pp. 539-40.
[15] *Brown Shoe Co., Inc. v. United States,* 370 U.S. 345 (1962).
[16] *Ibid.*, p. 346.

left to time to restore the control of the market over the structure
of the industry. In aluminum, the government took direct action
to create competitors.

In the petroleum industry, the competition sought through "deintegration" of its dominant organization was later effected by
re-integration. Competition in this industry did not appear until
the separate companies arising out of the court decision of 1911
started to branch out vertically and horizontally into each other's
fields of operation. Their growth hastened by the growth of the
automotive industry, successful crude oil producers emancipated
themselves by integration, from dependence on the refining facilities of former Standard Oil companies.

Obviously, a complete balance has still not been achieved. The
integrated "majors" enjoy strategic advantages of access to supplies and the market leverage that goes with far-flung interest at
all levels of production and distribution. Indeed, it is idle to speak
of free enterprise as something that remains fixed. From time to
time, the government will undoubtedly have to put its finger on
what it regards as disproportionate advantages or squeezes that
are bound to develop in such an industry. Nonetheless, integration, with the technological and market rivalries that it has stimulated, appears to have enlarged the scope of the competition in
petroleum and its satellite areas beyond anything that the dissolution itself could have done.

Of the steel story, perhaps the most significant aspect is the
price paid to escape government action. Under Judge Gary,
United States Steel adopted a policy of slow growth and soft competition. Other firms were allowed to establish themselves. That
policy clearly contributed to the success of United States Steel in
defending itself between 1911 and 1920 against the attempts of
the government to dissolve it. But, in consequence, it was left
behind in the race to capture markets for light sheets, stainless
steels, and other light alloys in the automotive and other industries. It remained heavily overburdened with unwanted facilities
for rails and heavy structural steel forms. It is notable that, even
after World War II, when other companies were spending their
capital funds to increase net capacity, United States Steel was still

206   BIG ENTERPRISE IN A COMPETITIVE SYSTEM

heavily engaged in replacing obsolete equipment in order to compete to advantage in the more rewarding areas of the steel business of today.

Over the first half century of its existence, United States Steel
appears to have increased its physical output by some 85 percent.
Competitor companies, meanwhile, increased their output by percentages of from 500 to more than 3,000. In a sense, the market
furnished the steel industry with the telling lesson—which the
courts did not deliver in that instance—of unprofitability of mass
integration in which competitive suppleness has been sacrificed
for sheer massiveness.

In aluminum, the public policy problem was created not by
merger, but from the comparative slowness of market forces in
breaking into the monopoly position of the firm with the head
start. While the rivalry with producers of other metals was real,
it did not eliminate the monopoly power stemming from lack of
competitors in the production of primary aluminum. In addition,
this control over aluminum ingot gave Alcoa substantial leverage
as a fabricator.

Few would deny that independent fabricators of aluminum
products shared in the growth stimulated by the campaign of
Alcoa to win recognition for aluminum. Nonetheless, the fabricators at any one stage, from sheet or bar to finished consumer
goods, were dependent on the one main ingot producer and owner
of the bulk of the ore supply. When the primary producer entered
successive stages of fabrication, the opportunity for discrimination against customer-competitors, whether or not exercised, existed. However fair or wise the primary producer in adjusting
margins from one stage of production to the next, the structure
of the aluminum industry precluded well-balanced competitive
opportunity, except as other materials were effective as actual or
potential alternatives to aluminum. If the monopolist leaned
backward not to squeeze his customers while competing with
them, the ultimate consumer might suffer from the very hesitance
of the dominant firm to drive for market through lower prices
and smaller margins.

Legal proceedings directed at Alcoa's monopoly beginning as

early as 1912 did not materially alter this situation. However, when the government at the end of World War II disposed of its aluminum-producing facilities, it seized the opportunity to give preference to the bids of potential competitors. Moreover, as an additional method of increasing the number of potential independent suppliers of ingot in the American market, a District Court in 1950 ordered a complete separation of ownership ties between Alcoa and Aluminium Ltd. of Canada. Thus, the problem of bringing or keeping the aluminum industry in line with market-oriented competition was met in part by the limitations that other metals or nonmetallic materials imposed on the monopoly of aluminum; in part by government attack on specific practices deemed in restraint of trade, from which Alcoa agreed to desist; in part from the company's general experience in developing tenable market relations with users of aluminum; and in part by circumstances that enabled the government to bring two large competitors into the field by offering extremely favorable terms for the purchase of government-owned facilities.

A situation similar to that in aluminum has long prevailed in nickel production. In that industry, the bulk of the ores and ore-reduction facilities is in Canada. There was no opportunity for the United States government to offer surplus war plants to competitors of the corporation holding the monopoly—International Nickel Company of Canada. The American subsidiary of International Nickel was essentially an integrated rolling mill operation. The government therefore had to confine its suit under the Sherman Act to the company's alleged anticompetitive discriminatory practices *vis-a-vis* buyers and fabricators. Under the consent decree ending the United States government's suit, International Nickel was required to cooperate over a period of twenty years with existing and potential rolling mill producers of nickel products, by making materials and equipment parts available to them without restriction or discrimination, under terms as favorable as those afforded within International Nickel itself. In addition, the company agreed to make available to technical institutions and potential competitors a manual of the processes employed as of 1947 in the production of rolled nickel products. These requirements may be lifted at any time during the twenty-year period if it is shown to the satisfaction of the court that International Nickel and its subsidiaries have met with substantial competition, rendering unnecessary any further government intervention to enforce competition.

Direction for Public Policy

These cases suggest the advantage of flexibility in government action to correct monopolistic situations, particularly those which the market itself has not eliminated within a reasonable time.

What is a reasonable time, under the broad mandate of the Sherman Act, has been left to the judgment of the administrative or enforcement agencies and ultimately to the courts. Naturally, the corporation that the Department of Justice or the Federal Trade Commission selects for a test of competitiveness in big business will protest against being made the guinea pig. What rationale is available to the management of big business concerning the understandable position expressed in the following testimony?

> Let me make it clear from the beginning that we have no quarrel with the antitrust laws as such. We believe sincerely that such laws are good—that they are essential safeguards for our free enterprise economy.
>
> But changing interpretations often leave modern business in the dark as to what honest course it can pursue. Frequently, it finds itself attacked for things done years before in complete good faith, and such attacks raise grave doubts as to the future propriety of present actions. These are difficult questions against which to weigh the commitment of millions of dollars of stockholder capital.[17]

In part, the preceding discussion of moves and countermoves, private and public, points to the direction of an answer. The essential question regarding the tenability of further integration is whether the advantage is temporary and may be expected to

[17] Testimony of Crawford Greenewalt, president of du Pont, *Study of Monopoly Power,* Hearings before the Subcommittee on Study of Monopoly Power of the House Committee on the Judiciary, 81 Cong. 2 sess. (1950), Pt. 2-A, p. 543.

work itself out as the resourcefulness of rivals is mobilized, or whether the market will be frozen by continuous exploitation and accretion to a point where only public intervention can pry it open. Each situation must be examined to determine what alternatives to a monopolized product have already become available that may lessen the importance of whether a competitor will emerge to duplicate the product. It must also be determined whether, in a persistently dominated market, competitors do not enter the field because of limited demand or opportunity, or because of restrictive tactics effectively employed by the dominant producer to retain market control. In the last case, the indicated step is public action to eliminate the artificial barriers created by a specific monopolistic practice. Beyond that, after a period long enough to demonstrate the little likelihood of readjustment without further government intervention, additional steps may be justified to open a market to potential competitors. Among such steps, the last and most drastic is dissolution.

Governmentally enforced dissolution may be the only available step when integration has gone so far as to weaken the force of competition. But it is clear that enforced dissolution is justifiable only as a last resort. The free enterprise system would have little to recommend it—indeed the very reason for its being would be destroyed—if continual government-forced reorganization were required to keep it competitive. Freedom of enterprise is a futile concept if it excludes freedom to expand and to grow. This freedom should be restricted only after taking fully into account whether dissolution entails any substantial weakening of the market incentives relied upon for economic efficiency and progress.

Obviously, dissolution is not the answer unless the separated members acquire the ability and incentives to grow and develop into viable firms, and, in short, to compete vigorously both within and without the industry.

Voluntary Divestment

Integrated corporations cannot be expected to abstain from further integration when it appears to advance their interests. Nor can they be expected voluntarily to "de-integrate" to the detriment of their total operation. On the other hand, it has been shown that integrated giants can misconceive the means and objectives of their development, or confuse mere expansion with efficient growth. In a dynamic economy, where innovation also speeds obsolescence, divestment of unessential or unprofitable components is a logical corollary to freedom of integration.

That agglomeration is not synonymous with progress is from time to time demonstrated by the sloughing off of product lines by integrated companies. A large petroleum corporation discontinues production of cosmetics; an aluminum producer of furniture; a film manufacturer of vitamins. Store-to-store retailing is abandoned and transferred to wholesalers by the leading soap maker. Meat packers have dropped local plants when they have seen that the business could be better handled through fewer channels, and chain store outlets have reduced the number of their stores and increased the importance of their individual outlets. Cases can readily be cited in which particular items of the product mix of the big business have been abandoned as others have taken their places. Experimental departments or processes may be abandoned within a comparatively short time if they fail to justify the cost and effort involved.[18]

The importance of giving enterprise, large or small, free rein to use its resources in developing opportunities for new products, processes, or markets, has been repeatedly noted in this discussion. The condition for such a free rein is that successive integrations must represent improvement rather than mere consolidation. The problem of streamlining, of relinquishing as well as acquiring, has to be faced. The principle is applicable to quasi-integration as well. When an automotive company pools its know-how with a petroleum company to produce an antiknock preparation, when a petrochemical company combines with a coal company to explore

----

[18] Michael Gort shows the following rates of total product abandonment for the 111 companies he examined: 1929-39, 5.7 per year; 1939-50, 12.6 per year; 1950-54, 16.8 per year. He suggests that the high rate could reflect "the trend of diversification away from related production processes and products," and that "possibly this introduces increased risks and consequently greater frequency of product abandonments." *Diversification and Integration in American Industry* (Princeton University Press, 1962), p. 51.

the gasification possibilities in coal, or when a copper company and a zinc company link know-how in mineral extraction to develop a new metal, the combination can be more readily countenanced as consistent with competitive efficiency if, when the new venture has been put on its feet, the offspring is allowed to go off on its own and prove itself in the market, free from the inhibitions of overlapping company interest.[19]

However desirable it may be in terms of efficiency, the firm may nevertheless find it difficult to relinquish what is not essential to the total corporate operation. Inertia in this regard can be attributed to a natural tie to traditional operations, to identification of personnel with the existing corporate bureaucracy, or even to dependence on the corporation on the part of customers and suppliers as well as employees. It is also true that offers to dispose of product lines or patents under apparently liberal conditions have sometimes lacked takers. Many proposals registered with the Department of Commerce have received little or no response. The importance of this feature of business behavior readily justifies increased attention to the possible aid that government fiscal policy could provide in encouraging the separation of business pieces that no longer require attachment to the parent organization.[20] The discretion exercised in achieving growth by integration promises to be crucial to the survival of big business as an essential and profitable instrument both of progress and efficiency.

---

[19] The situations here used for illustration include the collaboration of Standard Oil of New Jersey with General Motors in the development of the Ethyl additive; of Gulf Oil and Kopperex in research of gasification; of Kennecott Copper and New Jersey Zinc in titanium exploration. But these are merely indicative of many similar situations in which units have been formed to combine the specialist's know-how and the physical facilities of the parent company. See, for example, Alfred P. Sloan, Jr., "Evolution of the Automobile," in *My Years with General Motors* (Doubleday, 1964), pp. 219-37.

[20] A liberal tax policy for recapitalization of divested units might well be considered in a public policy of encouraging voluntary separation in the interest of efficiency and competitive balance. The importance of this factor was explicitly recognized in the compulsory du Pont-General Motors divorcement. Its relevance to voluntary divestiture should be no less real. Special tax treatment of du Pont stockholders was embodied in H. Res. 8847 of Aug. 22, 1961 (see Legislative Reference Service, ed., *Digest of Public General Bills and Selected Resolutions*, 87 Cong. 1 sess., U.S. Government Printing Office, 1961, p. E-493) and was passed by both Houses of Congress on February 22, 1962.

11

Summary and Conclusions

SINCE BIG BUSINESS emerged as a national issue at the close of the nineteenth century, it has been regarded both as a symbol of national capacity for economic advancement and as a threat to the survival of a competitive system. Public policy toward big business has been predicated on the general assumption that Americans want competition and abhor monopoly. That premise was the basis for the passage of the Sherman Act, designed to combat the monopolies sought by the early trust and holding companies. It was implicit in the Wilson campaign against the money trust, culminating in passage of the Clayton Act, the Federal Reserve Act, and the Federal Trade Commission Act.

Fear of business concentration pervaded the work of economists during the depression years. Particular stress was placed on the finding that a substantial percentage of the nation's business assets was held by a limited number of the largest corporations, and that a few dominated some of the most important industries. Studies by economists appeared to demonstrate the presence of "administered pricing," by which the established leaders tended to drain the price system of its flexibility as they met declining demand by reducing output and employment rather than by lowering prices and profit margins. The length and severity of the depression were for a time attributed in part to the rigidities introduced by big business. Indeed, the Temporary National Economic Committee set up by Congress appeared to confirm this general trend of thought and to call for the freeing of markets from control by the oligopolies. In more recent years, the charge of "administered prices" has been used in an attempt to show that the price rise following World War II was due in large measure to the arbitrary pricing decisions of big business.

These developments have been matched by support for public policies inconsistent with a competitive system. Apart from the policing and umpiring that must be associated with any orderly economic system, public measures for protection against the uncertainties of the market have increased with the growth of big business. This emphasis has been reflected in fair trade laws legalizing the fixing of resale prices for retailers, in the programs of crop control and parity prices for farmers, and in various forms of special licensing, tariffs, and other barriers to free business entry.

These measures do not, however, amount to the abandonment of competition. On the contrary, Americans appear to agree that the competitive process is worth preserving. It provides an opportunity for choice, decentralization of economic power, and freedom of opportunity; it does not depend on *noblesse oblige* to produce socially desirable behavior. Any fruitful discussion of the compatibility of big business with a competitive system must, on the other hand, reckon with the existence of conflicting objectives. Americans want to enjoy the technological advantages that large size frequently offers, but fear the power that is associated with "excessive" size. They prefer to invest their savings in strong, stable, well-known corporations with proven management, but deplore the difficulties that small businessmen have in obtaining risk capital. They admire the capacity of big business to introduce new products and make them household items, but view with alarm the position thus acquired and the tendency for many smaller enterprises to become satellites, looking to big business rather than to themselves to determine the products they service or distribute. They seek an economic system that promotes efficiency commensurate with the preservation of basic social values. Big business serves that system only to the extent that it contributes to the achievement of these concurrent objectives.

In the final analysis, two central questions underlie the issue of big business and competition. The first is that of *structure*. Has the growth of big business tended to narrow the opportunities for new enterprise by concentrating employment, assets, and market control in the hands of a few industrial giants? The second is that of *performance*. Is the behavior of big business regulated in the last analysis by the market forces?

Concentration of Power in the Business Structure

The structure of the economy consists of a relatively small number of extremely large organizations and a very large number of extremely small ones. A few large firms account for a disproportionate share of national employment, output, and investment. One or a few large, multiplant, multiproduct firms has the dominant share of a number of industries. Nevertheless, an analysis of the statistics of concentration, whether of employment, production, or financial resources, suggests an over-all pattern of continued mobility and change.

Distribution of Employment

The big industrials, with which this study is mainly concerned, share the production of goods and services in a diversified economy of more than 60 million persons gainfully employed in public, quasi-public, and private activities, in agriculture and the professions, in government and nonprofit organizations, in domestic services and in small and medium-sized business enterprises, proprietary and incorporated. Among the 4.4 million business firms in 1956—all but 37,720 of which had fewer than 100 employees each—the 3,100 largest corporations (with 1,000 or more employees each) had an aggregate of 15.5 million employees on their payrolls.

At the opposite extreme, the number of self-employed workers, as given in the 1960 census figures, was 7.9 million, or one-eighth of the total labor force. This figure would be substantially increased if the owner-managers of the smallest business corporations were recognized as being self-employed enterprisers who had incorporated their businesses.

Self-employment outside of agriculture has continued to increase during the period of big business growth. The great decline in the percentage in agriculture has been accompanied by an increase mainly in trade and services, both typically small business areas. Opportunities for the entrepreneur are reflected also in the number of business firms in operation, since the vast majority are proprietorships. The rate of increase in the number of businesses exceeded that of population between 1900 and 1940, and has grown about in proportion to population since 1940.

Businesses generally have been growing larger, and the number in the higher-size brackets may be expected to increase. There were 6,410 businesses with 500 or more employees in 1956, against 4,900 in 1939. The 6,410 accounted for 46 percent of total business employment in 1956; the 4,900 accounted for 40 percent in 1939.[1] The giant industrials—those with 10,000 or more employees —numbered about 223 in 1958. In manufacturing, 181 such firms accounted for nearly 6 million employees; in retail trade, 37 accounted for close to 1.3 million. The concentration of employment in firms of this size is impressive. Nevertheless, the predominant portion of gainful employment (about 75 percent in 1956) is still in business firms with fewer than 1,000 employees, or in the nonbusiness field. Both concentration and opportunity for self-employment have persisted side by side in the American economy.

Concentration of Output

The 1958 Bureau of the Census study of concentration in American manufacturing reports concentration ratios of more than 60 percent for 90 of the 443 industries considered. In 29 of these, concentration was more than 80 percent.[2] These statistics are, of course, consistent with other information suggest-

[1] Howard R. Bowen, Donald W. Paden, and Genevieve B. Wimsatt, "The Business Population in Wartime," *Survey of Current Business* (May 1944), p. 12.

[2] *Concentration Ratios in Manufacturing Industry, 1958*, Report prepared by the U.S. Bureau of the Census for the Subcommittee on Antitrust and Monopoly of the Senate Committee on the Judiciary, 87 Cong. 2 sess. (1962), Pt. 1, Table 2, p. 42; Pt. 2, Table 9, p. 457.

ing that, at any given time, a substantial proportion of the economic activities of the business sector is controlled by a relatively few large firms.

On the other hand, when these concentration ratios are compared with those of earlier periods, a significant element of instability is encountered. The inability of the Bureau of the Census to compare more than 198 of these with earlier data for 1,800 product classes for which 1935 data are available is striking evidence of the fluidity of modern market situations. Newcomers have steadily penetrated markets earlier dominated by patents or the power of industrial giants. Substitutes from other industries have exerted continuing pressure on conventional markets. The leading aluminum company stood alone in the industry for many years, but aluminum has waged a constant fight for markets with other metals, with glass and with building materials. It replaced steel in the automobile industry and was in turn replaced by steel. Linoleum, a product of another highly concentrated industry, competes with an ever-growing list of floor coverings, and rivals of linoleum companies include powerful companies in apparently unrelated industries such as that of rubber. Pressure to compete may be exercised by distributive organizations; powerful buyers and their threat of entry may force competition in markets where producers are few. There is no substitute for tires, yet even the tire industry, with roughly 70 percent of the replacement market for new tires controlled by four firms, is not immune from this kind of competition. It is not the number of participants producing the bulk of a single product, but the number of participants in the market in which the product must compete that determines the significance of concentration ratio.

Concentration of Financial Resources

There is probably no aspect of big business that suggests concentration so dramatically as the financial strength of the large industrials. By comparison with big business, the percentage of total assets attributable to the smaller units of business enterprise is small. The total assets of unincorporated businesses are estimated to be less than one-fifth of the assets of the corporate sector.[3] The figures for unincorporated enterprise are not, however, reliable. Large and small enterprises have such different capital requirements that asset accounts are misleading as a measure for comparing the economic importance of the corporations, particularly the giants, and the many proprietorships. The large corporations are the very firms that require the pooling of investments because they operate in industries requiring heavy capital investment—steel, petroleum, transportation equipment, and electrical machinery, for example. The small business, on the other hand, is typically one that does not require a large investment to achieve relatively high sales and income and in which entrepreneurial skill is an important, but not a bookkeeping, asset.

More significant than the size of corporate assets as a measure of financial power is the extent to which the concentration of these assets has affected the distribution of income across the economy. Corporations have generally originated slightly over half of the national income and nearly two-thirds of the national payroll over the past quarter century. The payrolls of unincorporated business (including the unincorporated farms and professions) have amounted to about 25 percent of corporate payrolls; although declining in recent years, their net income has generally exceeded that of the corporations before taxes.[4]

Although there has been an increase during the last two decades in the percentage of the total business product originating in the corporate sector, the distribution of corporate income as reported by large and small corporations over the same two decades indi-

[3] See Raymond W. Goldsmith, Robert E. Lipsey, *Studies in the National Balance Sheet*, Vol. I (Princeton University Press, 1963), p. 43. Assets shown for nonfarm unincorporated businesses in 1958 are roughly 18 percent of the assets of nonfinancial corporations.

[4] U.S. Office of Business Economics, *U.S. Income and Output, 1958*, Supplement to the *Survey of Current Business*, Table I-8, pp. 126-27 and Table I-12, pp. 134-35; and *Survey of Current Business*, Vol. 43, No. 7 (July 1963), Table 2, pp. 12-13 and Table 8, p. 17.

cates little change in the distribution of corporate income by size of firm. The rise in the financial power of big business has apparently been accompanied by comparable gains in the rest of the economy.

Composition of the Corporate Sector

Undoubtedly the corporation is the predominant form of business organization in the economy. Yet the corporate sector is not homogeneous. Of the 1,140,574 corporations submitting balance sheets to the Internal Revenue Service in 1960, 43 percent had total assets under $50,000 with an average net worth of $6,500.[5] For the most part, these small businesses are independent entrepreneurs in corporate form.

In the category of industrial enterprises, the total financial resources of the small, medium-sized, and giant firms are approximately equal. Of the $535 billion of total assets for all industrial enterprises in 1960-61, $190 billion is held by the unincorporated industrial firms and by the 662,188 corporations with less than $500,000 in assets. The 400 industrials with $100 million or more of assets held $173 billion, slightly less than half of the total. The middle group of corporations, with assets ranging from $500,000 to $100 million, reported assets totaling $172 billion.[6]

The 100 largest industrials in 1960 accounted for about 15 percent of all before tax income originating in American private business. Their assets amounted to over $125 billion. Fortunately, these 100 largest do not form an integrated whole. They represent many branches of industry, from retail trade and electronics to foods and petroleum. Nevertheless, if the list of the ranking members remained essentially unchanged over a long period, there would be much greater reason for alarm than if the group exhibited substantial evidence of turnover in leadership. Comparison

---

[5] U.S. Internal Revenue Service, *Statistics of Income, 1960-61*, Table 3, pp. 60-61, and Table 47, p. 306.

[6] *Ibid.*, Table 4, pp. 62-92.

of the list of the 100 largest industrials of 1909 with the 100 largest at various periods down to 1960 discloses significant turnover in ranking. The 1960 list contains only 31 companies that were among the 100 largest in 1909. Similarly, the lists for the intervening years, 1919, 1929, 1935, as well as 1948, show numerous replacements and marked changes in the rank of those that remained.

Industries heavily represented in big business in the early part of the century—coal, shipping, leather—have yielded to more recently developed industries, including the automobile and aircraft, chain retailing, and electrical equipment industries. The companies that have retained their positions of leadership are those that have not hesitated to embrace opportunities in growing industries. Few that have limited production to their traditional lines, and none that has adhered to traditional methods, have increased their stature in the family of the 100 largest or in the economy as a whole. The outstanding companies have helped to revamp their industries and have even created new ones.

In the structure of the economy as revealed by conventional statistics of business concentration, the notable feature is the wide variation in the character and number of economic opportunities and of the means to exploit them.

The Character of Big Business Performance

The large corporation develops pricing policies for the longer term covering a multiplicity of transactions and reflecting its own costs and production goals. This is in contrast to the seller who sets his sights on single transactions and current market conditions. But if the large company can pursue a price policy independent of immediate market conditions, how does the market enter the picture?

The decisions of the large company, representing a calculated adjustment to broad markets, undoubtedly exert an influence on the market. This does not, however, mean that the market has thereby yielded to the giant firms the final power of determination.

The administered price is essentially a considered guess as to the terms that will command continued and profitable acceptance of the product. The responsiveness of the market must be watched. No administered price will stand against the unwillingness of the market to accept it. Miscalculation incurs the heavy penalty of a decline in sales and an increase in unused capacity.

In the 1930's, many writers suggested that the advent of the giant industrial, capable of influencing prices by substantially raising or lowering the total market supply, had drained the system of its essential price flexibility. The unwillingness of big business to price fully up to immediate demand following World War II was also noted as indicative of big business discipline over the market.[7] Yet the price behavior of different commodities, as far back as price movements can be reliably traced, indicates little change in price flexibility or inflexibility. Durable goods in general have remained more stable than nondurable, consumers' goods more stable than producers' goods.

Big business has, on the other hand, developed new centers of competition, adding to the complexity of price making. The large corporation has become sensitive to pressures for expansion inside its organization; to the offerings of business rivals; to the market responses to its innovations. Frequently the multiproduct firm incorporates a variety of brands, models, and price lines that are themselves directly competitive in the open market.

As labor, managerial staff, and shareholders press for larger shares, central management is compelled to find new means of reconciling and meeting these various claims. They can be satisfied only by devising less costly processes, compressing margins, innovating, improving products, and increasing volume. The market effect of these pressures on the large company is visible in the range of substitutes, and the familiar whetting of consumer appetites with model changes.

---

[7] Prices of many consumer durables immediately following World War II were set below those prices that consumers were willing to pay for the quantities available. This aspect of pricing policies was evident in the shortages and waiting periods characteristic of the early postwar years.

The most effective expression of large-scale enterprise is seen in the many and varied forms of innovation, crossing product and industry boundaries. While the search for newer high-margin items may be instinctive among business firms, whether large or small, the large corporations have not only the urge to discover them but also the facilities to produce them. Original ideas may come from individuals or independent small firms, but it takes the technical and financial resources that big business can afford to convert them into market realities. If not big business, it would take government to develop, outside the market process, the continuous major innovations requiring large capital investment over a considerable period.

As product and industry boundaries are extended, not one but many groups may be affected and compelled to increase their know-how. Thus the range of metal alloy industries is profoundly influenced by the chemical industry, with consequent reaction on the markets for basic metals. Petroleum refiners, distillers, manufacturers of rubber goods, paint, film, and foods compete with the chemical firms. Synthetic fabrics and detergents disturb the tranquillity of the markets for organic raw materials. End products are less readily classified in terms of the particular materials that go into them. The span of the market for a product, geographically and over time, is frequently determined by the means of packaging and preserving.

Analysis of performance thus tends to bear out the indications in the structural analysis, that market behavior is determined more by the number and variety of independent products and of the available substitutes than by the number of corporations making a particular product in a narrowly defined industry. Innovation, in extending the number and variety of products that may be purchased, can also give rise to challenging price competition. Substantial reductions in the prices of a long list of commodities produced by big business — rayon, dyestuffs, aluminum and electronic products, tires, sound-reproducing machines, drugs, and other important consumer items — can be traced to the impact of innovations.

It is not suggested that all big business is always in a fever of innovation or that the growth follows a uniform pattern. Innovations are usually superimposed on a base of established products, market positions, skills, and business relationships. The customary response to price changes or new substitutes may be immediate in fats and oils and sluggish in building materials. But in few markets can a company trust its established position to perpetuate profitable margins. The ease with which industry and product boundaries can be crossed by firms of large resources and know-how has lessened the likelihood of successful insulation against competitive markets.

The Competitive Prospect

Thus far the ingenuity of American business management has, on the whole, been able to cope with the mounting problems of corporate size. The outstanding cases of growth are those in which increased size has apparently been attended by improved efficiency and continued innovation. Credit may be given to an increased willingness of large corporate management to decentralize operational responsibility among its units as a way to cope with the increasing size and complexity of the multiproduct, multiplant corporation. In addition, management has become aware of the crucial importance of ensuring continuity of managerial competence by encouraging new talent. Finally, the general emphasis on research and new product development, which has given high place to pioneering in the growth history of the business enterprise, is perhaps the decisive factor in allaying the fears for survival of the free enterprise system that have attached to big business ever since the merger-monopoly era.

These related developments have also served to stay attempts to establish government-imposed specific size limits on the business corporation. But they have not eliminated, nor should they be expected to eliminate, the instinctive resistance to any entrenchment of the final decision-making power of business in a few vast organizations. These developments do, however, indicate that big business has had a measure of success in remaining compatible with the competitive tradition.

The great variety of small and medium-sized enterprises that have heretofore flourished along with big business does not provide a completely satisfying answer to those who fear further expansion of big business. The big business will be asked, as before, whether it is becoming too big. The larger big business becomes, the greater will be the need to make sure that it is not becoming bigger and more ramified than is essential for maximum efficiency within the frame of competition.

Big business growth has sometimes been a process of agglomeration—of adding new branches, new products, and new techniques to the established enterprise—not adequately offset by streamlining established operations to retain only those elements that clearly contribute to the efficiency of the whole enterprise. More intensive study is required of the internal structures of the largest companies to test the impression of overextended product mix that has been gained from study of the growth histories of only a few large companies.

The current situation is one in which big business frequently contributes an element of dynamics in older and more traditional markets. Nevertheless, there is opportunity for further exploration of how this stimulus of big business may be kept alive or even increased. To ensure healthy survival, business enterprise must retain the urge to grow that has served it so well in the past. Looking to the future, two developments may be envisioned. It may be that the growth of population and national production will continue to provide ample scope for the general expansion of the large industrials in a climate of ever-evolving opportunity. But it may also be that the progressive expansion of the big business will intensify its problem of how to carry great overall size without becoming economically sluggish or without impeding the maintenance of those conditions conducive to effective and desirable competitive behavior.

Americans can view the future with some degree of optimism because of the achievements of their economy during the era of big business growth. Each sector of organized business, large and small, is dependent on the other in contributing to the composite performance of the economy. Each grows to some extent at the expense of the other. Yet each also creates new opportunities for growth of the others. Big business draws on the specialized abilities, flexibility, and individual services that small business can best supply and thereby creates opportunities for their number to increase.

However, this does not imply that the present allocation of responsibilities among the sectors, or the organization within those sectors, is the best attainable. Nor does it follow that the division of fields is, or ought to be, clear-cut or unchanging. The sectors must operate side by side, challenging as they cooperate. No field is, or should be, irrevocably closed as the exclusive domain of one type of organization.

In the United States, big business undertakes a major role within the business sector for the coordination of individual effort and resources. So far, at least, it has been possible to rely chiefly on private markets for control of the economic power vested in these giant corporations. Big business has not only been kept subject to the constraints of the market; it has also made an essential contribution to the vitality and effectiveness of economic activity in this country.

Index

Index

A & P. *See* Great Atlantic & Pacific Tea Company

Adams, Walter, 166n

Adelman, M. A., 23n, 50n, 128n

Administered prices (*see also* Big business, pricing in; Price policies of big business; Prices), 5, 7, 8n, 212-13, 220; on cost basis, 156, 159; rigidity of, 166-68

Agriculture (*see also* Food industry), Controls in, 26; decline in, 66; employment in, 63, 169, 214-15; prices in, 167, 169; production in, 69

Airplane industry, 33n, 34, 80; growth of, 134, 219; increased use of aluminum in, 94

Alchian, Armen A., 50n

Aldrich Committee, 18

Aluminum Ltd., 35n, 207

Aluminum Company of America, 34, 35, 35n, 39n, 92, 94n, 95, 95n, 186, 206-07

Aluminum industry, 35, 35n, 90, 159n, 205, 206, 216; "deintegration" in, 210; influence of substitute products on, 92-96, 100-01; integration in, 191; pricing in, 95-96, 222; properties of, 93, 93n; use of, in transportation industry, 93-95

American Bicycle Company, 11n

American Cement Institute, 36, 36n

American Rolling Mill Company, 195

American Sugar Refining Company, 9, 9n

American Tobacco Company, 11, 13, 13n, 15, 36, 36n, 134

Ammonia, anhydrous, 160-61

Anti-trust laws (*see also* Clayton Act, Federal Trade Commission Act, Interstate Commerce Act, Sherman Act), 6, 7, 12, 19-21, 33, 35, 40, 125, 208; changes in, 30-31; revival of activity under, 28; violations under, 37

Apparel industry: concentration in, 91; large firms in, 69

Armstrong Cork Company, 188

Ashley, W. J., 55n

Asphalt industry, 11n

Assets: as a measure of financial importance, 110-13, 216-17; as a measure of size of firm, 69, 120-21, 123-24; debt offsets to, 110; fixed *vs.* liquid, 110; of one hundred largest corporations, 118-22, 123-24, 134n, 212; ratio of sales to, 121; of small corporations, 218; of unincorporated business, 111

Associated Oil Company, 133

Automotive industry, 34, 56; consolidation in, 22 38n, 91; effect on tire industry, 98; equipment, price concessions on, 178n-79n; growth of, 134, 135, 181, 199, 205, 219; and integration, 189, 210; intracompany competition in, 172; price differentials in, 160; use of aluminum in, 94, 216; use of steel in, 94, 201

227